ST. PETERSBURG

INSIGHT *City* GUIDES

Project Editor: Wilhelm Klein
Introduced by Yevgeny Yevtushenko
Principal Photography: Fritz Dressler
Art Direction and Design: Villibald Barl and Hans Höfer
Editorial Director: Brian Bell

A P A

PUBLICATIONS

ST. PETERSBURG

First Edition
© **1992 APA PUBLICATIONS (HK) LTD**
All Rights Reserved
Printed in Singapore by Höfer Press Pte. Ltd

ABOUT THIS BOOK

This is a unique book about a unique city. All cities are unique, of course, but few have recast themselves as often or as fascinatingly as this one, which has been known by three different names during this century. Even as this book was being edited, the city's population was voting on whether to change the name Leningrad, which had succeeded Petrograd, back to its original name of St Petersburg, the City of Peter.

What makes this book's approach unique is its daring departure from the customary guidebook practice of sending writers into a country or city to observe, explore and report their findings. Instead, Apa Publications sought out expert writers within the USSR, pairing their valuable insights with Apa's proven expertise in producing an internationally renowned series of guidebooks. What is on offer, therefore, is not St Petersburg as filtered through the sensibilities of foreign observers, but St Petersburg as seen through the eyes of Soviet writers. It is the next best thing to staying with a family in the city, sharing their joys and frustrations about the place they know and love.

Together with two companion volumes, *Insight Guide: The New Soviet Union* and *CityGuide: Moscow*, this book represented a milestone in East-West cooperation – but also, at times, a trial in patience. Although the authors of the proposed chapters were initially identified with the assistance of Russian friends, it was never simple, because of the state of communications within the USSR, to contact them and coordinate their efforts. Also, editorial priorities kept changing to take into account the storm of change brought about first by *perestroika* and *glasnost*, then by the consequences of the attempted coup against Mikhail Gorbachev in August 1991.

Hans Höfer, Apa Publications' publisher, assigned **Wilhelm Klein** to manage the project. With the assistance of **Konstantin Likutov**, deputy editor-in-chief at Moscow's Novosti Press, Klein set about identifying possible local authors and photographers. In addition, conscious of the award-winning photojournalistic tradition of this series, he secured the services of a top German photographer, **Fritz Dressler**, professor at the Academy of Arts in Bremen and a regular contributor to Insight guides.

Russia's greatest names

To set this book in the context of the dynamic changes taking place in the USSR during the 1990s, **Yevgeny Yevtushenko**, the country's most outspoken contemporary poet, introduces the western reader to this city that had been not only the centre of Czarist Russia but also the cradle of the Bolshevik Revolution (or coup, as they now call it). Yevtushenko's profound insights into Leningrad's cultural background make us understand that the dramatic developments we see today are part of a historical continuity. Leningrad is again becoming that window to Europe that it was designed and destined to be.

The next exceptional contributor is **Dmitry Likhachev**, a native of Leningrad. Now in his eighties, he is the most venerated member of the Academy of Sciences of the USSR

Klein

Yevtushenko

Likhachev

and, having been a victim of Stalin's purges, has been dubbed "the conscience of the nation". Like Yevtushenko, he is also a People's Deputy, a member of the USSR's new parliament that looks set to change the course of history. For this book, he wrote about the city's architecture.

Next on the list of outstanding contributors is **Anatoli Sobchak**, an often controversial figure. After holding a chair as professor, with a doctorate of law, at Leningrad University, he became a People's Deputy and was later elected Leningrad's mayor. In 1990, together with Gavriil Popov, chairman of the Moscow City Soviet (and later Moscow's mayor), he left the Communist Party in protest. By this act, the two men attracted worldwide publicity and boosted the process of democratization. During Sobchak's mayorship, we might witness Leningrad's third change of name, if the Supreme Soviet ratifies the wish of the majority of the city's population to restore "St Petersburg".

Igor Zakharov studied Philosophy at his native Leningrad University. He was secretary to the Politburo member Alexander Yakovlev and is now editor in a Moscow publishing house. In this book, he wrote about Leningrad's colourful history and about the parks and palaces in the suburbs, and provided the valuable insider's advice contained in the fact-filled *Travel Tips* section.

Lidiya Ginzburg was a historian of literature and a survivor of the blockade. She died in 1990 at the age of 88, before this book was published.

The chapter about the "People of Peter" was written by **Fyodor Dmitriev**, who has lived in Leningrad since he was five. He works and writes for the *Leningradsky Literator* and translates from Scandinavian languages.

The cultural aspects of this book were covered by various writers. Two women wrote the main part. **Elvira Kim** is a geographer and art critic who writes frequently in major publications. **Olga Kalinina** is also a geographer and lecturer on art with a similarly long list of publications to her credit.

Georgi Katayev, a graduate of Moscow University, spends most of his time in Leningrad. He specializes in the city's cultural heritage and writes frequently about it in periodicals such as *Ogonyok* and *Rodina*.

N. Zorkaya, a leading Soviet film critic, is author of a series of books about the history of Soviet cinema. **Andrei Karaulov** is also a well-known dramatic critic who has written several books about art and politics.

Then there is **Leonid Ivanov**, whose painstaking researches and love for the city on the Neva enabled him to provide the detailed information in the Places section. He studied the Russian language and also contributed to *Insight Guide: The New Soviet Union*.

The final touches

The final touches to the book were provided by **Villibald Barl**, Apa's Yugoslav-born art director, and by **Christopher Catling,** who edited and indexed the final English text. Production was supervised in Apa's London office by **Brian Bell**.

Welcome, then, to St Petersburg. We hope you will be as captivated by its splendour as we were when we put together this book.

Kim   *Kalinina*   *Katayev*   *Karaulov*   *Ivanov*

History

Features

Places

Maps

THE CITY WITH THREE NAMES

*The poet **Yevgeny Yevtushenko** traces the city's changing identity through history.*

The St Petersburg poet Georgi Adamovich found himself, after the Revolution, in one of the world's loveliest cities, Paris – yet he still used to sigh bitterly for the lost beauty of the city on the Neva whose beauty and spirituality he regarded even more highly:

On Earth there was but one capital.
The rest were merely towns…

None of the émigrés like Adamovich who tried to preserve this stone fantasy of Peter I in their memories ever called it Petrograd or Leningrad; when asked, they would always say they came from St Petersburg.

The origin of such a conspicuously foreign name is explained by the fact that Peter I's associates and drinking companions were mainly German and Dutch. The Czar himself insisted that they call him Peter, not Piotr, his Russian name. St Petersburg was renamed Petrograd at the beginning of World War I when anti-German feelings were running high, and thousands of people took part in attacks on the city's German bakeries. The city was renamed Leningrad after Lenin's death in 1924. At that time 32,000 Leningradians joined the Communist Party in just one year. Now members are leaving it in their thousands.

In 1991, Leningrad's citizens voted by referendum to return the city to its original name. In a television interview the Mayor of Leningrad, Sobchak (who, like his Moscow counterpart, Popov, has now left the Communist Party), said that the city's main priority today was not the decision to change its name (which will inevitably cost millions) but, first and foremost, raising its people's standard of living. He did not, however, reject outright the idea of changing its name

in the future. The radicals demanded this be done immediately, as they considered the October Revolution – and that means Lenin as well – to be the worst misfortune ever to strike the City of the Czars and of the Muses.

But are they right, these romantic purists who are trying to preserve only their cherished image of St Petersburg, in regarding all the other aspects of the city's life as a historical imposition, a nightmare with which they do not wish to be identified?

Pasternak wrote the following quatrain on the nature of tragedy:

…in the double meaning
Of life, impoverished to observe,
But great in light of
The losses borne.

Of course, it was tragic – revolutionary Petrograd losing the essence of St Petersburg when raging crowds cleared the thoroughfares of the shadows of the Decembrist aristocrats in what was primarily a just, but also a filthy, stream. It was the Decembrists who, sipping French champagne, had once dreamed of embodying the ideas of pampered French liberalism. And it was tragic that Leningrad lost the essence of Petrograd where, in the Stray Dog literary café great poets like Blok, Mayakovsky, Mandelshtam and Pasternak could be seen sitting in the same room – true, usually at different tables – and where Chagall, who had not yet emigrated, used to decorate the streets during demonstrations, and where Gorky could still get Lenin to agree not to have some freethinking intellectual or other arrested.

Ever so, the City on the Neva became even greater "in light of the losses borne". There was the October Revolution, the sailor's gruff phrase, "The guard's tired", which broke up the Constituent Assembly. There was the terror of the 1930s when thousands of Leningradians were arrested and annihilated. There was the terror of the Fascist siege when people made soup from old belts or shoes. And all these tragedies made the city even greater in history. These three different names, it turned out, were not like the masks a resourceful actor could change with a magician's sleight of hand. On the contrary, they proved to be three great roles which history had bestowed with cruel generosity upon an actor no less great.

St Petersburg: Pushkin, in his poem *The Bronze Horseman*, retrospectively eaves-dropped on the secret thoughts of Peter I, who had conceived the idea of building a new capital of Russia overlooking the world's open seas:

By nature we are fated here
To cut a window through to Europe…

Peter, the first Russian Westerniser on the throne, studied ship-building in Amsterdam transforming the thousands of stonemasons, carpenters, soldiers and state criminals who had been driven to these marshy, mosquito-ridden parts into obedient instruments of his will, Peter himself became an instrument of the political and economic imperatives, which dictated the need for a new capital on this site. Of that new capital, Pushkin said:

And before the younger capital
Ancient Moscow has paled
Like a purple-clad widow
Before a new empress.

Peter was compelled by another impera-tive, a psychological one, resulting in his urgent need to leave Moscow. In his child-

and London, levied a tax on beards and forced all his courtiers to smoke tobacco; he could not have carried through his Western-ising plans without a powerful port where, as Pushkin had him say, "ships of every flag" would indeed "come to visit us".

In fact, notwithstanding all his innova-tions, Peter only built upon the ethos of the free city of Novgorod, which once had a sea watch on this very site from which Novgorodian sea pilots guided German ships across Lake Ladoga. Peter won this site back from the Swedes who had taken control of it, and founded St Petersburg in 1703. By hood a frenzied, bloodthirsty mob had burst into the Kremlin, and he had been saved only by a miracle. Plots were constantly being hatched against him there. And he person-ally had cut off the heads of the *streltsi* (members of the military corps established by Ivan the Terrible who enjoyed special privileges), grasping the blood-stained axe between his young hands, and trembling with hatred and fear. The Moscow boyars' beards were just the place for all Peter's reforms to get entangled in. And what better place for rebellions and murders than Mos-cow's winding back streets?

The straight streets of the City on the Neva, on the other hand, were perfect for the promenades, parades and masquerades Peter enjoyed so much. The streets of St Petersburg looked just like a series of cuttings in the forest. They were so straight that it seemed they had been cut through the wooded marshes exactly as his eyes had directed, and not with axes.

Fearless though he was in his battles against foreigners, Peter feared Moscow as he would fear an old witch with an evil eye. The marshes on which he built the new capital seemed firmer to him than the stone-patterned floors of the Kremlin.

prising and intrepid but also rather light-fingered, evidently as a legacy of his childhood peddling.

The "birds of Peter's nest" were his *oprichniks* (the special administrative élite established by Ivan the Terrible) but with the important difference that they not only tracked down and executed enemies of the state but also built St Petersburg alongside the Czar. In the Table of Ranks introduced by Peter, 14 rungs of the ladder separated the serf from the highest state officials but Peter also made it possible for a person to climb to the top in one go. True, this took a fair degree of good luck as well as talent.

Henchmen: While constructing St Petersburg, Peter was naturally afraid of relying on people who regarded Moscow as their hereditary nest. He made Alexander Menshikov his right-hand man; he, rumour has it, previously earned his living as a peddler of hot pies. Menshikov's luxurious palace still graces the banks of the Neva and the Czar often used to spend the night there after friendly drinking sessions. He also sometimes thrashed his host, who was enter-

<u>Left</u>, Schlüsselburg, where the city originated.
<u>Above</u>, czarist splendour in Pushkin.

Peter's companions helped him not only to chop off heads but also to hew the masts of ships and fashion the shape of the state. The Russian navy was built with Peter's own hands and it was no accident that the first battleship of this fleet was named *The Poltava* after the town where Peter had defeated the Swedish King Karl XII. The Russian naval flag – a dark blue cross on a white background – was hoisted for the first time ever above this ship. A dispatch from the British emissary, James Jeffreys, recorded the eve: "They have launched a battleship with ninety cannons, ten ships are on the stocks... The ships are built here no worse than in Europe..."

Jeffreys had forgotten that Russia was also Europe. But Peter never forgot his first English boat which he had found in a barn and mended, and which, as a 15-year-old lad, he had learned to manoeuvre on the River Yauza. On his orders this boat, which was named *The Grandfather of the Russian Fleet,* was sent by cart from Moscow to St Petersburg. For 16 months it stayed on dry land until finally, in May of 1723, it was lowered into the Neva.

With an escort consisting of nine galleys plus the imperial yacht Peter sailed the boat

You will also be amazed by the many different items in the cabin, of the highest quality, that Peter made with his own hands, including furniture, a boat and boots. Just as he used to drink, and make others drink, a huge amount of vodka from the Great Eagle Cup, he also used to do a huge amount of work, and made others do so as well.

Built on bones: For many, this massive workload proved fatal. St Petersburg is a marsh paved with human bones. As there was no suitable building land, the first migrants dragged earth from far-off places to the city bastions in old sacks, bark matting and even in the hems of their coarse hemp

down the River Neva from St Petersburg to Schlüsselburg. All the ships and boats on the river formed up and saluted *The Grandfather of the Russian Fleet* with gunfire, fanfares and fireworks. "From small causes may come great results" was written in blazing letters in the sky.

When in Leningrad, make a point of visiting Peter's Log Cabin. You will be amazed how tiny a structure could accommodate such a giant of a man. In 1756 the poet Alexander Sumarokov sung the praises of this log cabin thus: "As this house be small, so Peter in the world be great."

clothes. Fever and disease claimed a great many lives. When a person died, he was wrapped in the matting in which he had just dragged earth and buried in the earth he had brought himself.

St Petersburg is a Russian pyramid. But Peter was a proletarian Pharaoh who lost as much sweat as his slaves. He used to get up at five o'clock and spend half an hour walking about his room, thinking. Then for half an hour his secretary used to read him various business reports and hand him papers to sign. After breakfast, at six o'clock he used to set off on foot or horseback for the wharf,

Senate or Admiralty, work until late, and then celebrate with a feast.

He was both a Spartan and an epicurean but talented and inventive, not senselessly oppressive, tasteless and dull. Wishing to make St Petersburg a "paradise", he had palaces built in and around the city, presented his wife, Catherine I, with the country house of Saaris Moisio (later renamed Tsarskoye Selo), his daughter, Elizabeth, with a palace at Strelna, and had Peterhof, with its famous cascade of fountains, built for himself where he greatly loved the small palace of Mon Plaisir.

From a graveyard of its first builders, St

When Peter was close to death, he wrote, "Give it all away…" but he did not manage to say to whom. Peter's remains were to have been buried in Moscow but his companions objected to this plan and had him buried instead in the Fortress of St Peter and Paul which he had founded.

In the autumn of 1728 Moscow became the capital once again, and the Imperial Court moved back there. St Petersburg began to fall into decline and its unfinished buildings started collapsing alongside the unfinished ships. Peter's stone fantasy, whose wings were made from the canvas sails of his ships, seemed to be doomed.

Petersburg gradually grew into a beautiful city, as a Finnish folk legend of those times records: "Many kings from different countries tried to build a town on the Neva's marshes but each time the marshes swallowed up the first houses. Then a Russian giant came along and built a house and it was sucked under, then he built another and it, too, vanished. Then he went into his smithy and forged an iron town in a great fire and put it all on the marsh at once."

Left, the former Kunstkammer. Above, golden youth in Petrodvorets.

A tremendous personality, Peter had a great gift for deploying numerous resourceful foreigners in the service of Russia. He appointed them to high state office with complete confidence; sensing that his solicitous gaze was upon them and appreciating his friendly, business-like disposition, they did not let him down. But when the solicitous gaze vanished, so did many of the talented foreigners. After the deaths of Peter I and Catherine I the remaining talentless careerists from abroad formed a foreign mafia around the Imperial Court which was to go down in history as the *Bironovshchina*, or

the rule of Biron, named after the German favourite of Empress Anna.

Extravagant city: In 1732 Empress Anna made St Petersburg the capital again but life in the city, which had once been so creative, now became parasitic. Peter had also been fond of fireworks but only when the smithies' fires were blazing nearby. Now there were again fireworks but the fires in St Petersburg's smithies – along with the fires in the torture chambers – were for forging tongs which, when white-hot, were used to tear apart people's nostrils.

An ice mansion, which was later to figure prominently in Lazhechnikov's historical novel, was built between the Winter Palace and the Admiralty for the wedding of the court jester, Prince Golitsyn. It consisted of luxurious reception rooms, grottoes, numerous sculptures, an elephant spraying hot oil out of its trunk, and even plates of ice piled high with black and red caviar and glasses of ice for the French champagne.

It was not just the common folk but also many of the nobility who grumbled at this extravagance, for such luxury was enjoyed only by those members of that high society who mixed with the second-rate foreigners. As most of the latter were of German extraction, Germanophobia disguised as Francophilia increased among the nobility. St Petersburg became well and truly Frenchified when, in 1741 the palace guardsmen removed the regent Anna Leopoldovna, (who had ruled after Anna and Biron and was also pro-German) and placed Peter's energetic, fun-loving daughter, Elizabeth, on the throne.

With her light feminine touch, Elizabeth wiped clean the window into Europe which had been smeared with *Bironovshchina*. The rights and liberties gained by the nobility were instantly transformed into palaces and country estates, no less magnificent than the Imperial ones, and into the exclusive Corps of Pages along with several other higher educational establishments.

The St Petersburg Academy of Sciences, which had been founded by Peter but which had then "stood idle" for some time, resumed

Catherine the Great.

its activities. The Academy of Arts was founded. The vast potential of the so-called "simple" Russian was seen in Russia's first academician, the illustrious *Archangel muzhik* (peasant), Mikhailo Lomonosov, who, in true Renaissance style, harmoniously combined the talents of a scientist, poet and artist. The Italian sculptor, Rastrelli, designed a bust of Peter while his son built the Smolny ensemble and the Winter Palace.

St Petersburg's greatness lies in the fact that it is not only Russian but the first Russian European city. Peter's daughter, Elizabeth, was, however, a patroness not only of the arts and sciences but also of her numerous favourites. But where the latter were concerned, she was still no match for Catherine II who, supported once again by the palace guardsmen, seized hold of the Imperial sceptre which her husband, Peter III, had held in his weak hands for only a short while.

Catherine the Great: This German-born, French-speaking woman, who once managed to make four mistakes in a three-letter Russian word, slipped into the role of an Orthodox believer like a gifted actress. In order to change from the provincial Princess of Anhalt-Zerbst into the Empress of Russia, she made a perfect study of the Russian character.

Subjected to the insults of her ruling aunt, Elizabeth, and her husband Peter, Catherine once even attempted to commit suicide but the knife caught in her corset; who knows, perhaps she was only play-acting. With her intelligence and perseverance she eventually won Elizabeth's favour and this intelligence subsequently earned her the title of "Catherine the Great", an honour accorded to nobody else but Peter and herself, either in their lifetime or posthumously.

Catherine had been a bibliophile since her early youth and her reading of Voltaire, with whom she later entered into a correspondence, radically changed her political views. Voltairian liberalism and the monarch's position, which were mutually contradictory, produced a bizarre blend of enlightened absolutism against a backcloth of the most benighted slavery.

Contemporaries noted that in her case ambition gave way to industry. With unequalled industry, for instance, she created her *Instruction*, a compilation of the works of Montesquieu and Beccaria and the first attempt at a Russian constitution. Paradoxically, the deputies of the Legislative Commission to whose verdict Catherine had submitted her free-thinking work, began ruthlessly censoring the Empress, deleting with particular zeal all the parts dealing with measures to prevent the abuse of Imperial power and ways of emancipating the serfs.

The historian Kliuchevsky left this brilliant description of Catherine: "Autocratic mained a constant object of her affection. Today his name is remembered in connection with Eisenstein's film *Battleship Potemkin* and the expression "Potemkin's villages". This phrase has been used to symbolise official lies and pomp ever since Catherine went on one of her tours of the countryside and the prince had theatrical props decorated with village scenes erected along her route.

Potemkin was a gifted army commander but an even greater sybarite and the designer of numerous St Petersburg masquerades and feasts that turned into gastronomical orgies. The historian Pyliayev cites the following

power acquired a new aspect, as was her intention, and became something akin to individual constitutional absolutism. In a society which had lost its sense of the law, even such a fortuity as a monarch's felicitous character could pass for a guarantee."

In her private life Catherine sought revenge for the many years she had spent living in obscurity at Elizabeth's court, and she tried to surpass her "dear aunt" both in lovers and feasts. According to some sources, she had 20 favourites during her 34-year reign from 1762 to 1796.

Only Prince Potemkin, however, re- menu of a refined meal in Potemkin's day: "Hazel-grouse soup with chestnuts and Parmesan cheese. Large fillet *au sultan*. Eyes of beef in 'morning awakening' sauce. Pallet of beef stuffed with truffles. Tails of veal tartar. Crumbled ears of veal. Fine slices of lamb's leg. Pigeons *à la Stanislavski*. Goose in a shoe. Turtle-doves *au Noyaliev* and snipe with oysters. Green grape gâteau. Thick 'handmaiden' cream".

Fortunately, however, Catherine the Great and her court also devoted considerable time and attention to architecture, to which the city on the Neva owes its inimitable beauty.

There are certain sights you must see in Leningrad if you are to understand what St Petersburg was really like: the Hermitage, the Winter Palace, Peter's Log Cabin, the Pushkin House-Museum and the equestrian statue of Peter the Great by the French sculptor Etienne Falconet.

Story of a stone: The rock for this statue was found seven miles from St Petersburg and nicknamed the "Thunder Stone". The old folks used to say that Peter had actually climbed on top of it when he was surveying the surrounding countryside. It weighed 1,600 tons, and a wide cutting had to be made for it through the forests. It was pulled by

a terrible eyesore. Shortly afterwards a scruffy and, moreover, drunk peasant rolled up in a cart pulled by a scrawny horse to clear the block away. The crowd started jeering at him. He took no notice of them and started digging a pit with an ordinary shovel.

He dug all day, and all the next, and the next after that, carting the earth away to the Neva. Then, on the fourth day, something extraordinary happened: the massive block rolled gently into the pit all by itself. Then the little peasant started chucking earth on top of it until the rock was completely covered. So, when you stand near the statue of Peter, remember that, somewhere beneath your

rope along runners by the ancient Egyptian method and when it reached the Gulf of Finland several months later, it was loaded on board a scuttled barge.

After the water had been pumped out, the barge rose to the surface and carried the rock the rest of the way. Thousands of spectators, including Empress Catherine, watched in wonder as the rock was unloaded. Then the part needed for the pedestal was cut away. The block that was left was also massive and

Left, winter scene in Pushkin. **Above**, the Czarina travelling during winter.

feet, there is a block of rock which is a kind of underground monument to the ordinary Russian who, neither under the czars nor under the Soviet regime, has ever had a monument erected to him above ground.

In his poem *The Bronze Horseman* Pushkin made this monument a symbol of the state in the shape of a massive horse, thundering on the heels of a defenceless man who is running away from it, and rearing on its bronze hooves over his head.

These bronze hooves did not spare the prodigal children of the Russian aristocracy, the Decembrists, who organised an uprising against the autocracy in December 1825: they were executed or exiled to Siberia. These Decembrists belonged to a generation who had been educated not by quasi-hairdressers and quasi-lackeys from France but by genuine French free-thinkers who had fled to Russia and instilled their heretical ideas in the children of the aristocracy.

In essence, all the great Russian literature initiated by Pushkin can be seen as the ordinary person's defence against the State's bronze hooves. These hooves loomed over Gogol's poor Akaky Akakievich who was stripped of his wonderful new greatcoat by thieves. These hooves did not spare the head

shorter than the previous one because the name "Petrograd" itself lasted for only 10 years: from the beginning of World War I in 1914, when anti-German feeling instigated the renaming of St Petersburg, until Lenin's death in 1924 when the city was renamed after the leader of the October Revolution. Only nostalgia for all that had vanished made Andrei Bely entitle his novel *St Petersburg*, for his work is the portrait of a city which had already changed irreversibly from St Petersburg into Petrograd.

Here is a characteristic extract from the chapter entitled *Meeting*: "They were sitting in the hall, one body on top of another, body

of Fedya Raskolnikov, the unfortunate murderer, and protagonist of Dostoyevsky's novel *Crime and Punishment*, the man who killed an old woman, no less unfortunate in her greed, with an axe, imagining himself to be Napoleon. All classical 19th-century Russian literature originates from St Petersburg's White Nights and dreams, swirling like the mystical vapours on the marshes that existed before the time of Peter I and which, it seems, had remained only hidden under the thoroughfares' cobblestones. St Petersburg is the birthplace of the Russian classics.

Petrograd: This section will be much

huddled against body; bodies swaying to and fro; and shouting to one another about there being a strike in such-and-such a place and about a strike being got ready in such-and-such a place and about people being on strike here and here and here; and about them striking right here, and, wait, don't move! First some intellectual Party official spoke about it and then a student said the same thing over again; next came a girl student; and then some politically aware proletarian, but just when a politically ignorant proletarian and representative of the lumpenproletariat was about to say the same thing over again, a voice boomed right across the room, and it was so deep, it sounded like it was coming from a barrel, and it made everyone jump... Thunderous applause. 'That's right! That's right! Don't let him speak! It's a disgrace! He's drunk!'

'No, I'm not drunk, com-rathes! Ssso... yer mean, yer ssslave an' ssslave away on thisss 'ere bourgeoisssie... In ssshort: grab 'em an' pusssh 'em under; that'ss it... ssstrike...' "

This was no longer St Petersburg, this was Petrograd, even though Andrei Bely clung feverishly to its old name. But maybe he called it that as a gibe. The city's face was

style of Peter and Catherine, just as envious maids, trembling awkwardly, will try on their mistresses' expensive gowns while they are away.

The new Russian bourgeoisie was certainly not all alike: some merchants became patrons, supported Russian avant-garde artists, bought up Van Goghs, Gauguins, Matisses, Picassos, and even surreptitiously gave donations to the Bolsheviks, while others mercilessly worked their workers to the bone, vindicating the popular saying that there is no worse master under the sun than an ex-slave.

The city's landscape was definitely de-

changed rapidly, not so much by the World War I as by the 20th century which came crashing down on Russia like an avalanche, just at the time when the aristocracy's authority had begun to dwindle and that of the rising merchants and manufacturers had begun to increase.

Merchants' mansions suddenly started popping up here, there and everywhere like mushrooms. They were sometimes lacking in taste but they mostly tried to imitate the

Left, *The Bronze Horseman*. **Above**, Lenin shows the way.

meaned by the intruding factory chimneys, just as classicism in art was by decadence. The latter coincided, or, rather, was closely connected with the tremendous public outrage that followed the mass shooting in 1905 of a group of workers who were on their way to the Winter Palace with a petition. This day became popularly known as "Bloody Sunday" and very likely marked the beginning of the end of autocracy.

In an attempt to justify his far-from-liberal rule, the young Czar Nicolas once said, perhaps not without some foundation, that the Decembrists' uprising in 1825, which had aimed at assassinating the Czar, had thrown Russia back about 50 years. If this is true, then it is equally true that the bullets the Czarist army fired at the workers hurled Russia into a revolution for which it was unprepared, and prevented it from turning into a developed power with peacefully elaborated social liberties.

St Petersburg, and then Petrograd, was destined to become the bridgehead of these two tragic accelerated processes. The first was the fault of the country's hot-headed "progressives" and the second of its "reactionaries" who had been frightened by the terrorist acts of members of the *Narodnaya*

burg's past, conjured up a vision of a Petrograd blizzard in which he saw 12 Red Army men as the Twelve Apostles, only with blood-stained hands, and Christ following behind like a white spectre. He saw a certain expression in the eyes of the soldiers on their way back to their barracks:

That fatal "couldn't care less"
Which paves the way
For a turn of world events,
If only by not preventing them.

Blok was prophetically right. The empire's weariness, coupled with weary liberal disillusionment, proved to be that fatal "couldn't care less" which resulted in the

Volya (People's Will) organisation.

In this context the following words of Piotr Chadayev, Pushkin's spiritual teacher, writing in 1851, sadly spring to mind: "When speaking of Russia, they always presume that they are speaking of a state which is similar to the others: in actual fact this is not true at all. Russia is an entirely special world, obedient to the will, arbitrariness, fantasy of one man whether he be called Peter or Ivan is of no import: in all cases it is the same – arbitrary rule personified."

Alexander Blok, who had an astounding inner sense of the destruction of St Peters-

outbreak of World War I, and the Revolution was a direct consequence of the war. Before the war a foreboding of a world cataclysm, as of impending retribution, penetrated every corner of the capital like a disquieting draught before a storm.

Degenerate city: Count A.N. Tolstoy gave the following eye-witness account of Petrograd at that time. "During the past decade vast enterprises had been created with incredible speed. Fortunes worth millions had emerged out of nowhere. Banks, music halls, skating rinks and marvellous taverns had been built in cement and cut glass where people were held spellbound by the music, mirrors' reflections, scantily clad women, light and champagne. Gaming-houses, meeting houses, theatres, cinemas, amusement parks were hurriedly opened. On an uninhabited island not far from St Petersburg engineers and capitalists worked on a new construction project of unprecedented luxury. There was a spate of suicides.

"The court rooms were packed with hordes of hysterical womenfolk, avidly listening to nerve-racking, gory trials. Luxuries, women; you could get anything. Debauchery was rife, and it spread like a plague to the Palace. And Rasputin, a powerfully

anticipating that dreadful fatal day. And there were also prophets – something new and incomprehensible seeping from every nook and cranny…"

The words evoke the scene before the eruption of Vesuvius and subsequent destruction of Pompeii: life, already degenerate and totally out of control, with its masochistic, provocative coquetry actually bringing the volcanic lava upon itself from the fiery depths into which it is so afraid to gaze. The poetic apostles of Pompeian Petrograd likewise invoked the lava to descend upon them: "Coming Huns, I greet you… March across us!"

built illiterate peasant with crazy eyes, gained access to the Palace and Imperial throne, and began ruining Russia's good name with his mockery and insults…

"Girls made a secret of their innocence, and wives of their faithfulness. Destruction was considered good taste, neurasthenia, a sign of sophistication… People made up vices and perversions for themselves so as not to seem insipid. Such was St Petersburg in 1914… It carried on as though it was

The eruption did not have to be prevailed upon for long, and the revolutionary lava came gushing out of the crater of war. Kerensky, who represented the centrist liberals, made the unforgivable historical mistake of insisting that the war must be continued until victory was achieved. Returning from exile abroad, Lenin, previously little-known to the broad masses, won the workers', peasants' and soldiers' hearts with the slogans "Peace to the peoples", "Land to the peasants!" and "Factories to the workers" and was soon given a tumultuous welcome in the city of Petrograd.

Left, Smolny in 1917. **Above**, the Revolution has succeeded.

Revolution: During this wave of social hatred the craze for creating new values was soon replaced by another for redistributing those already in existence. The idea of "constricting" the bourgeoisie resulted in the occupants of basements, sometimes several families at once, moving not only into the mansions of aristocrats but also the apartments of writers, composers, scientists, doctors and university professors. The slogan "Steal what's stolen" turned into an orgy of self-robbery on a hitherto unprecedented scale nationwide.

Here is what Maxim Gorky, a living witness and herald of the Revolution, wrote of

this: "People are stealing in a wonderfully artistic manner: there is no doubt history will describe this process of Russia's self-robbery with the greatest enthusiasm. Churches and military museums are being robbed and sold, cannons, rifles, quartermasters' supplies are being sold, the palaces of grand princes are being stolen, everything plunderable is being plundered, everything sellable is being sold..."

Petrograd lost the treasures of St Petersburg – not only from museums and churches but human ones as well. Gumiliev, the first chairman of the Union of All-Rus-

sian Poets, was executed. Many eminent representatives of the intelligentsia emigrated while they were still able, and a miniature St Petersburg was formed in Paris.

There were also many who stayed behind, including, for instance, Gumiliev's first wife, Anna Akhmatova, the great St Petersburg poet, who said that she clamped her hands over her ears when she heard a voice urging her to leave. Those who had stayed behind tried to preserve St Petersburg in their souls but it had vanished like Atlantis. Many unwittingly turned into snails curled up and hiding in the shells of their memories at a time when, to quote Veniamin Kaverin, "courtiers carried round carrot tea, a bald cashier blew on his chilled hands, and huge black tears fell from stove pipes onto the chilled intelligentsia".

It would be unfair, however, to say that the Revolution merely annihilated everything within its reach. Such was its dual effect that, while irrationally uprooting mighty age-old trees of culture with its feverish breath it also raised from the depths of the earth numerous young shoots, which then stretched towards the Revolution in spellbound wonder.

The writer Victor Shklovsky recalls how, in 1921, the composer Glazunov came to Gorky to ask his help in obtaining a bread ration for a very young musician. Gorky asked, "Is he a violinist – they come young – or a pianist?

"A composer."

"How old is he?"

"Fourteen. He's a music teacher's son. Accompanies films in the Select Cinema. Recently the floor caught fire under his feet but he went on playing... He's brought me his compositions..."

"Any good?"

"No, awful. It's the first music I can't hear when I read the score."

"Why have you come to me, then?"

"I don't like it but that's not the point, the age belongs to this young boy, not me."

"What's his name?"

"Shostakovich."

Petrograd's intelligentsia stopped heating their Dutch stoves decorated with painted tiles because they were uneconomical. Instead they started using homemade iron stoves whose pipes stuck out of windows. Most likely on account of its squatness this oven was nicknamed a *burzhuika* (bourgeois woman). The intelligentsia did not stop creating great art; however, this art reflected that magnificent and awesome epoch of history like an old Venetian mirror tarnished by the smoke and grime of a *burzhuika* stove. One of the geniuses of the revolutionary period was the artist Filonov whose paintings were later heroically saved during the Leningrad siege by his sister.

Pasternak, who attended the First Congress of Soviets in revolutionary Petrograd, gave this eye-witness account of Lenin:

Leningrad: When the NEP was in force (the New Economic Policy that Lenin introduced in 1921 to revive the collapsed economy), it seemed as though old St Petersburg might yet return to Leningrad: private shops, restaurants and variety shows were opened. Once again the streets resounded with the clip-clop of the hooves of dray-horses, which had miraculously not been made into sausage-meat during the Civil War.

The cinemas were showing films starring Adolfe Menjou and Douglas Fairbanks, as well as films by experimental Soviet directors in an entirely new idiom. Censorship in the 1920s was relatively lax, and did not

And suddenly he loomed on the rostrum,
Loomed, even before he had appeared...
And I thought of the origin
Of the age of shackling burdens.
A genius comes, a portent of privileges,
And avenges his departure with
oppression.

Peter's creation was renamed Leningrad after this man. Once Lenin had gone, everything turned out to be as aggressive and vengeful as the poet had predicted.

Left, the poet Mayakovsky in 1917. <u>Above</u>, Gorky and literary friends.

apply to the form of works, as it did later. In Leningrad avant-garde artists still held exhibitions, cooperative publishing houses put out the works of Formalist authors and the skinny young Shostakovich, whose music Glazunov could not hear when he read his scores, was now turning into a giant of world music. He had no idea then that the floor was going to catch fire under his feet again, and in a more daunting manner than it had that day in the Select Cinema.

In what could be interpreted as an act of self-preservation, an attempt to fill the void which had been left after the emigration of the St Petersburg intelligentsia, there appeared a brilliant Pleiad of young Leningrad writers known as the Serapion Brethren. Their number included Veniamin Kaverin and Victor Shklovsky (who was quoted earlier in this chapter), Lev Lunz who was later to die in one of Stalin's labour camps, and Nikolai Tikhonov and Konstantin Fedin who were talented in the 1920s but who gradually turned into literary officials. Who could have foreseen then that the intelligentsia would be split, and that not all of its members would be able to withstand the test of fear in a dignified manner?

Later there appeared a group of eccentric

Leningrad reprisals were meted out wholesale. The 30-year-old writer Boris Kornilov was one of the numerous victims of the Revolution which devoured its own offspring. Hailed by Bukharin at the First Congress of Writers as the hope of the nation's poetry, Kornilov was later shot as an enemy of the people in 1938.

Kornilev's ex-wife, the poet Olga Bergholts, also had a tragic life. She was pregnant when she was arrested and was beaten so badly during the interrogations that she suffered a miscarriage. Later, during the Fascist siege of Leningrad, she read her poetry over the radio and appealed for

poets in Leningrad who through their own special brand of naivety or, as they put it, "detachment" succeeded in protecting themselves from the Orwellian animal farm which Leningrad and, indeed, the country's entire life, was gradually becoming. All of them, with the exception of Zabolotsky, were to die in prisons or behind the barbed wire fences of labour camps.

Whereas the authorities of Czarist St Petersburg had dealt with free-thinking writers on an individual basis (Radishchev had been exiled to Siberia; Dostoyevsky had been sentenced to hard labour), in Soviet

courage, in the process becoming one of the city's best-loved heroines. She is the author of the austere lines engraved in the granite and marble war memorials in Leningrad and many other Soviet cities: "No-one is forgotten and nothing is forgotten."

Allow me also to quote one of my own verses here: "Victory has the face of much suffering of Olga Fedorovna Bergholts." This great woman was subsequently denounced during the "witch hunt" in the 1930s which flared up after the murder of Kirov, the leader of the Leningrad Communist Party, in 1934. The murder had been organised on Stalin's secret orders to justify the mass terror which was to follow. Stalin stood by Kirov's coffin and shed crocodile tears, and Zhdanov was elected instead of Kirov – Zhdanov who in 1948 was to become the infamous author of the report in the journals *Zvezda* and *Leningrad*, sanctioning the Party diktat in art and ridiculing the top writers, Akhmatova and Zoshchenko.

His choice of these writers for reprisals was not accidental. The old St Petersburg aristocratic poetry of Akhmatova had infuriated the plebeian ideologists for some time, just as the aspect of an old cathedral infuriates rampant atheists.

low that they could not see otherwise.

Here is how the mind of a Zoshchenko character works: "I was always in sympathy with centrist convictions... Even under War Communism when the NEP was introduced, I did not raise objections... But, by the way, my heart sank in despair when the NEP was introduced. It was like I had a premonition of the sharp changes that lay ahead. And sure enough, under War Communism things were much freer, I mean, where culture and civilisation were concerned. I mean, in the theatre you were free not to take your coat off – you could sit there in whatever you had come in. That's what I call an achievement."

Zhdanov also had a special account to settle with Zoshchenko. In his satirical short stories Zoshchenko had depicted the new masters of old St Petersburg as triumphantly self-assured nonentities and the proud bearers of insolence and ignorance. With deadly precision Zoshchenko had showed how pathetic and miserable these people really were. So convinced were they that they were examples for the whole of humanity to fol-

Left, face of an innocent victim of the blockade and the same generation today. **Above**, today's Leningrad ladies.

The war years: The human species was being destroyed. But then World War II, which in the USSR is called "The Great Patriotic War", demonstrated the phenomenal moral resources of those Russian people who had miraculously survived the relentless war being waged against them by Stalin and his stooges.

Besieged Leningrad became the centre of this morality. The significance of the 900 days and nights of the Leningrad siege was far greater than the 10 days which shook the world in 1917. The diary entries of the little Leningrad girl, Tanya Savicheva, is an epic account of the freezing, starving city's tragedy: "Granny died on 25 Jan… Uncle Aliosha on 10 May… Mummy on 13 May at 7.30 a.m… Everyone's dead… Only Tanya's left…"

A doctor by the name of Samovarova recalls: "They ate all the cats and whatever dogs there were. Men died first because men are brawny, and do not have much fat. Women – even small ones – have a thicker layer of fat. But women also died, even though they were tougher. People turned into old folk because their layer of fat had been destroyed and all their muscles and veins showed through, and they were all

goose-foot rissoles; cabbage-leaf schnitzels; oil-cake liver; fishbone-flour sauce; casein fritters; yeast soup." Children worked at factories to get workers' ration cards. Many of them were so weak with hunger that they were tied to the machines to prevent them from collapsing. When people could stand it no longer, they made soup from wallpaper, leather belts and gloves.

The diary of Yura Ryabinkin, a young Leningrad boy who died of hunger and cold, makes sad reading: "The cold… is driving us out of this room. But there used to be a stove here on which we cooked omelettes, sausages and soup, and mother used to sit at a

terribly flabby. You could tell the cannibals by their glowing pink faces."

A Bechstein piano could be bought for a few loaves of bread. Once again the *burzhuika* stoves came to the rescue of the people of Leningrad. But this time there was no firewood and so they were sometimes heated with antiquarian books and valuable Empire furniture.

The maximum daily bread ration was 125 grammes. Here is the menu of a Leningrad workers' war-time canteen – in summer, what's more, not winter: "Plantain soup; nettle and sorrel purée; beet-leaf rissoles;

table and work far into the night by the light of a lamp… Sometimes the gramophone would play, and there'd be joyful laughter, and we'd have a huge New Year's tree, as high as the ceiling, and we'd light the candles… There'd be piles of sandwiches on the table (with all kinds of fillings!) and lots of sweets and spicy biscuits hanging on the tree (and nobody ate them!)… The flat's empty now. And completely silent. It seems to have frozen and turned into an icicle, and it will only melt in the spring…"

Perhaps, if Yura Ryabinkin had survived, he would have become a fine writer – perhaps even a contributor to this book. The survivors tried to support each other by sharing their last crumbs of food and their hopes. Out of these hopes grew Shostakovich's celebrated symphony which was first performed in the besieged city and was named *The Leningrad*.

Old employees of the Hermitage have this almost incredible but actually true story to tell. When the museum's main paintings were evacuated, the empty frames were inscribed with the artists' names and the titles of their paintings were left in the halls to make it easier to set up the displays again after their return. Servicemen, many of

Ladoga and lorries, often sinking through the ice, brought bread to their besieged compatriots. As soon as Hitler, whose idea it had been to destroy the City on the Neva, was forced to lift the siege, the outcome of the war was decided. Leningrad's Piskaryovskoye Cemetery is a gigantic memorial to the victims of the siege.

Gogol has described Nevsky Prospekt thus: "There is nothing better than Nevsky Prospekt, in St Petersburg at least: it is everything for it. What isn't this street, our capital's pride, blessed with?" More sceptical of the beauty of St Petersburg-Leningrad, the present Mayor, Sobchak, has set up an

whom were not from Leningrad, came to see this wonderful museum before they left for the front. Guides took them round the freezing cold halls and, in front of the empty frames, did their best to describe the beauty and grandeur of the paintings which had hung there before the war.

Despite the Fascist bombings the "Way of Life" was opened across the icebound Lake

Left, Shostakovich working on his Seventh Symphony in besieged Leningrad, 1941. Above, Soviet soldier buying a ticket for the premier of Shostakovich's Leningrad Symphony in 1942.

international restoration fund. Despite its dilapidation, this city is still uniquely beautiful and it would be an irreplaceable loss if the city were to be destroyed by neglect.

Europe without Leningrad is unimaginable. As Dostoyevsky wrote of Moscow and St Petersburg: "What, indeed, would seem more contradictory than St Petersburg and Moscow. From a theoretical viewpoint, St Petersburg was, in principle, founded, as it were, in contrast with Moscow and its entire concept. And yet these two centres of Russian life essentially constitute a single centre..." It could scarcely be better put.

Moscow is in the middle of Russia. But the physical heart, St Petersburg, built by Emperor Peter I in the northwest corner of the country, was conceived as – and indeed became – a window into Europe. Window: a dwelling's eye; the eye is in the head. Hence St Petersburg is the head and the mind, while Moscow is the heart and the soul. They also call Moscow the mother and St Petersburg the father of Russia.

A city of stone: Russia, as one contemporary writer put it, is, for the most part, a land of "dissipated being", an endless expanse. Suddenly, almost three centuries ago, it got the totally uncharacteristic city of stone (*petra* means stone in Greek; *burg* is German for fortress). St Petersburg became the fist, the swordpoint, the transceiver tuned in to Europe and the waves of Western influence, the collector of raw Russian power, which civilisation harnessed and communicated to the world at large. This, by the way, is the reason why the Revolution could only have started here – as a response to the West.

It would be wrong to think of St Petersburg, then or now, as synonymous with Russia. Yet the rest of the country would not be Russia without St Petersburg. Russia, as the author Georgy Gachev remarked, "is realised as a permanent dialogue between St Petersburg and Rus".

An ancient trade route: The Neva was Russia's traditional outlet into the Baltic. A thousand years before the city was founded, Lake Nevo (Ladoga) was the northern border of the territories of the Ilmen Slavs, the tribe that lived on the banks of the River Volkhov, Lake Ilmen and the rivers that flowed into it. The Volkhov, which connected Ilmen and Ladoga, was the main route from the Varangians to the Greeks, as the chronicles called it, the route that started on the Neva and ended in the mouth of the

Dnieper, on the coast of the Black Sea. This is not merely a legend: recently, in the area of Leningrad's Galley Harbour, where "guests from beyond the sea" were received in the old days, a buried treasure – a collection of 11th-century coins – was found.

Early in the 11th century, these northern lands, known as Upper Rus, were claimed by the united state of the Eastern Slavs, the Kievan Rus. Its borders ran to the banks of the Neva and the rapids of the Dnieper, and

Russian ambassadors visited the courts of the emperors of Byzantium and the State of the Franks in the 830s.

Nevsky's times: The young state soon entered a time of internal strife and fell apart. Upper Rus no longer belonged to Kiev – it was now part of Novgorod, an autonomous state where Karels and Finns lived together with Slavs. Roughly at the same time, these lands saw the first conflicts between Rus and Sweden, which continued for the next seven centuries, with success passing from side to side (the final war ended in 1809 after Russia annexed Finland). The first famous battle

Preceding pages: the Decembrist uprising of 1825. <u>Left</u>, the face of a stern ruler, Czar Peter the Great. <u>Above</u>, Alexander Nevsky, the ancient hero of Rus.

took place 750 years ago on the Neva; Birger, the earl of Sweden, was routed by Alexander, the prince of Novgorod, who is known in the country's history as Alexander Nevsky ("of the Neva").

Villages in the delta: To undermine the resistance they encountered from Novgorod, the Swedes built the Landscrona fort on the Neva in 1300. The Russians destroyed it and built, in 1323, a fort of their own – Oreshek. The fort, which stood further inland on the Neva, was part of the northern defensive chain of Muscovy together with Ivangorod, Ladoga, Yamburg and Koporye (Muscovy annexed Novgorod in 1471–78).

forts were claimed by Sweden. On the site where Landscrona once stood, the Swedes built a new fort, Niensants.

Reconquering the land of the fathers: By the end of the 17th century the Swedes controlled the entire Baltic Sea, whose shores belonged to the feudal absolutist Swedish Kingdom. This both irritated Russia and contradicted the interests of other countries. In 1700, Russia, Denmark, Poland and Saxony started a war against Sweden. The goal of Peter the Great's Northern War was to reclaim the lands of the "fathers and grandfathers", the old Russian forts and outlets to the Baltic.

By the 16th century, there were several dozen villages (over 1,000 houses in all) in the delta of the Neva. The village of Spasskoye stood where the Smolny Palace was later built; the village of Palenikha was situated where Liteiny Prospekt runs today. There were two villages on the bank of Bezymenny Erik (Fontanka) – Usadische and Kalinkina (the latter gave its name to Kalinkin Bridge); further up the river Neva lay the villages of Verkhny and Nizhny (Upper and Lower) Dubok.

After Russia, under Ivan the Terrible, lost the war of Livonia (1558–83), the northern

Undaunted by early defeats, Peter proceeded to renovate old fortifications, replenish the armed forces and create an artillery force almost from scratch. In November 1702, Noteburg (Oreshek) fell to the Russians after a 30-hour assault. Peter gave the fort a new name, both sufficiently belligerent and understandable to his enemies – *Schlüsselburg* (Key Town). On 1 May, 1703, the Russians took Niensants. They now controlled the entire length of the Neva: Russia held the "key" and the "lock" to the Baltic Sea.

The founding of the city: But to "stand on

shore with steady foot", these forts were clearly not enough. In the search for a new and more reliable stronghold, the Czar explored the isles in the Neva. A site was chosen in the delta, on the small Hare Island. Here, on 16 May 1703, Peter founded the new Russian fort, which he named Saint Peter Burgh. That autumn, over 120 cannons were installed on its bastions; in November, the fort was visited by the first peaceful merchantman sailing from the Netherlands.

From the first, Peter wanted his creation to be grandiose and glamorous: in the autumn of 1704, he wrote to his closest supporter, Alexander Menshikov, that he was going to

tumn of 1705. Its shipyard became the first enterprise in St Petersburg and the birthplace of Russia's first "sea-going" battleship, the 54-cannon *Poltava*. The Admiralty became the gravity centre for urban construction, which started with 100 *izbas* (cottages) for naval officers. On the right bank of the Neva, not far from the fort, was Peter's own house or log cabin (built in 1703 and surviving to this day), made of squared logs painted to resemble brick. Not far away, in Troitskaya Square, the builders erected a wooden cathedral. Several hundred wooden stores made up the Gostiny Dvor. The first streets of the city's early settlements (Pushkarskaya,

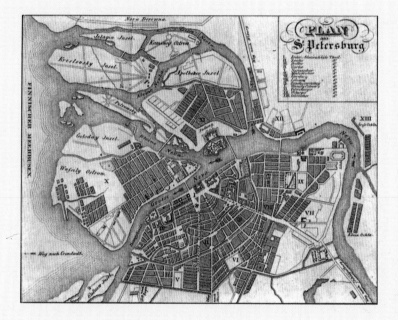

his "capital Peterburgh". Meanwhile, the Swedes still threatened the fortress from land and sea. But not for long: several years before the end of the Northern War, the Russians seized all lands to the north and west of the fortress within at least a 100-km (60-mile) radius; from the sea, the mouth of the Neva was protected by Fort Kronshlot on Kotlin Island (later to become the sea fortress Kronstadt).

The Admiralty was completed in the au-

Ruzheinaya, Grebetskaya and Rybatskaya) were oriented towards the fortress. Many streets in the district still bear their original historic names.

The early years: In the autumn of 1703, the number of workers sent to St Petersburg from various Russian towns reached 20,000. This figure doubled the following year. But the city needed trained construction workers. Peter issued a decree concerning the "eternal settlement" of masons, brick-layers, carpenters, metalworkers, joiners, tailors and book-keepers in St Petersburg. These workers were given houses and veg-

Left, Ivan III and Tartars at the court. <u>Above</u>, plan of St Petersburg, early 1800s.

etable plots. Roughly 1,500 of them came every year; in the end, they formed the basis of the city's working population. There were also hired hands, soldiers and Swedish prisoners-of-war. In the beginning, construction was headed by the first governor of St Petersburg, Alexander Menshikov, and the city's first architect, Domenico Trezzini.

In 1710, construction work began on the Church of Isaac Dalmatsky. That same year, the Alexander Nevsky Monastery was founded. The opening cut in the woods between the Admiralty and the monastery, was called Great Perspective (Nevsky). In 1712, Trezzini started work on the stone Peter-and-

largest industrial enterprise. To the east of the Foundry lay the Tar Yard, which produced tar for the Admiralty.

The Capital of the North: St Petersburg became the capital in 1712, when the Imperial Court moved from Moscow to the banks of the Neva. Several months later, the Senate, too, moved there (the Senate was a collegiate body that succeeded the Boyar Duma). Young Russia celebrated victories not only on the field of battle, it also carried out fundamental internal reforms which ushered in a new era of development.

Construction was booming. Peter himself presided over construction work on the

Paul Cathedral inside the fortress. As the cathedral rose above the ground, the fortress gradually became known as Peter-and-Paul.

Next came the turn of private residences. Menshikov ordered a magnificent three-storey stone palace with a large garden on Vasilievsky Island. The Summer Palace was built on the left bank of the Neva for Peter himself. The Summer Garden surrounded the palace. On the same bank, but closer to the Admiralty, a winter palace was built for the Czar (not to be confused with today's Winter Palace!). Further upstream, there was the Foundry – St Petersburg's second

Vyborg Side, Vasilievsky Island and at Peterhof and Oranienbaum (his summer palaces and parks). In 1714, almost 10 million bricks were produced for the city. Yet more was needed, and Peter banned construction in stone all over the country with the sole exception of St Petersburg. Masons and other "artists of the building trade" were sent to the new capital by force.

Many foreigners were invited. Architect Jean-Batiste Leblond, stucco-moulder Bartholomeo Carlo Rastrelli, oak-carver Nicolas Pinaud, fitter Jean Michel, caster Pierre Sauvage, metal-worker Theodore

Belen, masons Bethalier and Cardasier, and many others. Each of them was given a shop with 10 Russian apprentices. This turned St Petersburg into a unique training centre for builders, who were shown the most advanced methods and absorbed the latest word in their trade. Progressive ideas stood behind the general plan of the city, notably the master layout of the "House of Nobles". Stone edifices designed by Leblond (which have mostly been redesigned since then) are still regarded as the architectural backbone of many of the older quarters, with the matchless rhythm and harmony of Leblond's proportions.

Russia gained the right to join the circle of northern countries, traditional exporters of timber, leather, lard, fish, grain, and iron (Tula factories produced up to 800,000 pods of pig iron). Peter's Persian War (1722) strengthened Russia's presence on the Caspian Sea, with its trade routes connecting Central Asia and Western Europe.

But exports and the transit of Oriental goods were not the only factors of the economic boom in Russia. The country now had a well-developed industry. The number of industrial enterprises grew more than tenfold during Peter's reign and most of these innovative and previously unheard-of facto-

The Northern War ended in victory for the Russians in 1721. It lasted for over two decades and cost Russia the lives of 40,000 soldiers and at least 70,000 civilians. But the country did not pay this terrible price in vain: the gap between the Middle Ages and the new times was bridged. Russia emerged as a developed and mighty European power.

Industrial development: With outlets to the Baltic Sea and lands to the north of St Petersburg providing access to the Baltic Region,

The architects of St Petersburg: left, Rastrelli and Veldten, above, Quarenghi and Rossi.

ries were concentrated in St Petersburg.

The scale of reform, which taxed Russia's strength to the limit (Peter often fought barbarity with utter ruthlessness), bred a new ideology, created new economic and political needs and promoted the dynamic development of education, science and culture – primarily in the new capital.

In 1711, the first print shop was opened in St Petersburg, producing the country's first newspaper, *Vedomosti*. Peter's library was moved to St Petersburg from Moscow. It was opened to the public. Next door, a collection of rarities was on display – the first museum in town (the Kunstkammer). The volume of printed matter grew 20 times in Peter's lifetime. Ninety percent of this output was secular literature concerning navigation, shipbuilding, mathematics and medicine as well as calendars, manuals and translations from foreign languages.

Many hitherto unknown things came to Russia: new uniforms and new firearms for the regular army regiments, huge naval vessels, libraries, a public theatre, museums and the Academy of Sciences, parks and park sculpture, fountains and canals, "exemplary houses" and the avenues of St Petersburg, new clothes, new manners and a new style

ferred from St Petersburg back to Moscow – but for a short time only. Then the officers of the Guard put Peter's daughter, Empress Elizabeth, on the throne.

The rise of the gentry: Meanwhile, the gentry was expanding its influence, particularly its right to own estates and serfs, and concentrated on ridding itself of the rigidly proscribed duty (in accordance with Peter's decree) of state service. The gentry won the day: *On Bestowing Liberty to the Gentry of Russia,* the manifesto signed by Elizabeth's successor, Peter III, finally freed them of state duties. This essentially turned the gentry into a class of parasites, which controlled

for daily intercourse, amusements and festivities. It was only natural that all these novelties were more concentrated in the new capital than at any other place in Russia.

The post-Peter years: Unfortunately, many of Peter's projects fell under the shadow of oblivion with his death in 1725. In a little more than 14 years, Russia had four monarchs: Catherine I (Peter's last wife), Peter II (his grandson), Anna Ioannovna (his niece) and the infant Ivan Antonovich (Anna's nephew). Every time the throne stood empty, political rivalry split opposing groups of gentry. At one point the capital was trans-

the entire might of the empire's military-bureaucratic machine. Their positions grew stronger with each new military success: the war for the Black Sea with Turkey in 1735–39, the war for Finland with Sweden in 1741–43, the Seven-Year War with Prussia in 1756–63.

By the middle of the 18th century the population of St Petersburg reached the 100,000 mark (less than 40 percent were women). There were 2,000 aristocrats, as many merchants, and entire quarters filled with foreigners – Englishmen lived on the Neva behind St Isaac's Church, Germans and Frenchmen on Vasilievsky Island, and Italians between Sadovaya, Nevsky and the Fontanka. The first floating bridge across the Neva was put into place in 1727; several decades later, the city had 40 bridges spanning its assorted rivers and canals.

A centre of art and science: St Petersburg attracted financial capital, wealthy clients and the "educated class" of the imperial court. It also offered a unique opportunity for architects, artists, actors and scientists. The court orchestra appeared in 1729; many aristocrats kept orchestras and choirs of their own. In the 1730s, an opera and ballet theatre was put together in the imperial palace. In 1738 ballet-master Jacques Landais opened a ballet school which founded the famous Russian tradition of choreography. In 1756, there appeared The Russian Theatre for Comedies and Tragedies (it was founded by actor Fyodor Volkov and its first director was Alexander Sumarokov, the famous poet and playwright).

It was at that time, in the middle of the century, that Mikhail Lomonosov, the "father of Russian science", reached his prime. He was a professional chemist, mathematician, physicist, geologist, astronomer, botanist, philosopher and historian. He made important discoveries in metallurgy, mining, the production of glass, porcelain and dyes. He was the author of *Russian Grammar*, the mastermind behind "Russian classicism". He and his supporter, Count Ivan Shuvalov (who helped Lomonosov found the Moscow University in 1755), initiated the creation of a new centre of education and the arts – the "Academy of the Three Noblest Arts" – painting, sculpture and architecture in St Petersburg.

Catherine the Great: In 1762, Peter III was removed from the throne after another palace coup. The reins of power passed into the hands of his wife, Catherine II, the daughter of an insignificant German landowner. Catherine ruled Russia for a third of a century. She presided over the retrieval of Byelorussian and Ukrainian lands from Poland and over the war with Turkey, which

gave Russia the Crimea and the northern coast of the Black Sea. Georgia and Armenia asked for Russia's protection. The empire spread over 17 million square kilometres, and its population topped 28 million.

St Petersburg, the political centre of Russia, was turning into one of its largest cities. By the end of the century, it had a population of 220,000, and it remained on a par with Moscow until the 1930s.

New enterprises were under way – Berd's Iron Foundry, Potyomkin's Glass Factory, the Admiralty's giant Izhorsky Complex. The number of hired workers grew, even though a third of the population of the capital

was made up of bureaucrats and army and navy officers. The growing might of the state was adequately represented by the majesty of monumental architecture. Cultural life, science and education thrived. In 1764, the country's first educational establishment for women, the Smolny Institute, was founded. In 1774, the Mining College was opened and in 1783 the popular pedagogical school. New educational establishments, academies, theatres and libraries all required buildings which would reflect the ideals of the "enlightened monarchy", notably its devotion to "universal well-being". The stern

Left, Petrodvorets' Golden Hill cascade. **Above**, Peter III.

and majestic classical architecture, which replaced mid-century baroque, expressed these socio-aesthetic ideals with the utmost elegance and simplicity.

Stone embankments were built on the Neva and the Fontanka. The Hermitage buildings went up near the Winter Palace. Creations by Yury Felten, Antonio Rinaldi, Jean Batiste Vallen de la Mothe and Giacomo Quarenghi were numerous and pleasantly different. In 1782, St Petersburg got what is probably its most famous masterpiece – the *Bronze Horseman* (the statue of Peter the Great). In this way, the end of the century produced the unique, majestic and

beautiful city known as the Northern Palmyra – the symbol of eternal values, expressed through architecture.

The new century: Emperor Pavel ascended the throne in 1796. He felt a profound hatred for the memory of his empress mother. During his short reign, he made spasmodic attempts to restore the austere might of Peter's epoch in new social conditions, to turn the gentry into a mechanically exact, powerful apparatus, which could successfully face a revolution comparable to the one in France. The gentry responded with yet another conspiracy: no sooner had the emperor moved to

his new, impenetrable Mikhailovsky Castle than he was assassinated in the early hours of 3 March 1801. His son, Alexander, ascended the throne, and with his succession Russia entered the 19th century.

The liberalism and reformist intentions of Alexander's first decade on the throne and his profound belief in the firmness of the Russian monarchy were reflected in an architecture of grandiose proportions and serene beauty. Outstanding architects, with their new understanding of the city ensemble, aimed for openness and organic harmony with the city's layout. St Petersburg gained the ensemble on the tip of Vasilievsky Island (de Thomon), the new Admiralty (Andreyan Zakharov), and the Kazan Cathedral in Nevsky Prospekt (Andrei Voronikhin); it was from this monument to Russian military glory on 11 August 1812, that Count Mikhail Kutuzov, who had been appointed commander-in-chief, left to join his army; it was here that the remains of the great general were buried after the war with Napoleon had been won.

Mirror of the Czars' might: The 1812 war, in which a 14,000-strong volunteer corps from St Petersburg took part, unleashed an unprecedented wave of patriotism. The victory over Napoleon, the victorious march of the Russian army, and the taking of Paris boosted Russia's international prestige. The new phase of construction in St Petersburg was marked by growing national sentiment. It was the time for "High Classicism", the art which, as the greatest master of the school, Carlo Rossi put it, "was designed to leave everything that Europeans of our era created far behind in its majesty".

The city that elevated all spheres of human endeavour to unprecedented heights now expressed itself in the perfect harmony of architectural masterpieces. The rare compatibility of expanses of water and open spaces, the balanced novelty of architecture and the unforgettable light of white nights made St Petersburg, the world's northernmost capital, one of the most beautiful cities ever seen by the human eye. The city reminds you of its might with every step you take. Helmets, shields and javelins are ubiquitous ornaments on the innumerable walls of palaces and administrative buildings. They are repeated on the rich facades of private mansions. Laurel wreaths and military symbols are often incorporated into iron grilles. St Petersburg would allow no one to forget that it was the capital of the empire, the seat of the all-powerful sovereign.

And if a foreigner chanced to find himself in this Russian city and marvelled in awe at the poverty of the serfs who wore straw *lapti* on their feet, there were usually clever people to tell him, "Don't be fooled, stranger! These poor serfs will take to the axe if another Napoleon tries to burn down their wooden huts again. Don't be fooled, stranger, when you admire the nature of Russia, don't be fooled by the slow, unhurried flow of Russian rivers, by the eternal calm of the endless Russian steppe…"

St Petersburg is the mirror of the Czars' might. Canals cross its straight paved streets, and the waters of the Neva wash the granite of its quays. All this gives the city the appearance of a northern Amsterdam, the only difference being that there are no windmills, no ephemeral European-ness of scenery. The walls of the luxurious palaces, arranged into architectural ensembles as if by someone's divine hand, are washed by frequent rains. Low clouds hang over the city like a threatening omen.

The city is rich, proud, haughty in the Czar's way. The iron grilles, lace made of metal, illustrate the skills of the people who made them. Yet they speak nothing of freedom and airiness. The entrances to many edifices have stone arches, yet their only purpose is to commemorate a military or triumphal peace.

Austerity, geometric harmony and military might are the distinctions of this city. This frowning force cannot be made friendlier even by the domes of innumerable cathedrals, resplendent in their gold attire. Poets and dreamers have not found life comfortable here. They have looked at the city with a stranger's eye, listening to the wind howl around the spacious parks and seeing relentless Father Time march by. Only poets

daydream of different worlds, different skies, different suns; the aristocrats, the golden favourites of fate, found this city cozy and snug – it was theirs. Yet not all of them thought this way.

There was no other place where social contrasts were felt so acutely. In the golden epoch of aristocratic culture, the apex of clamour and splendour, protests thundered in St Petersburg, voices which condemned the evils of serfdom and monarchy, voices which brought the Revolution to life. In 1816, the "Union of Salvation" was founded in St Petersburg by radical officers, veterans of the 1812 war. The goal of this small secret

society was to destroy monarchy, adopt a constitution and eliminate serfdom.

Two years after that, there appeared the "Union of Prosperity", which had as many as 200 members. In 1820, after riots in the Semyonovsky Regiment and the government's vicious reprisals, the leaders of the union dissolved it, and formed a secret society in its place. The "North Society" was set up in St Petersburg in 1821, and its counterpart, the "South Society", appeared somewhat later in the south of the country.

The Decembrists: Emperor Alexander died late in 1825. The members of both societies

Left, Napoleon in Moscow. **Above**, the victorious Alexander I.

decided to play upon the indecision in the highest corridors of power concerning the nomination of a successor to the throne. The coup was planned for 14 December 1825. On that day, the Decembrists fired the first shot against czarism in Senatskaya Square behind the statue of the *Bronze Horseman.* They lost. The leaders were executed on the wall of the Peter-and-Paul Fortress on 13 July 1826 – Pavel Pestel, Kondratiy Ryleev, Piotr Kakhovsky, Sergei Muraviev-Apostol, and Mikhail Bestuzhev-Riumin. That year, the Emperor Nicholas created the ominous Third Department of his Chancellery; the *gendarmes* in its employment started their

by well-trained worker cadres and supervised by professional engineers.

The first steam engine was installed in the Admiralty in 1800. The first steamship, the *Yelizaveta,* came out of the shipyards in 1815. The Kronstadt Iron Mill was transferred to St Petersburg in 1801; known as Putilovsky and later Kirovsky, the mill is still the city's largest enterprise.

The first locomotive was produced in 1845. St Petersburg was also the first city involved in the railroad business. Russia's first railway connected the capital with the suburbs – Tsarskoye Selo and Pavlovsk – and opened in the autumn of 1837; in 1851,

campaign of terror which struck against freedom of thought in Russia.

The total domination of the empire's military-bureaucratic machine, whose only purpose was to perpetuate serfdom, should have stopped the process of economic, political and cultural development in a country racked by profound conflicts, conflicts that were especially apparent in the capital. Yet it did not, and St Petersburg evolved to become the industrial centre of backward, feudal Russia, the national leader in many industries. Its enterprises were frequently equipped to state-of-the-art level, manned

the Moscow to St Petersburg railway came into operation. At the same time, the city gained its first cast-iron bridge across the Neva (today called Lieutenant Schmidt's Bridge).

Industry and transportation required qualified engineers. In 1828, the St Petersburg Technological Institute opened its doors, followed by the Civilian Engineers' School four years later. The Academy of Sciences opened new branches. The Pulkovo Observatory (located near today's Leningrad international airport) was opened in 1839. In 1842, there came another important scientific event – the foundation of the Depot of Standard Measures and Weights (where the famed Dmitry Mendeleev, the father of the periodic table, worked later). During these years, such greats as Alexander Pushkin, Mikhail Lermontov, Nikolai Gogol and Mikhail Glinka lived and worked in St Petersburg.

St Petersburg's magazines – especially *Sovremennik* and *Otechestvennye Zapiski* – printed heated articles by the new generation of revolutionaries, the men who founded the revolutionary-democratic movement in Russia: Vissarion Belinsky, Nikolai Dobroliubov and Nikolai Chernyshevsky. Liter-

ary criticism, which was a legal form of expression, was used, in effect, to criticise the social order. As new revolutionary ideas spread, underground circles appeared. The Czar took immediate action. In 1849, for instance, a mock execution was staged for the 21 members of Petrashevsky's circle on the parade-ground of the Semenovsky Regiment in St Petersburg. Among them was 21-year-old Fyodor Dostoyevsky, who was condemned to forced labour.

Left, the Neva embankment during the 1800s. **Above**, Alexander II, who was later assassinated.

In 1855, shortly before the fall of Sevastopol, the largest Russian fortress on the Black Sea, Nicholas I died in his Peterhof residence. Before he died the emperor observed the ships of the British fleet, which were blocking Kronstadt, on the horizon. Russia was about to lose the Crimean War – "payment", as Russian historian Sergei Soloviev put it, "for 30 years of lies, 30 years of suppressing everything that had life and spirit, of popular force."

Times of terror: A new stage of the struggle for liberty started in the 1850s and the 1860s. It was marked by mass activity, a change of leaders (from aristocrats to people of common origins, democratic-minded intellectuals and students). The government of Alexander II was forced to proceed with reforms, which had the effect of opening the way for capitalist development in Russia yet preserved the foundations of authoritarian rule intact. Serfdom was abolished; administrative management reorganised; self-management was allowed at grass-roots level; a judicial reform was carried out.

Yet society wanted more: the government lost popularity and appeared more and more conservative. *Narodniks* (populists) tried to provoke a peasant uprising through terrorism. In April 1866, Dmitry Karakozov, a student, attempted to shoot the Czar near the wall of the Summer Garden. He failed, but there was no stopping the revolutionary terrorists. This upsurge of tragic heroism was accompanied by the birth and gradual development of an organised proletarian movement: the working class was becoming conscious of its decisive role in history.

The first worker leaders in St Petersburg did not yet dissociate their goals and means from the populists' terror tactics. In February, 1880, Stepan Khalturin placed a bomb in the Czar's apartment in the Winter Palace. The emperor once again, miraculously, escaped death. One year later, however, on 1 March 1881, the death sentence passed on the Czar by the populists was carried out. On the embankment of Yekaterininsky (now Griboyedov) Canal, he was mortally wounded in a bomb attack; the blast also killed his assassin, Ignaty Grinetsky. Six years after that, on 1 March 1887, the conspirators who were preparing to assassinate Alexander III were arrested and executed. Among them was Alexander Ulianov, Lenin's elder brother.

Lenin himself first emerged as a political activist in St Petersburg in 1895, when he presided over the creation of the "Union for the Struggle to Liberate the Working Class", which later evolved into the proletariat's revolutionary party.

The Revolution draws close: The defeat suffered by Russia in the war against Japan (1904–05) accelerated the Revolution. On 2 January 1905, the workers of St Petersburg's Putilovsky Factory went on strike. This grew

duced 15 percent of the national industrial output. The capital had almost 600 banks; 40 percent of the capital invested there belonged to monopolies.

Art flourishes: Spiritual life was also full of contradictions and tension. It assumed a great many forms. The Russian Museum was opened in 1897. Its creative approach to the artistic heritage brought the artists into the centre of public attention – including the works of Alexander Benua, Konstantin Somov, Yevgeny Lansere, Mikhail Dobuzhinsky. Traditional painting by Ilya Repin and Valentin Serov was still quite popular. The radical left-wingers rallied around the

into a general strike by 8 January. On 9 January ("Bloody Sunday"), a peaceful worker's demonstration was met by gunfire. The first barricades appeared that same day. The first Russian Revolution had begun. It lasted for two years and covered the entire country. Nothing was gained. Reaction and police terror set in.

By 1913, the volume of industrial production had increased tenfold over the previous 50 years; the city's 1,000 factories and plants employed half a million people, of whom 70 percent worked at enterprises employing more than 500 persons. St Petersburg pro-

"Youth Union" and its stars – Kasimir Malevich and Vasily Kandinsky. Plays by Anton Chekhov, Maxim Gorky and Leonid Andreev enjoyed immense popularity. The stage of the Mariinsky (now the Kirov) Theatre was graced by Fyodor Shaliapin and Leonid Sobinov, Anna Pavlova and Matilda Kseshinskaya. Russian music was enriched by the works of Alexander Glazounov, Alexander Scriabin and Sergei Rachmaninov.

The search for new forms and decisions in modern-style architecture, and the development of the St Petersburg architectural tradition by the neoclassicists (which continued

even after the Revolution) brought new architectural solutions, and these served to determine the image and layout of the city for the following decades.

World War I became history's great accelerator. St Petersburg was in the centre of things (it was then given the more Russian name of Petrograd). The ruling circles were losing their hold on power, workers and the other have-nots lived in want and the bourgeoisie got rich on manufacturing supplies for the military. The war took more and more lives, fuelling pacifist and revolutionary sentiment among the workers. In 1917, they numbered 400,000.

In 1916, the revolutionary movement in Petrograd became a tangible threat to czarism; in 1917, Russia was caught in a nationwide crisis, which led to the bourgeois democratic revolution in February. Emperor Nicholas II abdicated. The country was ruled by two entities, the bourgeois Provisional Government and the Soviets of Workers', Soldiers' and Peasants' Deputies.

The Bolshevik coup: Lenin returned to the city in April, and immediately called the

Left, the last Czar, Nicolas II. Above, Lenin's face by Ilja Glasunov (1984).

workers and peasants to struggle for a socialist revolution. The conditions for this revolution were ripe by autumn. On 24 October (6 November, according to the modern calender), an armed struggle for power began. The Bolsheviks ordered soldiers and workers from the Red Guard to take control of bridges, the telegraph system, railway stations, and the central power station.

The next morning Lenin, who headed the uprising from the Bolshevik headquarters in Smolny Institute, and Leon Trotsky, the head of the Petrosoviet, ordered the State Bank and the central telephone exchange to be seized. The shot from the revolutionary battleship *Aurora* on the evening of 25 October signalled the beginning of the attack on the Winter Palace, where the Provisional Government was meeting. The palace was taken, and the majority of delegates to the Second Congress of Soviets, which convened in Smolny, adopted Lenin's *Decree on Peace* and *Decree on Land*.

This congress also elected the new Executive Council and the soviet that was to govern the country – the Council of People's Commissars, chaired by Lenin.

In January 1918, the commissars dispersed the Constituent Assembly, which worked for one day only (the Bolsheviks did not have a majority there); the new state system was then legalised by the Third Congress of Soviets at the end of January.

On 6–8 March 1918, the Seventh Congress of the Communist Party convened in Petrograd. Lenin addressed the congress no fewer than 18 times. He managed to come out on top of the heated debate: the Brest peace with Germany, Austro-Hungary, Bulgaria and Turkey, which was concluded on 3 March, was approved. This was the last party congress to take place in Petrograd – on 10 March the government and all central authorities moved to Moscow, which once again became the capital of Russia.

Soviet times: The city of three revolutions, Petrograd remained at the front edge of the revolutionary struggle. The people of Petrograd fought on all the fronts of the three-year civil war. In May and October, 1919, they managed to defend their city from advancing White Guard volunteers.

But Petrograd took a long time to heal its war wounds. Where there were 2.5 million people in February 1917, only 740,000 remained in 1920.

In January 1924, after Lenin's death, Petrograd was renamed Leningrad. From the first days of socialist construction, the working people of Leningrad were in the front ranks. In 1925, Leningrad started producing the first Soviet tractors. The first generator for Volkhov Power Station, the first in the ambitious chain planned for the entire nation, was manufactured here. That year, the country's first palace of culture was built in Leningrad. Together with new housing, the

palace became an illustration of how Soviet power planned to implement its principles of social justice.

Leningrad factories became a school of advanced methods involved in new, ultracomplex industries. In 1931, the first Soviet blooming mill was manufactured at the Izhorsk plant. The Kozitsky Factory produced the first Soviet TV set in 1936 (mass production started in 1947). The city grew and prospered, and the new residential areas embodied the principles of socialist urban construction. Late in the 1930s, a development plan was put together for Leningrad.

Times of war and suffering: In 1939, the population topped 3 million. But their peaceful labours were jeopardised by war. In the winter of 1939–40 Leningrad became a frontline town: a mere 25 km (16 miles) to the north lay the Finnish border. The USSR's proposals to exchange territories were rejected, and a difficult winter war began. The USSR was the aggressor, difficult as it may be to admit. In March, 1940, a peace treaty was signed with Finland, in accordance with which the border was relocated to over 100 km (62 miles) from Leningrad.

On 22 June 1941, Germany invaded the USSR, starting what is known in Russia as the Great Patriotic War. On 18 July 1941, the first Nazi bombs fell on Leningrad. The first German artillery attack came on 4 September. On 8 September the blockade of Leningrad began, a 900-day struggle the likes of which history had not known.

Hitler's group of armies code-named "North" (30 divisions) stopped and formed a 200-km (125-mile) siege ring around the unbending, impenetrable city. The enemy dropped over 100,000 bombs and fired 150,000 artillery shells. The death toll was 16,747; 33,728 were wounded. Hunger killed 641,803. Another 716,000 were left without roofs over their heads. But the foot of an enemy soldier never stepped into Leningrad. This thought gave life and strength to the exhausted people, who were always hungry and cold, yet did not stop working.

The blockade was broken only in January, 1943. Another a full year passed before the soldiers of the Leningrad front finally routed the Germans late in January 1944.

Leningrad's industry and municipal facilities were quickly repaired and restored. By 1948, the city's industry had reached the prewar level, which was exceeded 2½ times by 1955. At that time, Leningrad had 250 large enterprises. Its research and cultural potential consisted of 300 research institutes, 46 colleges, 96 technical colleges and 420 secondary schools, 19 theatres, over 60 cinemas, 125 palaces of culture and clubs, 48 museums and over 620 mass libraries. The city was coming back to life, and growing.

In the first two decades after the war, 18 million square metres (200 million sq. ft) of housing space were built in Leningrad – more than during the entire history of the city before 1917. In the ensuing five years, an additional 11 million square metres (120 million sq. ft) were added. In 1955, the first subway line was opened. The city reclaimed its position as the country's biggest industrial and cultural centre after Moscow.

Present times: The past decades of Soviet history have left their mark on Leningrad, which has been reduced to the state of a rank-and-file provincial centre with its habitual decay, poverty and drab everyday life. Architectural monuments fall apart, dirt mars even the central avenues, there are empty

architect of perestroika, changed the game again. But, as ever, the inherent optimism of the Russian people refuses to be quenched.

The first real changes for the better have already taken place. Let us mention only one of these changes – the ambitious yet quickly fulfillable task of restoring Leningrad and making it the USSR's foremost centre for foreign tourism. A special fund has already been set up with millions in foreign, primarily American, capital. There are plans for dozens of projects, including the restoration of historic buildings and the construction of new hotels. The people of Leningrad begin to feel their spirits rise. Leningrad is working

stores and angry people – all this becomes apparent to any visitor who come to see the Palmyra of the North. Yet the city, despite everything, survives. And just as perestroika gave the country a new lease on life (or hopes for a new life, in any case), so Leningrad developed several hopeful signs of the coming resurrection. The signs are still faint, and many hopes faltered after August 1991's attempted coup on Mikhail Gorbachev, the

Left, Stalin, the initiator of a reign of terror.
Above, Boris Yeltsin confronts Mikhail Gorbachev after the 1991 coup attempt.

towards the restoration of its former glory as a great city, a city open to all the best that Western civilisation has to offer. It looks to the future with growing confidence.

In the light of this, it seems possible to believe in the words of what Dmitry Likhachev, who is probably the most famous celebrity living in Leningrad today (and who writes in this book). He has said that "Leningrad is destined to replay its role as a window into Europe." The people of Leningrad have never lost a sense that that is their historic role, ordained by the visionary founder of their city, Peter the Great.

Notes Of A Blockade Survivor

*Memories of the 1941–43 siege by the writer and historian **Lidiya Ginzburg (1902–90)**.*

There was no peace, ever. Even at night. Normally the body should calm down at night, but the fight for warmth continued even in one's sleep. It wasn't that people hadn't the means to keep warm – they certainly piled enough warm things over themselves before going to bed. But this made the body struggle – all these heavy things were quite a load; what is worse, they slipped and constantly fell off. In order to hold the entire pile in place, one had to make insignificant yet ultimately tiring muscular efforts.

One had to train oneself to sleep without moving, with one leg twisted in such a way as to hold the base of the pile. Otherwise everything would relentlessly slide to the floor. Then, the pile, unsteadier than ever, would have to be remade in the dark, freezing room. One could not afford to throw one's arms wide, or to lift one's knees beneath the blanket, or to turn and hide one's face in the pillow. This meant that the body and the nerves never got a complete rest.

People fought for their lives in their own apartments just as polar explorers do in emergencies. In the morning they woke in a sack or in a cave constructed from every conceivable material they could pile up. People woke at four, at five. They managed to get warm during the night. Yet all around, there was cold, which continued to torment them all day long.

Still, people waited with impatience – not even for morning, because morning (light) came much later – no, they waited for a suitable reason to get up together with the beginning of the new day, 6 a.m., when the stores and bakeries opened.

This does not mean that everyone went to the baker's at six in the morning; on the contrary, many tried to stave off the moment

for as long as they could. But the 6 o'clock mark was a comfort line, which brought awareness of new possibilities. In a way, it was the best moment: all the bread of the day is still ahead, yet it is not the reality of the day. Hungry impatience got the upper hand over fear of cold. It pushed people out of their little caves, warmed with their own breath, into the coldness of the rooms. It was easy to get up, much easier than in the life where scrambled eggs were waiting for you and

hardly required a second thought. Later, the transfer grew even simpler – people hardly ever took their clothes off, and the only thing one had to do on waking was to shove one's feet as quickly as possible into the rolled woollen boots standing near the bed.

The typical day started with a visit to the kitchen or the service staircase, where firewood had to be prepared for the temporary stove. Night was only just starting to disperse, and the walls of the building opposite did not yet carry even a hint of their yellow colour; they loomed darkly through the broken glass of the staircase window.

Preceding pages: after an air-raid in 1941. <u>Left</u>, vegetables grew everywhere. <u>Above</u>, relief at the Piskarevsy Memorial.

So one had to work by touch, driving the axe at an angle to the wood, and then striking. Hands were the greatest problem. Fingers tended to close and remain in some chance position. The hand lost its ability to grasp. It could only be used as a paw, a stump or a stick-like tool. People groped in the dark as they collected splinters from the stone floor of the landing, lifting them between two stumps, and placing them in a basket.

The next thing to do was to bring water from the frozen cellar. Ice covered the steps of the laundry, and people slid down on their haunches. On the return trip, they went up with a full bucket, searching for dents in the

negotiate. Far away, a ceiling with an alabaster knob… head thrown backwards, people measured the rise of the staircase, through which they were about to carry the rock-heavy water using sheer willpower.

The day would bring many more spaces. The largest was the space separating one from dinner. The best place for dinner was a departmental canteen, where porridge tasted more like porridge. People would run, spurred on by the cold, through the insultingly beautiful city, snow crackling underfoot. Alongside, other people would run (or crawl – it was always either/or) with bags, with covered dishes suspended from the

icy surface to put the bucket in. A kind of mountaineering exercise.

The resistance of each thing had to be negotiated with one's will and one's body, without intermediate tools or devices. People went down the staircase with empty buckets, and in the broken window could see the narrowing expanse of the yard, which would have to be covered with full buckets on the way back. This sudden realisation of space, its physical reality, bred anguish.

One could rest on the lower steps with full buckets. Head thrown backwards, people measured the height they were about to

ends of their stick-like arms. People would run in the cold, conquering space that had suddenly become material.

The more educated remembered Dante and that circle of his Hell where everything is covered with ice. In the canteen, it is so cold that the fingers that froze in the street will not open; people hold spoons between the thumb (the only digit that works) and the frozen stump.

Dinner itself is another hassle with space; the spaces of dinner are small yet agonisingly condensed with queues of people. A queue before the door, a queue before the inspector, a queue for an empty seat at the table. Dinner is something fleeting and ephemeral (a plate of soup, and so many grammes of porridge). Yet it was overestimated and decelerated in accordance with the classic canons of literary plotting. If asked what they were doing, the people would answer, "We are having dinner".

Then there was a period of successive air raids, which came one after another. On the way to dinner one had to hide in cellars or continue through the noise of the anti-aircraft guns and the whistles of the militia. People hated the militiamen, who saved them from the bombs, and thought of the

closer to the stove and warmed frozen hands. Until the day's supply of splinters burned out, nothing could tear that person away from this exquisite pleasure. In the room behind, cold was raging and darkness reigned. It was only near the small door of the stove that the life-giving circle of light and warmth shone. The circle of life. The only thing one could warm were one's palms. The palms absorbed the flames. It was sheer ecstasy, which was invariably spoiled by the swift end.

It was waiting for the end and the realisation of the ebbing of our vital forces which spoiled any joy and the very sense of life. The

bombing as of something that kept them away from dinner.

Some people left home at eleven in the morning and sometimes came back at six or seven in the evening. It was absolutely dark at home. The stove was lit and, in its smoky light, the soup from the canteen was poured into a pot. Bread was cut into 40-gramme pieces. Then the person who came from the outside world, the world with dinner, moved

Left, warning of shells at the General Staff building. **Above**, the "Way of Life" across frozen Lake Ladoga in 1942.

blockade made this formula self-evident. As for the inevitability of the end, the blockade made it as predictable as running along a closed circle.

What takes place is the displacement of suffering with suffering, the mindless sense of purpose of the doomed, which explains why people survive in an isolated cell, a forced-labour camp, in squalor and in the lowermost depths of humiliation. This is something that the more fortunate people find difficult to understand; it is people in comfortable cottages who blow their brains out without any apparent reason.

THE PEOPLE OF PETER

The city known as St Petersburg, Petrograd and Leningrad over the short 290 years of its history, years which have, nevertheless, absorbed entire epochs, has always been referred to as "Peter" by its inhabitants. Having once walked its streets and breathed its air, moistened by the closeness of the Baltic, it is impossible to shake the initial feeling that you are touching something eternal and holy, yet, at the same time, something earthly and fleeting.

Leningrad is the Soviet Union's second largest metropolis. Its population is approaching five million; it has huge ports, factories, research institutions and educational establishments. Still referred to as the "northern capital", it has lost much of its former glamour. Founded by Czar-reformer Peter the Great, St Petersburg bore, not without pride, the title of capital of the Russian Empire between 1712 and 1918. Since that time, when fears for its safety made the government of the fledgling Soviet state transfer its seat deeper into the country to Moscow, the glitter of Petrograd waned. Its best minds fled the country. Civil War and World War II caused irreparable damage to the once-great city.

Now provincial, Peter is going through hard times. The once-splendid facades are decaying and collapsing. As a result of impotent city management and idiotic economic decisions, houses that have survived innumerable floods and the war now give way to modern structures. We are witnessing the death throes of the last shreds of that very St Petersburg culture, which, as Leningrad's star newsman, Alexander Nevzorov, put it, was "violently interrupted in its development in October 1917".

One could go on forever about whether St Petersburg's culture has disappeared once and for all, about the fate of the city's famous intelligentsia, about the causes of the present plight of what used to be one of the world's most beautiful cities. As the people of Leningrad realise with sinking hearts, one thing that is definitely not coming back is the old Peter atmosphere, so precious to all who had even a once-in-a-lifetime whiff of it. Because neither the huge residential areas with their supermarkets, schools, kindergartens and outpatients' clinics, nor the recently-erected industrial districts, are old Peter.

The city of Peter the Great, Rastrelli, Quarenghi, Rossi, Stasov and Voronikhin lies elsewhere, behind the old gates. It is spread across 42 islands and the mainland, crisscrossed by 40 rivers and 20 channels. There is the majesty of the Winter Palace, St Isaac's and the austere beauty of the Peter-and-Paul Fortress. There is the tourist wonderland where millions flock every year. There are the majority of Leningrad's 60 museums (of which the most famous are the Hermitage and the Russian Museum) and 17 professional theatres, including the famous Kirov (getting a ticket to a Kirov opera or ballet is regarded as incredible luck by both locals and visitors).

The tip of Vasilievsky Island offers the best overall view of the city from a square with a magnificent collection of architectural gems. Once the subway, bus or trolley takes the people of Leningrad to their mundane "sleeping" districts, they leave the charms of the old city and become the "population" – standing in interminable queues, hurrying to identical apartment blocks with inferior living conditions.

Problems of the day: Come to think of it, life in the old city is nothing much to write home about, either. Many inner-city residents still live in "communal" apartments (sharing kitchens and bathrooms with neighbours). And where students, artists and unrecognised poets find a certain Bohemian charm in the corners, rooms or apartments they rent in the old town, the majority of native locals find them too "exotic" to live in.

Leningrad is one of the oldest towns in the nation in terms of the age of the people: 1.2 million inhabitants are past retirement age.

Preceding pages: when spring comes, faces gladden. **Left**, winter can be frosty in Leningrad.

The majority of them suffer housing problems. They are also burdened by food shortages and a lame social security system. It is not a pretty picture. Senior citizens and people who are a generation younger still remember the war, the 900 days of the blockade, the bombs and shells which destroyed 3,000 buildings and damaged another 7,000. As they repeat the habitual "Let there be no war – that's the main thing", they still cherish faint hopes of someday living in apartments of their own, even in old age.

World War II occupies a special place in people's souls here. Hunger claimed 650,000 lives; air and artillery raids another

and yearns for a hair of the dog in the mornings; Ivanov, carried away by the writings of Sartre in a cramped tram, is fined by transport officials and tormented by the other ordinary people around him, who tread on his feet and step on his…wings.

Depicting Ivanov as a person unlike everybody else, Grebenschikov, in spite of himself, came up with the image of an entire generation of Leningrad natives. The external distinctions (cheap wine and communal apartments) are not at all important, especially if we bear in mind that everyone in Leningrad loves "tea in midnight kitchens", as the poet phrased it. It is rather that the

17,000. Many who'd seen frozen corpses in the streets and the lawns near St Isaac's turned into vegetable plantations, are still alive. Come Victory Day (9 May), the veterans march along Nevsky Prospekt. Every year, however, their column inevitably gets that much shorter.

Ivanov lives: The typical face of the new city is Ivanov the ordinary man, the hero of the famous ballad by Boris Grebenschikov, a rock star (recently emerged from the underground). Ivanov lives in a communal flat on the Petrograd side, drinks cheap wine with faithful friends of either sex in the evenings,

people here, despite never-ending everyday disasters and the need to fight for everything, have retained the yearning for eternal values and faith in human decency and kindness.

A cosmopolitan people: Leningrad was always known as an educated town, a town of good manners and culture. Refined intellectuals from "Peter" have at times been unfairly attacked by jealous rivals (especially from Moscow) as snobs. In fact the influence of Europe, which is right on the doorstep here, and the best kind of cosmopolitanism (even in the worst years of the Iron Curtain) gave local intellectuals profound foreign-language skills and worldly knowledge.

Here, too, lie the roots of Russia's formidable culture of the 18th century – and succeeding centuries. St Petersburg gave us Alexander Pushkin, Nikolai Gogol and Fyodor Dostoyevsky. It has heard the music of Piotr Tchaikovsky, Mikhail Glinka and Nikolai Rimsky-Korsakov. Moscow was the hotbed of Slavophiles; St Petersburg was more open to Western influence and freely gave of its talents. It may be that the haughtiness one sometimes encounters in Leningrad is fuelled by the old but not forgotten insult – taking away the capital status from a city of such wondrous history! But

their doors to freshmen, whose destiny then becomes predictable – the merry years of college, living in a dorm, a hired room or family apartment.

Students get a small state subsidy – 50 roubles per month; even though the state does not want it back, ever, it is too small a sum to count. Dorm rates are minuscule, true, and you don't have to pay much for the food in a college café (if your palate can stand it, that is); still, money doesn't go far these days, and students have to rely either on their parents, or on themselves, for additional incomes.

Easy-going academic terms are inter-

surely Dmitry Likhachev, Academy of Science Member, one of the country's foremost intellectuals and an impassioned fighter for Russian culture, and Iosif Brodsky, the Nobel Prize-winning poet who now lives in America, could not be described as snobs.

There are many people who study in today's Leningrad – around 2 million attend assorted courses as well as higher and secondary schools. There are 40 colleges, including the university: every year, they open

Left, in spite of hard times, a happy face. **Above**, heroes of the Great Patriotic War.

spaced with excruciating exam periods with sleepless nights. Untold hours are spent in libraries (the city has several large ones and some 1,500 regular libraries). Then autumn comes, and the students take to the fields, helping the peasants to gather the crops (usually potatoes). To make up for all the suffering, there are the long summer months – time to go on vacation to the Crimea or the Caucasus, where the sea is so warm, or to stay with friends abroad – something quite usual nowadays. You can recognise a member of the student tribe anywhere – despite the varying quality of the clothes they wear, the students of Leningrad resemble their peers from Paris, Boston or Stockholm. Well, perhaps Leningrad students are paler and more prone to colds.

The only thing for which the people of Leningrad will never forgive the founder of their town is his choice of location (marshes and bogs) and, consequently, the climate (damp and stale). On the banks of the Neva, as generally on the shores of the Gulf of Finland, winter is unpredictable and spring and autumn are rainy and flood-prone.

The town has been devastated by floods many times; the city fathers finally decided to guard against future floods with a huge

tourists). The people were outraged when they learned that planners and the relevant authorities, who were obviously out to make a profit in hard currency, had decided to proceed with the project in Lisii Nos (Foxnose) even though they knew that the amusement park would endanger several freshwater deposits, already few and far between. Of the 2 million cubic metres of water that the city needs every day, nearly half goes for housing needs.

All in all, the political temperature is rising steadily. Meetings near the Kazan Cathedral and in front of the Mariinsky Palace, the seat of the city council, are commonplace. Since

barrier. But, as Nikolai Vorontsov, the Minister of Nature Protection (himself a Leningrad student) quipped, the only thing the flood barrier guards is the coastline of neighbouring countries, while Leningrad has traded in its floods for a huge and muddy wasteland right on its doorstep. Initiated by the Greens, ban-the-dam action quickly evolved into a mass movement for ecological purity in the aging city.

New times: Several years ago it would have been impossible, but today the people of Leningrad have managed to defeat the Soviet Disneyland project (aimed at foreign

perestroika, newspapers and leaflets to suit any political taste are on sale in the subway and in the streets. Heated debate takes place on the pavement – another sign of the times.

The current municipal council is not popular (even though it was elected via the most democratic, but, alas, not the most effective, procedure). Not so with the council's chairman: Anatoly Sobchak is the voters' darling, and not only in Leningrad. Sobchak does not want to trade his present position even for the post of prime minister, so grateful is he to the people of Leningrad.

An avid supporter of a free economic zone

in the Leningrad region, Sobchak lists the city's pros: proximity to Northern and Western Europe, road, rail and sea connections, and, of course, the city's high industrial and scientific potential.

Depoliticisation: One of the greatest worries of the day is that the once-hardworking proletariat has degenerated en masse owing to the long years of idling, guaranteed wages and suppressed initiative. The majority of workers just do not care anymore. True, perestroika partly revitalised the town's enterprises, including the giants – the Kirov Tractor Factory and the Elektrosila Plant, which produces the world's most powerful

regarded as one of the most sacred achievements of the revolutionary proletariat.

Getting around: At least 20 years ago, Vladimir Vysotsky, the popular actor and singer, wrote a song about Leningrad taxis. Even though the taxi park has grown many times since then (there are roughly 4,000 cabs), it is still not easy to get a taxi. Stories about getting to a station or the airport without paying exorbitant sums of money are told in bewildered tones. Foreign visitors are at times subjected to outright extortion: taxi drivers demand cigarettes, clothes or dollars. The most experienced travellers pay in dollars because, despite the hassle, Leningrad's

turbines for hydroelectric power stations. Depoliticisation is in progress; the party will no longer run the show. Many workers take an active part in assorted political movements, but the majority prefer to stay at home, watching TV (at best) or drinking with friends at home or in the street, near a beer kiosk. Incidentally, these kiosks, which boggle the minds of foreigners and sell *kvas*, a kind of weak beer, all year-round, are

Left, a doll leads the way to the Soviet altar.
Above, the spirits rise when street musicians begin to play.

taxis are still cheaper than those back home.

Most locals prefer municipal transport, which is always crowded yet reliable. First and foremost, that means the Metro (built in 1955), which is as comfortable and smart as the one in Moscow; then there are 3,200 buses and a large number of trolleys and trams. Transport fares in the USSR are so cheap they never cease to astound everyone, including the locals. Most would gladly pay more in exchange for greater reliability. So far, however, despite the eye-catching Soviet and foreign ads on buses, transport has clearly not been at its best.

No one is surprised at such small in-humanities anymore, not after the distribution of special ration cards for different kinds of food, and the demands to come to the liquor store with an empty bottle (only then can you buy a full one).

The first thing a visitor to Leningrad sees is its mixture of styles. It has pieces of Paris and Venice, Stockholm and Prague. There's nothing surprising about this: St Petersburg's houses reflect the St Petersburg way of life. The best designers and architects from all over Europe came here, and everything progressive was generously supported.

Take the centre, near Dvortsovaya Square,

for example: it was created by Russians, Frenchmen, Italians, and many other foreign masters – yet it is genuinely Russian. Every stone here breathes history. The palace walls saw three revolutions; today, the passers-by gape at a monarchist rally or a demonstration in support of giving the city back its old name. The former palace of the Czars now houses the famous Hermitage. Three million people visit this collection of world art every year. The museum illustrates another Soviet paradox: it employs experts with encyclopedic knowledge (philosophy, ancient civilisations, rare languages), whose salaries at times fall short of what a cloakroom attendant or watchman makes.

The black market: The average wage in Leningrad is 200 roubles per month. It doesn't go far these days, even with token rents, free medical care and education. Housewives increasingly turn to the free market in search of food, as state-run stores become emptier with each passing year. Against the background of the general plight, the so-called "majors" stand out. These people make money peddling foreign-made goods or selling hard currency. Recently, they've taken a liking to the Vyborg-Leningrad Highway, where they set up their currency exchanges and trading marts for foreign tourists. The police are clearly outmatched: the majors have new, often foreign-made automobiles with powerful engines and even computers, with which they keep track of the licence-plates of all undercover police cars.

Daily joys: Yet optimism runs high in Leningrad. There's more to life than everyday chores. Something new happens daily on the culture scene. Leningrad offers more than any other Soviet city to lovers of theatre, classical music, concerts, rock 'n' roll, or opera. Sports buffs can watch their heroes – the Zenith football club and the Army hockey club – in action and get a workout for themselves at one of the city's 36 stadiums or 20 swimming pools. Local people love the countryside: Leningrad has beautiful environs, made famous by the former residences of the Czars and pleasing to the eye by their forests and the lakes of Karelia. And if there's no time to get away to the still-pure beaches of the Gulf of Finland, you can enjoy the sun right in the city limits, on the beach near the Peter-and-Paul Fortress.

Making your way through the bustle of Nevsky, looking at the people, you realise the truth of what Boris Grebenschikov said: "I do not see that the city is dying. I do not know what is wrong with it, true, but I have no tragic premonition. Leningrad has suffered much. We must make life easier for the people, and the city will take care of itself."

Above, Russian bikinis. **Right**, selling fruit from a private garden.

Dmitri Gubin interviews **Anatoli Sobchak***, Chairman of the Leningrad City Soviet and People's Deputy of the* USSR.

You are the head of the Leningrad City Soviet, the majority of which supports radical economic and political reform. Other reforming city councils include those of Moscow and Sverdlovsk, but their number is quite small in nationwide terms. Aren't you afraid that the attempt, ascribed to you by certain critics, to build capitalism in single, isolated cities will end in failure?

No, I am not, because we have no intention of building capitalism. Our aim is, in fact, to reorganise the municipal government on the basis of common sense. We shall certainly be unable to cope with a crisis that is nationwide with only our isolated efforts, even with the help of the recently adopted laws on local economies, local self-government and individual taxation, though these will give us broader rights and more funds.

Leningrad is becoming so run-down, so rapidly, that I am amazed by the claims of the former municipal leaders that they handed over the city in perfect shape. The environmental disaster in Leningrad has not been exaggerated. Take the condition of houses, streets and our architectural monuments. Whole blocks of buildings are in need of repair and this is not being done, even in houses from which residents have been moved in advance of restoration plans.

Revolutionary measures are required to improve the situation. To begin with, Leningrad should be given the status of a free economic zone. This will enable its enterprises to end their state of subordination to ministries and departments and will enable them to operate as independent, economically and legally self-sufficient producers and it will create favourable conditions for the investment of foreign capital.

The first of the two most urgent tasks is to turn Leningrad from the centre of a military

industrial complex, which it is today, into a centre of culture, science and the manufacture of consumer goods. To this end it is necessary to sell off uncompleted projects, unprofitable enterprises and concerns which pose an ecological danger, on the best possible terms for the city.

We should also learn how to earn money from tourism. Although Leningrad is exceptionally attractive to foreign tourists we are short of hotels and we do not have a local

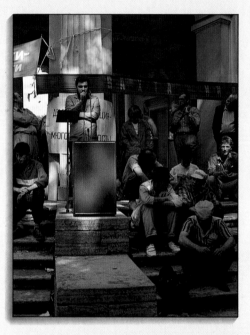

tourist infrastructure. The monopoly octopus, the state travel agency called Intourist, sucks practically all the hard currency Leningrad receives from the city, leaving us nothing but tourism-related problems such as prostitution and black market crime.

We have therefore to build our own infrastructure of international tourism, build new hotels to modern standards of comfort with the help of foreign capital and refit old buildings. The experience of other countries shows that tourism is a sure way of enriching a city and improving the municipal economy within a few years.

Speaking of the problems facing the city, you made no mention of the political one. It seems relevant to ask how, in your view, the regional Communist Party committee should act vis-à-vis the new Leningrad City Soviet?

While I cannot speak for the regional party committee, I think it should cooperate with the Leningrad Soviet and voluntarily eliminate the consequences of the party monopoly in the city. Party agencies should render maximum assistance to the city authorities if they wish to preserve their influence in the solution of municipal problems. If they

choose the road of resistance or sabotage, we shall have to resort to all necessary measures prescribed by law.

Will the Leningrad City Soviet respond in any form to the formally sympathetic warning of Boris Gidaspov, the leader of Leningrad's Communists, that the new Communist Party of Russia may be a very serious political opponent for the Leningrad City Soviet?

<u>Preceding pages</u>: breaking the chains. <u>Left</u>, peace campaigners. <u>Above</u>, Anatoli Sobchak.

As I have already said, should their platform include a thesis on the dictatorship of the proletariat, I shall personally propose to the Leningrad City Soviet that the activity of that Communist Party on Leningrad's territory be banned since the demand for a dictatorship is a demand for the forcible removal of the existing government, no matter behind whose name that dictatorship hides.

Do you think Leningrad people will support your plan to set up a free economic zone? Will they not boycott it on the pretext of preventing the sale of the national wealth?

In the course of the election campaign both our nationalist organisations and the conservative forces within the CPSU vigorously used this thesis, claiming that Russia was being sold out, etc. But I believe in common sense and I trust that people will understand that, far from intending to sell anything out, we aim to use foreign capital to build and promote here, in our city, things which may be an immense help to us; such as firms and enterprises to produce building materials, for the lack of which we cannot build a house even if we have heads, hands and money.

It is clear, of course, that our people will hardly be very pleased if we limit ourselves to setting up hard currency restaurants and bars. I think, however, that the developing tourist infrastructure should be oriented both to hard currency and to the rouble. Besides, the status of a free economic zone will enable everyone to take part in deals involving hard currency and get paid in that currency. It is well known that so far this has constituted a criminal offence.

Will you address the citizens of Leningrad with the traditional call of free economies: "Get rich"?

I can only promise that I will do everything possible to set up both private and mixed companies, at the same time taking into account the city's interests. Here is an example: at the moment, when leasing premises to an enterprise or cooperative, no one inquires whether it is profitable or whether it is of any use to the city. The fact that rental rates are the same for everyone opens up, I must frankly say, enticing opportunities for all kinds of shady dealings and bribery.

My view is that we should lease premises on a competitive basis and set rental rates depending on what goods or services an enterprise intends to produce and what prices it is going to charge. We may even lease premises rent-free to enterprises which will produce goods that are vital for the city and undertake to sell them at or below state prices. All this is at our own discretion. We will only welcome those who want to get rich if, at the same time, they enrich the city.

uted free of charge. This is one of the reasons why villagers move into towns.

Another and most important aspect is the fact that a person's respect for another begins with respect for his property, and his possessions. Not for nothing is the biblical commandment, "Thou shalt not steal", one of the foremost moral principles of human society.

We have forsaken this principle; daily contact with property that belongs to the state – hence anonymous, nobody's – has brought about what to me, as a lawyer, is a most horrifying shift in mass consciousness, a shift to a point where theft is not morally condemned. This attitude of the people is

I know you are a lawyer and a specialist in housing law. Therefore I would like you to talk in greater detail about your housing policy, which is a painful matter both for Leningrad and the entire country.

I have long been preaching the idea that a person should be the owner of his own home. In the first place this is in keeping with the principle of social justice. One aspect of social injustice is the difference between town and country. Many people outside the cities live in houses built at their own expense, while housing in the cities is distrib-

reflected by our language which has coined the innocuous word "carriers" when referring to the pilferers of state property.

One can imagine the reaction of conservatives to this idea. They are likely to exclaim: "Aha, tomorrow all these cooperators and all the underground millionaires will crawl out of their holes and get pushy, leaving nothing for us."

First of all, those who really have millions provided themselves long ago, without much ado, with all the housing they need.

We only pretend that housing is not sold and bought, while any broker at the housing exchange market can tell you exactly how much one square metre of housing space costs. What is supposed to be an exchange of housing space is in fact a regular trade in it, though this is, alas, very hard to prove in any court of law.

Second, it is proposed that flats are sold to those who already occupy them and to people on the waiting lists for housing. The evaluation will be based on amortised cost and take into account the type of house and its location in the city, and so cannot be high.

It is only when people on waiting lists and

tackle the problems not of Leningrad but of St Petersburg?

Though I know that many people would like to have the city revert to the old name of St Petersburg, I am generally not in favour of hasty decisions. The city lived through the cruellest period of its history, the siege, under this name, which has become near and dear to Leningraders regardless of politics. I think that we can restore the glorious name of the city's founder, Peter the Great, in some other way. The city's university, for instance, is today without a name.

The only change of name on which I will

existing tenants are satisfied and only once vacant flats become available in the city that the question of their sale to anyone wishing to buy may be decided. This will be a graphic demonstration of the principle that he who wants to have better housing should work better and earn more.

My last question to you as chairman of the Leningrad City Soviet is this: don't you think that you will very soon have to

Left, peoples' private exchange. **Above**, joyful children brighten up the day.

insist, and which I will propose to the Leningrad City Soviet, is the renaming of the Square of the Dictatorship of the Proletariat facing the Smolny Institute into Academician Sakharov Square, because this renaming is connected, for me, with the manifestation of the changes we are planning to make in the city. We intend to implement the ideas of Academician Sakharov, that great countryman of ours and great humanist, the ideas of party plurality, class cooperation and the priority of universal human values, which presupposes the rejection of any dictatorship, regardless of its name.

Recently a Leningrad newspaper conducted a poll among almost 1,000 foreign visitors. For some of them it was their first, for others their second or third visit. One of the questions they were asked was: "What impressed you most in Leningrad?" About 90 percent gave the same reply: "The architecture and the cultural wealth".

This is not surprising since it is indisputable that the former St Petersburg played a unique role in the history of Russian culture, a role that still fertilizes today's cultural scene. It was here that Alexander Pushkin wrote his greatest poems, that Mikhail Glinka composed his masterpieces, that Ilya Repin painted his best pictures and that Andrei Voronikhin designed his neoclassical structures. These are only a handful of the many geniuses of Russian culture who lived, and whose art prospered, in this city.

Geniuses of architecture: Genuine art is timeless – a truth confirmed by countless palaces, parks, bridges and embankments throughout Leningrad. Many Russian and foreign architects came, over a period of over 200 years, to work in the "Northern Palmyra", as St Petersburg came to be called. The architectural ensembles that sprang from their ingenuity are still cause for wonder. In spite of Peter the Great and Lenin, it is the architects of the 18th and 19th centuries who brought worldwide fame to St Petersburg, and not the statesmen. They came from France, Italy, Switzerland, England and Germany, as well as from Russia, to design some of the finest baroque and neoclassical structures of their age.

It all started with Domenico Trezzini (1670–1734), a Swiss by birth who came when the city was founded and worked there from 1703 until his death. In and around St Petersburg he built the earliest churches, government offices, palaces and country villas; on Peter the Great's instructions he even designed a series of standard houses for the different strata of society (houses for the nobility, for well-to-do families and for people of low birth).

Trezzini's structures are typical of early Russian baroque. Their distinctive features are streamlined silhouettes with modest interiors, and a combination of austere and baroque elements. Trezzini designed Peter's Summer Palace, (1710–14) and the Cathedral of St Peter and Paul (1712–33), one of St Petersburg's most magnificent structures. Towering over the cathedral is a belfry with a spire that was to be the tallest structure in the city and the symbol of the Russian Empire's new capital.

Artists and laymen unanimously regard the Italian Bartolomeo Rastrelli (1700–71), who worked in Leningrad in the mid-18th century, as the greatest master of Russian Rococo. His finest masterpieces are the Great Palace at Peterhof (Petrodvorets), the Smolny Convent (1748–59), the Vorontsov Palace (1749–57) in Sadovaya Street and the Stroganov Palace (1752–54) at the corner of Nevsky Prospekt and the Moika Embankment. These architectural ensembles, magnificent and impressive in their design and solemnity, were built, according to Rastrelli himself, for "the glory of Russia". Rastrelli's structures are distinguished by clear-cut architectural forms, complicated patterns of colonnades, and spaciousness combined with inimitable plasticity.

The founders of neoclassicism in Russian architecture are Vassili Bazhenov (1737–99) who designed the Mikhailovsky Castle (1799–1800) together with Vincenzo Brenna (1745–1800) and Ivan Starov (1745–1808) who built the Taurida Palace (1783–89) and the Holy Trinity Cathedral of the Alexander Nevsky Monastery (1778–90). Bazhenov was the chief architect of Emperor Paul I. His masterpiece, the Mikhailovsky Castle, became the last residence of the ill-fated czar who was strangled there on the night of 12 March 1801.

The buildings designed by Giacomo

Preceding pages: modern art on Ostrovsky square; art on the move. **Left,** Pushkin, the beloved master of Russian literature.

Quarenghi (1744–1817), another great Italian who worked in Russia, are distinguished by the lucidity of their plans and the monumental plasticity of forms achieved with the help of grand colonnades, which stand out against a background of smooth surfaced walls. The main building of the Academy of Sciences (1783–89), the former Assignation Bank (now the Financial-Economic Institute) in Sadovaya Street (1783–90), the Hermitage Theatre with the arch over the Winter Ditch (1783–87), and the Smolny Institute (1806–09) were built to his designs.

Russian neoclassicism reached its peak in the early 19th century when Andrei Voro-

Of great significance for St Petersburg were the ensembles and individual buildings designed between 1818 and 1834 by Carlo Rossi (1775–1849), especially the Arts Square ensemble (1819–25), which now houses the Russian Museum, and the building of the General Staff Headquarters (1819–29) with its monumental arch over Morskaya Street. The latter building rounds out the Palace Square ensemble.

Auguste Montferrand (1786–1858) created the inimitable St Isaac Cathedral (1818–58) and the Alexander Column (1830–34), remarkable for its massive monolithic proportions as well as for its austere beauty.

nikhin (1759–1814), born a serf, built such masterpieces as the Cathedral of the Kazan Icon of the Mother of God (1801–11) on Nevsky Prospekt and the Mining Institute (1806–11) on the Neva Embankment.

When Andreyan Zakharov (1761–1811) rebuilt the Admiralty he created a jewel of Russian and world architecture. Thomas de Thomon (1760–1813) designed the majestic building of the Stock Exchange (1804–10) which now houses the Central Naval Museum, and the two rostral columns (1806) on the Spit (Birzhevaya Strelka, now Pushkin Square) on Vasilievsky Island.

The essence of the city: Leningrad's residents deeply cherish the memory of their great architects. One would probably not be able to find in any other Soviet town so many streets and squares named after their city's architectural planners as there are in Leningrad. This is not accidental, because architecture is not only Leningrad's "calling card", it is its essence.

But, to be honest, it must be admitted that the monuments of Leningrad, like the culture of the city, and of the entire country for that matter, are having a hard time. Leningrad, the former capital of the Empire, always used to be a clean and tidy city whereas now, for example, the paint on the spire of the Mikhailovsky Castle has peeled off, and the whole building is covered with blemishes. Many residential buildings and even palaces are in a dreadful condition. Better times are on the horizon, however; the new democratic-minded city fathers have realised the urgency of the situation; some have spoken out strongly on it and a start has been made on tackling the problem of restoring the city to its old splendour.

Literary capital: There is scarcely a single Russian writer who, no matter where he was born or where he lived, has not cherished St

most of his time writing in St Petersburg. Except for a few influential years spent in exile and on trips to Boldino and Moscow, he was a true product of the atmosphere that prevailed in St Petersburg. Like nobody else, Pushkin loved "Peter's creation", and he himself created an impressive poetic image of the great city. Whole chapters of *Eugene Onegin* (1823–31), in which Pushkin described St Petersburg's high society and theatrical life, with its spectators and actors, were inspired by the city. His unfinished novel, *Peter the Great's Negro* (1827), depicts the city at the time of Peter the Great.

In Pushkin's mind St Petersburg symbol-

Petersburg, who has not written poems or prose about it and who has not rejoiced when thinking of the city on the Neva. In this sense St Petersburg is probably the most "literary" city in the world. A Leningrad literary critic once remarked that almost half of the outstanding writers and poets of all times and nations have written about St Petersburg. Quite possibly he was right.

The heart and soul of Russian literature, Alexander Pushkin (1799–1837), spent

Left, the Chesme church is now a museum. **Above**, windows at the Nevsky Monastery.

ised a new, "unshakeable" and powerful Russia. After the failure of the Decembrists' uprising in 1825, however, he thought of the city as a place of "ennui, cold and granite". It was here, in St Petersburg, after being mortally wounded in a duel with George d'Anthes, that Pushkin died, at No. 12, Moika Embankment.

The work of Nikolai Gogol (1809–52) is also associated with St Petersburg, where he lived from 1829 to 1836 before going abroad; here he wrote his best works, including *The Government Inspector*, *Marriage* and *The Greatcoat*.

"You can see the influence of St Petersburg," wrote Vissarion Belinsky, a prominent Russian critic, "on the greater part of Gogol's works, not in the sense that he owed St Petersburg his manner of writing, of course, but in the sense that he owed St Petersburg many of the characters he created." Gogol created an image of St Petersburg as a "smart European", a "dandy". But it was against the background of all this that "unusually strange happenings" took place, "everything breathed deception" and acquired a "fantastic tenor". Thus was Gogol's St Petersburg.

Fyodor Dostoyevsky (1821–81), born in

At various times Leo Tolstoy (1828–1910), who contributed his first works to the journal *Sovremennik* (Contemporary), the playwright Alexander Ostrovsky (1823–86), who also contributed to St Petersburg's literary journals, and Anton Chekhov (1860–1904), who had his plays staged at the Alexandrinsky Theatre, came to St Petersburg on short visits.

St Petersburg also figured prominently in the works of the great Russian poet Alexander Blok (1880–1921) who spent almost his whole life there. In the poem *Retribution* (1910–21), Blok wrote about the St Petersburg of the late 19th century as a city in

Moscow, wrote almost all of his novels in St Petersburg. With his brother he edited the magazines *Vremya* (Time) and *Epokha* (Epoch) here. In St Petersburg he saw "a mixture of something purely fantastic and perfectly ideal, and at the same time insipidly prosaic and common." St Petersburg's "dream" and "ideal" did not seem lofty for Dostoyevsky; he did not feel "a common unifying thought in the crowd, all were by themselves." For Dostoyevsky, St Petersburg was "the most abstract and imaginary city." A similar vision was later reflected in the works of the Russian symbolists.

which irresistible anti-autocratic forces were in the making:

In those dead and gloomy years
Somehow it seemed that Petersburg
Was still the heart and soul of Russia,
But doom was knocking at the doors.

No matter what Blok wrote about St Petersburg, he did so with a deep love. Anna Akhmatova (1889–1966), Osip Mandelshtam (1891–1938) and many other poets and writers also wrote affectionately about the city which, in opening out its heart and soul to them, itself became the heart and soul of Russian literature.

Russian music: Russian classical music is bound up with St Petersburg because it was here that the composers whose works constitute the musical treasure-trove of Russia created their masterpieces.

Mikhail Glinka (1804–57), who is the unchallenged founder of Russian classical music, the author of the brilliant operas *Ivan Susanin* and *Ruslan and Lyudmila*, and no less brilliant symphonic pieces and romances, wrote almost all of his works in St Petersburg. It should be remembered that after the premiere of *Ivan Susanin* in 1836 Vladimir Odoyevsky, the musical critic and poet, wrote: "What has long been sought

An extremely creative group of composers lived in St Petersburg in the 1860s. Three of them reached world fame: Modest Mussorgsky (1839–81) was author of many vocal pieces and the deeply emotional operas *Boris Godunov* and *The Khovansky Affairs*; Alexander Borodin (1833–87), author of such epic works as the opera *Prince Igor* and the *Second Symphony in B Minor* was also a master of chamber music; and Nikolai Rimsky-Korsakov (1844–1908) – who wrote many operas based on history, like *The Czar's Bride*, on fairytales, like *The Snow Maiden*, on epics, like *Sadko* and on satires, like *The Golden Cockerel* – was at

after and not found in Europe has come with Glinka's opera – a new wave in art and a new period in history has started, a period of Russian music." In hindsight these now seem prophetic words.

It should also be mentioned that a series of romances that Glinka composed, in 1840, as a setting for Nestor Kukolnik's lyrics were dedicated to his favourite St Petersburg. The series was called *Farewell to St Petersburg*.

Left, Gogol reading from his work *The Government Inspector*. **Above**, Mikhail Glinka, the founder of Russian classical music.

the same time a brilliant conductor whose music had a subtle lyrical character.

The Russian Musical Society, which introduced regular concerts, was established in 1859 in St Petersburg on the initiative of the composer and pianist Anton Rubinstein (1829–94). In the same year the Society started its first musical classes, on the basis of which Rubinstein organised Russia's first conservatoire in 1862. Among the first graduates of the conservatoire was Peter Tchaikovsky (1840–93), the greatest of Russia's symphony and opera composers, author of such masterpieces as the operas

Eugene Onegin and *The Queen of Spades*, the ballets *Swan Lake* and *The Sleeping Beauty*, and suites like *The Nutcracker*, not to forget his *Sixth (Pathétique) Symphony*. "Like Pushkin, he has become integrated into the very foundations of the Russian national conscience", wrote Dmitri Shostakovich (1906–75), the pre-eminent Russian composer of the 20th century and another graduate of the St Petersburg (Leningrad) Conservatoire.

Shostakovich lived in Leningrad until 1942. Many of his best works were written and performed here for the first time, in particular the opera *Lady Macbeth of Mtsensk* and the ballet *The Age of Gold*. He lived in Leningrad for the first months of the 900-day siege, during which he wrote his famous *Seventh (Leningrad) Symphony* which was performed in the besieged city by the Leningrad Radio Orchestra in 1942.

Igor Stravinsky (1882–1971), the outstanding Russian composer and conductor, who lived in the US after 1910, also began his musical career in St Petersburg, as did another classic composer of the 20th century, Sergei Prokofiev (1891–1953). Although Prokofiev lived in Moscow for most of his life, he often returned to Leningrad for premieres of his works.

Choreographers and famous dancers: St Petersburg produced not only great composers, but also splendid opera singers and brilliant pianists and conductors. The "Northern Palmyra" is, however, probably most famous for its ballet. As early as the beginning of the 19th century, ballets produced by the famous choreographer Charles-Louis Didelot (1767–1837) were performed at St Petersburg's Bolshoi Theatre. Alexander Pushkin, who often went to the theatre, highly appreciated Didelot's ballets and saw in them "a lively imagination of extraordinary charm". In the early 20th century, Anna Pavlova (1881–1931), Waslaw Nijinsky (1889–1950) and Michel Fokine (1880–1942) danced with enormous success on the stage of the Mariinsky Theatre (now the Kirov Theatre of Opera and Ballet).

Left, Anna Akhmatova in 1914, painting by Natan Altmann. Above, Leo Tolstoy.

But the best years of those inimitable dancers were spent abroad, where they performed in the ballet troupe, called the Russian Seasons, which was formed in 1907 by the prominent Russian choreographer Sergei Diaghilev (1872–1929). The Soviet ballerinas Galina Ulanova and Maya Plisetskaya started their careers in Leningrad, and it was also here that Rudolf Nuriyev, Natalia Makarova and Mikhail Baryshnikov, whose art is now known all over the world, won their fame. No wonder it is so difficult to get hold of a ticket at the Kirov Theatre; it was there that the Russian ballet came to flower and it is still thriving.

Though the great names of Leningrad culture are names from the past, especially from the city's heyday in the 19th century, a golden age for Russia generally, it does not mean that Leningrad today is devoid of great talents. There is spirit of renaissance in the air and the people of this city try hard to keep alive the essence of its splendid past. A visit to any of Leningrad's great theatres will reveal the truth of this. It is true that the city faces many problems today; even so, you cannot but feel the powerful spirit of its classical past still pulsating in its squares, streets and buildings.

For almost three decades, the best theatre in Leningrad was the **Bolshoi Drama Theatre** headed by Georgy Tovstonogov (on the Fontanka). The 1980s found both Tovstonogov and the BDT, as we call his theatre, in a crisis; today, after the death of its leader, the organisation seems to be falling apart, even though such productions as *Philistines*, *Khanuma* and *History of a Horse*, which have been preserved in the repertoire since the 1970s, are unsurpassed masterpieces.

The "hot" theatre is now the **Maly Drama Theatre**, which is close to the BDT in Rubinstein Street. It is nearly impossible to obtain tickets for a performance there. Lev Dodin, the theatre's young director, has rapidly evolved into a real master of the stage. His productions of Fyodor Abramov's novels *The House* and *Brothers and Sisters* were certainly the best to be seen in Leningrad in the first half of the 1980s.

These plays are still in the repertoire. Several new productions have been added of late, crowned by *Lord of the Flies*, in which Dodin seeks – and finds – bold solutions and new stage forms.

Yet he is alone in his search. There are many theatres in Leningrad, but, frankly, few of them deserve to be called theatres at all. For many years now the **Pushkin State Drama Theatre** has been experiencing problems, despite its status as the main "academy" of theatrical art in Leningrad (it is headed by the actor Igor Gorbachev). The wonderful, almost 200-year-long history of this theatre, its majestic building in midtown, on Nevsky, cannot make up for the faults of Igor Gorbachev's pompous productions from Russian history. His plays – take, for instance, *Kutuzov* – make one think of the past years of stagnation, when all Soviet theatres toed the line of "official patriotism", drawn by Brezhnev's ideologues. So, when 60-year-old Igor Gorbachev takes the leading role of the youthful Cyrano de

Bergerac in Rostand's famous play, one fails to find words…

Well, what is there to do? The theatre situation in Leningrad largely reflects social processes. Leningrad is not the capital, it is not Moscow, and the distance is felt. Yet the city does have its share of interesting productions. Igor Vladimov's **Lensoviet Theatre** attracts with the poetry of its plays; director Ruben Agamirzyan does interesting work in the **Komissarzhevskaya Theatre**: his production of *Fyodor Ioannovich* about Ivan the Terrible's son Fyodor is certain to be of interest to those guests of Leningrad who are fans of old Russia. Valery Gvozdikov, a young director, has recently become the leader in the **Leninsky Komsomol Theatre** – and attendance has gone up.

There are no venues for experimental drama in Leningrad; the avant garde is practically unheard-of; the only place where unusual approaches to the scenic art can be seen is the students' theatre owned by the Institute of Theatre, Music and Cinematography in Mokhovaya Street. Studio theatres are cropping up here and there, just as in Moscow, but it is too early to draw conclusions about the quality of their work.

There is no doubt that the famous **Mariinsky Theatre** (which, for some unfathomable reason, was renamed the **Kirov Theatre of Opera and Ballet** after the revolution (Sergei Kirov was a revolutionary and had nothing whatsoever to do with ballet) is the USSR's foremost music theatre today. This is true both for opera and for the ballet, which is headed by the famed Oleg Vinogradov.

Queen of Spades and *Eugene Onegin*, the two gems of Russian music by Peter Tchaikovsky, have been produced by conductor Yury Temirkanov as tragedies – which is not characteristic of *Eugene Onegin*, true, but there is also a profound lyricism and a poetic touch, the added combination of which charms. Conductor Vladimir Georgiyev has recently brought *Boris Godunov* (produced by Andrei

Preceding pages: at Leningrad's choreography school. **Left**, Fiodor Shaliapin as Boris Gudunov.

Tarkovsky for Covent Garden) over from the London stage. You can hear the famous tenor, Yury Marusin, in these productions. Boris Shtokolov, the celebrated bass, sings in Glinka's *Ivan Susanin*.

Oleg Vinogradov's ballets are an entire chapter in the contemporary book of Russian ballet. He has worked on several co-productions with Moris Bejar, and his *Petrushka* (Stravinsky) features Andris Liepa, who now works in the United States.

The imposing building of the Kirov is an entire palace; once inside, one remembers Meyerkhold's famous words, "How good it is for the soul to sit in this temple."

Opposite the Kirov is the **Leningrad Conservatoire**, where the best performers from all over the world come to play. Meanwhile, Yury Temirkanov, who worked at the Kirov for many years, now heads the famous orchestra of the **Leningrad Philharmonic**, which was created by the great maestro Yevgeny Mravinsky. Even though the orchestra spends a lot of its time playing abroad, it also remembers its loyal audience and plays frequently in Leningrad.

Theatre life is a unique thing. Changes occur every hour. Who knows, maybe a masterpiece is being born this very moment in one of the city's 50 or so theatres? There's good reason to hope for this – the city certainly has enough talented directors and actors. Come to meet them in the Actor's House on Nevsky Prospekt, whether just to talk or see them in action.

The cinema scene: Leningrad moviemakers are totally unlike their Moscow colleagues: in Leningrad, they are impeccable, elegant, restrained. They are more European than the simple souls of Moscow. They are aristocrats in their souls regardless of social roots or the fact that they live in a city that has been known as "the cradle of the revolution" since October 1917, the event which gave the "Palmyra of the North" (Leningrad) the name of the Bolshevik leader.

The great moviemakers, who made Leningrad famous, were all of that type. This is true of Grigory Kozintsev (1905–73), the man who founded the world-famous FECS **("Factory of the Eccentric Actor")** in the 1920s, created the three-part sequence about Maxim in the 1930s, which the public loved, and turned to Shakespeare in the 1960s and the 1970s (his *Hamlet* and *King Lear* have justly made it into the gold collection of world cinema).

This is also true of Ilya Averbakh, Kozintsev's pupil, who passed away long before his time (1934–86), the director of such psychological films as *The Monologue*, *Declaration of Love*, and *Voice*. Finally, this applies to the young generation of Lenfilm moviemakers as well.

Evenings and gala nights in the **Leningrad Cinema House** (in Tolmachev Street, formerly Karavannaya Street near Nevsky Prospekt) are ceremonious, strikingly similar to the style of reception that was in vogue during the days of the empire. It is a miracle how the city and its intellectuals have managed to retain their image in spite of all the suffering and hardships. The influence of arrow-straight avenues, thin spires and the glitter of grandoise palaces is clearly felt here. No, St Petersburg never really became the "city of Lenin" – at heart it still remembers Peter the Great.

As for the woes of Leningrad, they have been legion. They, too, have been recorded by the masters of the screen in both documentaries and fiction. The terrible documentary chronicles of the 20th century will forever preserve the images of the blockade of 1941–43: the city covered by huge mounds of snow; women standing in line near a hole drilled in the ice-covered canal (there was no running water); a woman, unsteady on her feet from fatigue and pain, dragging a sled bearing the corpse of her child.

People fell in the streets, faint with hunger, but they would not give in. In the freezing halls of a library, scientists pore over huge volumes. A great event takes place in the Philharmonic: for the first time ever, the orchestra plays the Seventh (Leningrad) Symphony by Dmitry Shostakovich. Filming was shot with constantly freezing equipment by people who shared the hunger and constant danger of artillery fire with the rest of Leningrad. The film is a heroic deed itself.

Leningrad moviemakers are proud of their studio. **Lenfilm** has an interesting history, which starts with a small *atelier* in Aquarium Summer Garden. Over the years, the studio became the second largest movie company in the USSR (after Mosfilm). The golden era of the studio fell in the period between the two world wars: great films of that era included *Chapayev* by Georgy and Sergei Vasiliev (1934), the *Maxim* sequence (1935–39), the *Deputy of the Baltic* (1937) and the *Member of Government* (1940) by Alexander Zarkhi and Iosif Heifits.

It is curious how, in Leningrad, people had little interest in the monumental epics that they loved so much in Moscow – films showing battles, the taking of the Winter

Palace and other czarist strongholds in their city. The movies about Lenin were mainly made in Moscow.

In Leningrad, the camera looked at the ordinary people, the rank-and-file participants in historic events. Chapayev, a partisan and Red Army officer in the Civil War; the St Petersburg professor of biology, who was elected people's deputy from the Baltic; the Russian peasant woman who made it into the USSR. Supreme Soviet – these characters,

Above, contemporary advertisement for the chronicle of 1911.

played by such Soviet stars as Boris Babochkin, Nikolai Cherkasov and Vera Maretskaya are part of the classic collection of the images of Soviet moviemaking. Leningrad films have a soft and humane intonation, a certain modesty and a marked preference for realism and psychology over formal experiments.

The tradition lives on in the work of the younger generation at Lenfilm (its best representatives are directors Vitaly Melnikov and Igor Maslennikov). The spirited, clever Dinara Asanova (1942–85) investigated the problems of adolescence and school education in her films: *Woodpeckers Don't Have Headaches*, *Key Without Right of Assignation*, and *Boys*.

A fresh look and profound analysis mark the films of Aleksei German: *Highway Inspection*, *Twenty Days Without War* (1977), *My Friend Ivan Lapshin* (1984). German is a remarkable director whose work suffered in the era of stagnation: *Highway Inspection* was kept from the public for 15 years, and was salvaged only in 1988 by the "conflict committee", which released over 200 films made in the period 1960 to 1980 that had not been previously shown in the USSR.

The fate of that film was shared by other Leningrad productions – for example, *The Second Attempt of Viktor Krokhin* by Viktor Sheshukov (about a boxer spoiled by the lies and falsity of professional sport). Aleksei German and his younger supporters ushered in a new era, the era of *The Burglar*, *Gunpowder*, *Forgive Me*, *Freeze-Die-Arise* (the producer of the latter, Vitaly Kanevsky, made his debut in motion pictures by winning the Golden Camera Award at the 1990 Cannes Festival).

Leningrad hosts the International Festival of Non-Fiction Films and a variety of symposia dedicated to the art of cinematography. Leningrad moviemakers are known in the country for their loyalty to principle, their non-conformism. It is not for nothing that the Chairman of the Union of Cinematographers of Russia was elected from their midst (director Igor Maslennikov); true enough, another chairman was elected from among the Muscovites (Sergei Soloviev), sealing the union of the two rivals.

It is, to put it mildly, unforgivable not to visit the Hermitage when you are in Leningrad. There are only a few museums of this class in the world – perhaps the Louvre in Paris, the British Museum in London and the Metropolitan Museum of Art in New York.

The facts and figures about the Hermitage are astounding: it has nearly 400 exhibition halls and is annually attended by more than 3 million visitors, who would have to walk over 20 km (13 miles) to view the displays in all the halls.

It is impossible to list all the treasures kept in the Hermitage, for they include 15,000 paintings, 12,000 sculptures, 600,000 works of graphic art, 1,000,000 coins and medals, 224,000 works of applied art. The Hermitage library, one of the world's largest depositories of books on art, runs into no less than half a million volumes.

But then, quantity in art means less than anywhere else. The important thing is that the Hermitage collections include top-class masterpieces. Judge for yourself. Among them are the M*adonnas* by Raphael and Leonardo da Vinci, *Judith* by Giorgione, Titian's *St Sebastian*, and 24 paintings by Rembrandt, including such all-time stars as *The Return of the Prodigal Son* and *Flora*.

The Hermitage boasts one of the world's finest collections of the French impressionists and post-impressionists. Classical sculptures, Egyptian mummies that lay buried underground for several millennia and superb pieces of Scythian gold are also to be seen here. In short, the Hermitage has unique exhibits dating from every period between the late Stone Age and our own day.

The finest architecture of its time: Now add to this the interior decoration of the Hermitage with its magnificent marble stairways and columns, parquet floors of rare beauty, ceilings ornamented with fancy gilt stucco moulding and period furniture. Vases, standard lamps and tables made of ornamental

stones – true *chefs-d'oeuvre* executed by Russian masters – alone number upwards of 400. The halls, the most famous among them being the Malachite Hall, are also decorated with coloured stone.

The architectural appearance of the complex of buildings housing the Hermitage today is majestic. The buildings were constructed in two stages, in the second half of the 18th century and in the mid-19th century. They reflect the changes in artistic taste and architectural style that took place with the transition from baroque to neoclassicism.

The embankment of the Neva offers a magnificent view of the grandiose **Winter Palace**, the small pavilion of the **Lesser Hermitage** standing nearby and the so-called **Old Hermitage**. The arch over the Winter Canal, well-known to lovers of the opera and traditionally associated with the scenery for Peter Tchaikovsky's opera *The Queen of Spades*, serves as a passage leading to the **Hermitage Theatre**. This splendid and world-famous ensemble was created by four outstanding 18th-century architects – Bartolomeo Rastrelli, Yuri Velten, Jean-Baptiste Vallin de la Mothe, and Giacomo Quarenghi.

A private collection: The Hermitage was initially set up as the private museum of the empress Catherine the Great. In the 18th century, the setting up of royal picture galleries was regarded as an affair of national importance in the countries of Europe. Catherine the Great started her gallery a year after her ascension to the throne in 1762. Having begun to collect art later than the other European monarchs, she spared no expense for the purpose.

Undoubtedly, not the least part in this was played by political considerations. It was one of the conspicuous undertakings which the empress needed to enhance the prestige of the Russian court. After the acquisition of the first lot of canvases by Dutch and Flemish painters in Berlin, systematic purchases of works of art at auctions in Paris and The Netherlands began. This task was given to

Preceding pages: the Winter Palace, home to the Hermitage. **Left,** the Jordan staircase.

Russian ambassadors to European courts.

Not just individual paintings, but also famous European collections were purchased, thus ensuring the high artistic level of the imperial collection. Soon Catherine the Great's gallery came to occupy one of the leading places in Europe. Sculptures, works of graphic art and carved gems were also bought for the Hermitage.

In the course of time, several other beautiful buildings – that came to be known as the Lesser Hermitage, the Old Hermitage and the Hermitage Theatre – were built next to the Winter Palace, the royal residence in St Petersburg. They were needed to accommo-

date the growing collection. Catherine wrote in one of her letters: "Although I am all alone, I have a whole labyrinth of rooms… and all of them are filled with luxuries…" She added ironically: "Only mice and myself feast our eyes on it."

The history of the Hermitage has some exciting and, sometimes, dramatic pages. It was here in the hall where paintings of the Italian and Spanish schools hang, converted into an interrogation room, that the arrested participants in the suppressed Decembrist uprising (14 December 1825) were questioned. Czar Nicholas I himself stayed in a

neighbouring hall amid pictures by Rubens and Van Dyck during the investigation.

It was also here in Voltaire's library, purchased by Catherine the Great in her day and kept at the museum, that the great Russian poet Alexander Pushkin worked on some of his books. Incidentally, he made a drawing of the statue of the celebrated philosopher in his notebook.

In December 1837 a great fire, which raged for more than a whole day, destroyed the Winter Palace. The inner passages linking the palace with the museum were dismantled and the museum's windows facing the palace were bricked up, and thus the Hermitage was saved. Fortunately, the palace was completely restored to its former grandeur six months later.

It was in the Winter Palace that the Provisional Government (which came to power after the overthrow of the autocracy – and whose sittings were held in the Malachite Hall) was arrested on 25 October 1917.

Restoration after the war: The 900-day siege of Leningrad from 1941 to 1943 was a bitter trial for the Hermitage, just as it was for the city itself. The museum's treasures were evacuated and thus, fortunately, saved. True, a large canvas by Van Dyck was lost. The buildings suffered heavy damage. Nonetheless, within a few years of the war's end they were completely restored.

Not long ago, in 1985, a modern vandal damaged Rembrandt's *Danae*. One of the visitors to the Hermitage, aiming to attract attention to himself, splashed the painting by the great Dutch master with sulphuric acid. It took Leningrad restorers four years to bring Rembrandt's masterpiece back to life.

As for the restoration of the whole of the Hermitage, which began in the same year, 1985, it will probably take more than a decade to complete. Fortunately, the Hermitage remains open to the public. And yet repair is repair, as the saying goes. Funds have been allocated and restoration work is in progress. But all the signs indicate that work may last many more years unless the assistance of foreign firms is available.

But the Hermitage cannot wait. Its buildings have been "worn out" over the centuries and its display area is far from sufficient.

Despite the fact that the former **Menshikov Palace** – the first stone building erected in the new capital of the Russian Empire – has recently been turned over to the collection (it now houses a display devoted to the early 18th-century period of Russian culture), the museum's exhibition halls can accommodate only a small fraction of what is kept in the exceedingly rich depositories of the Hermitage.

They say that a person would have to spend about 70 years of his or her life, working at it eight hours a day, in order to just glance at each Hermitage exhibit. Until such time as human beings extend their

It should be mentioned that Leonardo's famous *Madonna Litta* was bought by Stepan Gedeonov, the first permanently appointed director of the Hermitage, in Milan in 1864 from the family of the Counts Litta, related to the Russian imperial house. Later on, he bought Raphael's *Madonna Conestabile*, which arrived at the museum in 1881. Thus, it is Gedeonov whom the Hermitage has to thank for these two gems of its collection.

The Spanish collection of the Hermitage is regarded as one of the world's best. Its gems include *Boy with a Dog* by Bartolome Esteban Murillo and also the *Portrait of the Actress Antonia Zarate* by Francisco Goya,

longevity, we will restrict ourselves to picking out just a few of its masterpieces.

The best bits: A substantial share of the Hermitage collection is devoted to the history of Western European art. Paintings, sculptures, drawings and works of applied art dating from the 11th to the 20th centuries occupy 120 halls.

All the greatest masters of the Renaissance, such as Leonardo da Vinci, Raphael, Michelangelo and Titian, are to be seen here.

Left, *Pitcher and Bowls* by **Pablo Picasso**. **Above**, a gallery in the Hermitage.

presented to the Hermitage by the late US industrialist Armand Hammer. The Hermitage had no paintings by Goya before that. The museum does, however, boast a fine collection of drawings by the great Spaniard.

The art of Flanders, England and Germany is represented in the Hermitage by first-rate works. The Hermitage collection of works by French artists is the largest outside France itself. The paintings in this collection – ranging from Jean-Antoine Watteau and Jean Honoré Fragonard to Pierre Auguste Renoir, Henri Matisse and Pablo Picasso – are on display in more than 40 halls.

Monuments of the classic world – ancient Greek and Roman sculptural portraits and vases – occupy more than 20 halls on the ground floor in the building of the New Hermitage. The collection of the Oriental section, comprising 160,000 exhibits, is the largest in the Soviet Union. They include ancient Egyptian papyruses, sculptural pieces and other objects from Babylon, Assyria, India, China, Japan, Turkey, and other countries, embracing a period beginning with the 4th millennium BC.

The Hermitage collection of monuments and artefacts from the countries of the Near and Middle East includes the world's largest

collection of Iranian silver and carved gems dating from the period of the Sassanids (3rd–4th centuries AD), a collection that is famous all over the world.

By the way, when the Austrian writer Stefan Zweig came to the USSR in 1926, he visited the Hermitage. They say that he deliberately walked through 40 or 50 halls with his eyes closed so as not to see anything before he could stop near the canvases by Rembrandt and the collection of works by Watteau and Fragonard. Staggered by what he saw, Zweig asked to be shown something absolutely unique which was not to be seen

anywhere else. He was shown the Sassanids' silver and Scythian gold.

The Chinese collection: The section on the art of the countries of the Far East boasts the USSR's largest collection of monuments of Chinese culture and art. Its oldest exhibits include inscriptions on fortune-telling dice (there are some 200 of them) dating from the period of the Shang Dynasty (14th–11th centuries BC) and unique silk fabrics and embroideries (1st century BC) found during excavations at Noin-Ul in Mongolia in the 1920s. They are characteristic of the culture of the Huns of the period of the Han Dynasty. Also to be seen at the Hermitage are sculptural pieces and samples of wall-painting found at Qian Fo-dong (Monastery of the Cave of the Thousand Buddhas) near Tun Huang in Sinkiang in 1914–15.

Chinese art is also widely represented at the museum by porcelain, lacquerware, enamels, and paintings.

The lingering presumption that the Russian czars knew how to live in a grand way and were good judges of beauty is quite justified. Indeed, it would not be an exaggeration to say that each of the almost 400 exhibition halls of the Hermitage is very nearly a unique work of art created by talented Russian architects and artists and by the restorers who recreated their splendour.

The main staircase of the Winter Palace, built in the baroque style, is where every visitor to the Hermitage begins his acquaintance with the museum. Here everything is harmonious and exquisite. The same can be said about the antechamber with its famous **Malachite Temple** – a rotunda made of ornamental stones from the Urals – and about all the other halls of the Hermitage including, for example, the austere and majestic **Grand Hall** or the splendid **St George Hall**. Each of them is distinct from any other and each of them is truly inimitable.

It is hard to do justice to the enchanting beauty of the Hermitage halls. We will therefore conclude with a simple injunction: seeing the Hermitage is a must.

Above, Leonardo da Vinci's *Madonna with a Flower*. **Right**, a classical concert at the entrance to the museum.

The State Hermitage

Many tourists come to Leningrad with only one purpose in mind - to visit the Hermitage. No wonder that long queues in front of the booking office are quite common. The exposition was opened by Catherine the Great in the 18th century for the elite of Russian society. During the 19th century more and more people were permitted to see the collections in the Old, the New and the Small Hermitage. The Winter Palace, nevertheless, remained the residence of the Russian Czars until the Revolution of 1917. To see all the exhibits in one day is impossible. It's better to visit intensively those departments for which you have a special interest and just have a quick look around the remaining halls.

The Ground Floor of the Winter Palace

Different works of art and primitive household utensils

Central Asian art

Egyptian, Mesopotamian, Assyrian and Sumerian exhibits

The Ground Floor of the Small and the Large Hermitage

Antique art department

The First Floor of the Winter Palace

Western European art

Russian art and culture

The Second Floor of the Winter Palace

Medieval and Oriental art

Numismatic collection

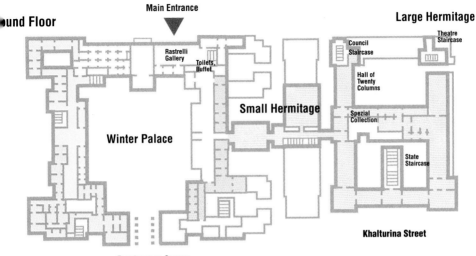

Ground Floor

Main Entrance

Large Hermitage

Rastrelli Gallery

Toilets, Buffet

Council Staircase

Theatre Staircase

Hall of Twenty Columns

Small Hermitage

Spezial Collection

Winter Palace

State Staircase

Khalturina Street

Dvortsovaya Square

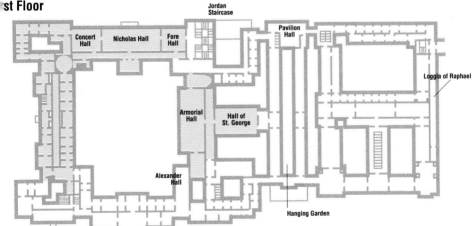

First Floor

Jordan Staircase

Pavilion Hall

Concert Hall

Nicholas Hall

Fore Hall

Loggia of Raphael

Armorial Hall

Hall of St. George

Alexander Hall

Hanging Garden

In a way, it is thanks to the Tretiakov Gallery that the Russian Museum exists today. This is how the story goes: in 1893, Emperor Alexander III (himself an avid collector of Russian painting) deigned to bestow his royal attention on the Tretiakov Gallery. Having examined the collection, Alexander exclaimed, "How fortunate Moscow is! We have nothing of the kind down in St Petersburg!" Soon afterwards, the decision was taken to open a museum of Russian art in the Russian capital.

And open it did – in 1898. The museum occupied one of St Petersburg's architectural marvels – the **Mikhailovsky Palace**. Built by Carlo Rossi for Alexander I's younger brother, Grand Prince Mikhail, in the first quarter of the 19th century, it became part of what we know today as Leningrad's **Square of Arts**.

Before inspecting the collection itself, have a look at the palace – it is certainly worth the trouble. The main facade, with its majestic Corinthian colonnade, is set back deep into the front garden. Rossi decorated the ground floor of the facade with symbols of Martian glory – armour, helmets, shields and swords. Mighty lions stand on guard at the main entrance.

The grounds are separated from the square outside by a wrought-iron grille. Laconic yet solemn, it is certainly one of the most beautiful in Leningrad with its rows of gold-pointed spears. Especially eye-catching is the combination of black iron and glittering precious metal. Rows of spears are interspaced with iron columns adorned with military trophies.

The opposite facade (looking out into the Mikhailovsky Garden) is altogether different: soft and mellow, it gives the impression of poetic harmony with the outlying scenery. Its serene beauty reflects the quiet, cosy thoughtfulness of the garden. Come autumn, the leaves of old Leningrad maples, which are of the same delicate yellow hue as the

Left, the crowning of Mikhail Romanov.

palace walls, gently fall on the sloping steps of the garden entrance.

The collection: It started with works of Russian art assembled from country residences of the czars, the Hermitage, the Academy of Arts and, of course, from private collections. There were about 2,500 of them – mostly paintings, sculptures and drawings. Today the Russian Museum is rivalled only by the Tretiakov Gallery as the world's largest repository of Russian and Soviet art: there are 370,000 items in its collection.

No other museum comes near to its collection of graphic and sculptural works. You will also find period furniture, samovars, carved stones, china and Russian gems. The section on Old Russian art displays icons, frescoes and mosaics. It would not be an exaggeration to call the Russian Museum a veritable encyclopedia of national art from its origins in the 10th century to the experimental works of the present day.

Portraits galore: Two supermuseums – the Tretiakov Gallery and the Russian Museum – complement each other: where Moscow (the Tretiakov) has more works by the democratically minded "unofficial" painters of the second half of the 19th century, Leningrad (the Russian Museum) is ahead with 18th-century works (mainly portraits) and early 19th-century painting. This can be explained by the fact that the Imperial Court resided in St Petersburg at the time and vogue painters, in search of lucrative orders, flocked to the capital where most aristocrats lived. The Academy of Arts was here, as well, serving as a magnet for academic, "official" painting.

The portrait genre came to dominate both painting and sculpture in the second half of the 18th century. The Russian Museum proudly displays the works of Fyodor Shubin (1740–1805), the greatest sculptor of the time, who created enough portraits of contemporaries to stock an entire gallery.

The most interesting paintings of the period are a suite of seven *Smolny Girls* by Dmitry Levitsky (1735–1822). Catherine the Great hired the artist to paint the seven top graduates of the Smolny Institute (a privileged school for daughters of the gentry). The girls are depicted showing off their talents and abilities. They act out a pastoral scene from an amateur play, dance and play musical instruments.

Icons: As the years went by, the Russian Museum swelled like a river with many tributaries. A special place in this full-flowing stream is occupied by northern icons, which are amply represented. In fact, icons are the first thing you see here.

The main prize of the early icon collection is the small 12th-century work, *Angel Gold-Hair*. It was part of a triptych of Christ flanked by angels. The unknown painter was clearly a person of not inconsiderable talent and poetic vision. He saw the angel as the embodiment of humaneness, undying beauty, purity and youth. This message from the distant 12th century reminds us of the eternal nature of the virtues of compassion and sympathy.

Another of the museum's outstanding icons is entitled *Boris and Gleb*. This 14th-century work by an unknown artist is a pearl of Old Russian art. It shows two young, early 11th-century princes, Boris and Gleb, sons of Kiev's Prince Vladimir. Both were murdered in the course of a dynastic dispute with their elder brother, Svyatopolk (*circa* 980–1019), whom the people stigmatised as "the Damned" for this foul deed. The church canonised Boris and Gleb. Russia's first saints are considered the guardian spirits of the country.

Sometime between 1360 and 1370, somewhere in Rus (the chronicles do not say where exactly) the greatest Russian painter of the Middle Ages was born. His name was Andrei Rublev. Only a few of his works survive. The Russian Museum has several Rublevs, including *Apostle Peter* and *Apostle Paul*. These huge icons (nearly double a man's height) were part of the grandiose iconostasis in the Assumption Cathedral in Vladimir, where Andrei Rublev and his friend Daniil Chyorny worked in 1408.

Prized pieces: Every museum has a *pièce de résistance*, an item prized above all other possessions. Such items are usually exten-

sively described in books, albums, postcards and booklets. Even though lack of space usually keeps a lion's share of works away from the eyes of the public, such works never see the inside of a storeroom – they are always on display in the best halls.

The Russian Museum has several such masterpieces. One of them is *Pompeii's Last Day* by Karl Bryullov (1799–1852). When it first appeared, the painting produced a bombshell effect in Russian society. Nikolai Gogol (then a young author) showered it with praise and called it "one of the most outstanding phenomena of the 19th century." Professors and students of the Acad-

emy of Arts gave solemn receptions and dedicated poems to the master painter. Even Alexander Pushkin wrote several verses about the painting.

Another masterpiece, which was created 40 years later, differs both in subject and plot. The picture is *Burlaks on the Volga* by Ilya Repin (1844–1930). Vladimir Stasov, the prominent Russian art critic, had the following to say about it: "Repin is as much a realist as Gogol, and quite as national. It was with a courage unheard-of in our land that he plunged headlong into the depths of folk life, the interests and the pains of the life our people live... Repin is a mighty artist and a thinker." Ilya Repin lived up to these words, and left a legacy of true masterpieces, many of which can be seen on a tour of the Russian Museum.

Russian landscape painting would be nothing without Isaac Levitan (1860–1900). Anton Chekhov, the writer and Levitan's close friend, called him "the best Russian scenic painter." One of Levitan's paintings – *The Lake* (1900) – has for almost a century now been an irresistible attraction.

Amongst the other paintings that you must see are the works of Mikhail Vrubel (1856–1910), the creator of the famed *Demons*, and,

of course, the paintings of Nicholas Rerikh (1877–1947), one of those artists whose vision, as Alexander Blok put it, "reaches beyond the foreground of the world to that which is hidden from view."

The Russian Museum also houses the works of one of the 19th century's outstanding sculptors, Piotr Klodt (1805–67). Visitors to Leningrad usually see his sculptures before they come to the Russian Museum –

Left, *Gymnasts*, a modern painting by D. Zhilinsky. **Above**, *Portrait of Chaliapin* by B. Kustodiev.

on the city's main street, Nevsky Prospekt (or, more accurately, on Anichkov Bridge), where four of Klodt's creations stand. The monument to fable-writer Ivan Krylov, in the Summer Garden, is also his work.

The museum also has an abundance of avant garde painting. The works of Natalia Goncharova (1881–1962), Mikhail Larionov (1881-1964) and Kasimir Malevich (1878–1935) exhibit a connection with folk art as well as medieval icons and frescoes. You would also do well to consider such works as Goncharova's *Sunflowers and Peasants* or *the Sailor* by Vladimir Tatlin (1885–1953).

Unfortunately, these painters were not fully appreciated in their homeland during their lifetime. Today, however, the Russian Museum has the world's largest collection of works by Kasimir Malevich – 136 paintings and drawings.

Fate was not kind to some other representatives of the Russian avant garde, including Vasily Kandinsky (1866–1944) and Alexander Rodchenko (1891–1956). As the Russian proverb says: "What we have, we don't cherish; once we lose it, we cry." Fortunately not all that many of their works were lost, thanks largely to the efforts of enthusiastic collectors. Now these riches are on display at the Russian Museum – the gloomy majesty of Kandinsky's fantasies and the strained compositions of Alexander Rodchenko along with the biological and physiological phenomena of creation by Pavel Filonov (1891–1941).

In recent years the opportunity has been provided to see other long-hidden masterpieces. The museum has now acquired two old palaces in midtown Leningrad – the **Stroganoff Residence** and the **Inzhenerny Castle** – hoping in this way to cope with the catastrophic lack of space.

But these are of secondary importance. The main thing is visit the Russian Museum, which remains an encyclopaedia of Russian life, Russian character, Russian soul. Come in and you'll see – besides the beauty of Russian nature, the charm of its women, the imaginativeness of its people – the spirit of the nation, which has, since time immemorial, found its reflection in genuine art.

The Russian Museum

It was Czar Nicholas II who ordered that the mixed collection
of Russian art and ethnographic items in the Mikhailovsky
Palace be opened to the public. The ethnographic exhibits were
later moved to the right wing of the palace and separately
named the Museum of Ethnography of Peoples of the USSR.

Russian art is now exhibited in the central building of the palace,
in the Rossi Wing (Fligel' Rossi) and the Benois Building to its left.
The ground floor of the central palace building and the Fligel'
Rossi contain the museum's collections of 19th-century Russian
paintings, decorative and applied art.

Masterpieces of Russian art from the 12th to the 18th century
are on the first floor.

You will find Russian art of the 19th and 20th centuries as well as
art from the Soviet period on both floors of the Benois Building.
The first floor of the Fligel' Rossi is occupied by contemporary
exhibitions.

Mikhail Palace

Benois Building

Nineteenth Century art

State Vestibule

Rossi Wing

Soviet art

Applied art

Main Entrance

Toilets

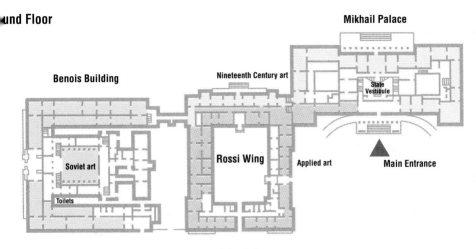

Iskusstv Square

Nineteenth Century art

White Hall

Eighteenth Century art

Nineteenth Century art

Early Russian art

Temporary exhibitions

Early Twentieth Century art

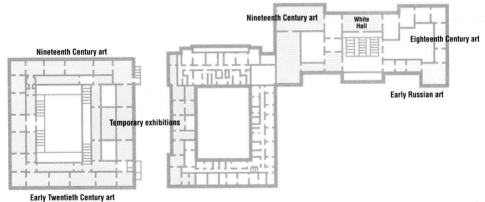

Academician Dmitry Likhachev writes about the eternal appeal of St. Petersburg.

The key feature of Leningrad's architecture is the predominance of horizontal over vertical lines. Horizontals form the basis on which all other lines are drawn. The predominance of horizontals is explained by the city's numerous water surfaces: those of the **Greater Neva** and **Little Neva**, the **Greater Nevka** and **Little Nevka**, the **Fontanka**, the

The shimmering line of rooftops seen against the background of the sky makes the buildings seem illusory or ephemeral. This impression is reproduced exquisitely by Dostoyevsky in his *Adolescent*: "Amidst this fog I was a hundred times beset by a strange but persistent dream: what if this mist disperses, goes up and away; will not all of this rotten, slimy city rise together with it and disperse like smoke, leaving behind only the original Finnish swamp?"

Moika, the **Griboyedov Canal** and the **Kryukov Canal**, for example.

Horizontal lines: The point of contact between water and land creates an ideal horizontal line. Leningrad's water seems to fill the city right to the brim. This invariably surprises those visitors more accustomed to cities that stand on tidal rivers or those with fluctuating levels.

Running above the two horizontals formed by water and embankment is a thinner, less definite line formed by the rooftops which never, in keeping with the often-repeated order, rose higher than the Winter Palace.

Perpendicular structures: Other characteristic elements of the city are the three spires, those of the **Peter and Paul Fortress**, the **Admiralty** and the **Mikhailovsky Castle**. They are viewed as perpendiculars to the horizontal lines, which favourably contrast and emphasise the latter. The spires are accompanied by tall belfries, such as that of the **Chevakinsky** on the **Kryukov Canal** (and once of the bell tower of the **church at Sennaya Square**, which, sadly, has been pulled down).

The enormous bulk of **St Isaac's Cathedral** with its gilt dome was meant to form the focus of Leningrad's second centre, fulfilling a town-planning function similar to that of St Peter's Cathedral in Rome. Other domes are evenly distributed all over the city and their spherical, non-rectilinear shapes sit like decorative flourishes, feminine in character, above the masculine lines of the city at large.

The city's main squares, **Palace Square** and the **Field of Mars**, stand near the Neva but are fenced off from it by a row of houses. The only square facing directly onto the Neva – **Peter's (Senate) Square** with the *Bronze Horseman* – exposes Peter the Great and his steed to a broad stretch of water.

In front of the Finland Station, on the other the **Leningrad Hotel**, built in an incoherent and unimaginative style like a box. Another major infringement of the city's image is the **Sovietskaya Hotel** in the old Kolomna District. Its isolated buildings of varying heights break Leningrad's typically coherent skyline and produce an impression of uninspired and gloomy confusion.

The colour spectrum: Of the other characteristics of Leningrad, I consider most important the following two: the city's colour spectrum and its harmonious combination of major architectural styles. The colour of houses in Leningrad plays so important a role that it would be hard to think of a major

side of the Neva and somewhat higher up the river, stands Lenin on top of an armoured car. The majestic gesture of the *Bronze Horseman* is a contrast to Lenin's oratorical gesture. The square is quite satisfactory in respect to town-planning terms, except for the unwieldy office building which ploughs the statue into one corner.

Modern violations: The dominance of horizontal lines in the city is badly distorted by

Preceding pages: a city of vertical and horizontal lines. Left, Atlantes carry a heavy load at the New Hermitage. Above, the Engineers' Castle.

European city worthy of comparison with it. Leningrad needs more colour than any other city because it is deprived of it by mist and rain. That is why brick masonry was not left unplastered, and plaster required painting. Watercolour tones prevail in the gamut of the city's colours.

The city's historical past, which is comparatively short (only three centuries long), may be viewed as a completed stage production, since it is quite obvious that the city's historical drama has been played out, no matter what its future significance for the country may prove to be.

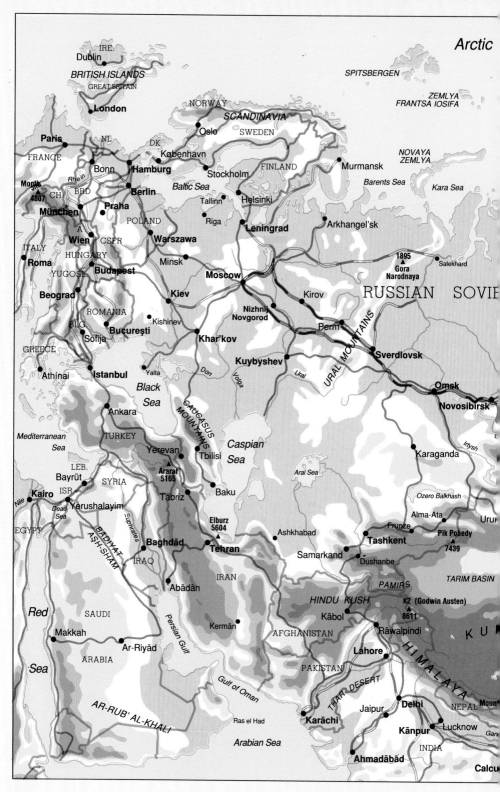

Ocean

NOVOSIBIRSKIE OSTROVA

RNAYA
YA

Laptev Sea

OSTROV
TAYMYR

'sk

SIBERIA

DERATIVE SOCIALIST REPUBLIC

Anadyr'

Ambartschik

Bering Sea

ALEUTIAN ISLANDS

KHREBET CHERSKOVO

Verkhoyansk

VERKHOYANSKIY KHREBET

Yakutsk

Sea of Okhotsk

Kiyuchevskaya
Sopka
▲ 4750

Petropoavlovsk-
Kamchatsky

Kap Lopatka

OSTROV SAKHALIN

KURIL ISLANDS

STANOVOY KHREBET

Amur

Yuzhno-
Sakhalinsk

Khabarovsk

Pacific Ocean

ssiberian Railway

Ozero Baykal

YABLONOVY KHREBET

GREATER KHINGAN

Nakhodka

Vladivostok

HOKKAIDO

Sapporo

Irkutsk

CHANGAJN NURUU

Ulaanbaatar

Harbin

Changchun

HONSHŪ

MONGOLIA

Shenyang

NORTH
KOREA

Sea of Japan

JAPAN

Fuji-san
▲ 3776

Tōkyō

Peking

P'yŏngyang

Soŭl

Osaka

G O B I

Tianjin

Yellow Sea

SOUTH KOREA

Pusan

Kitakyūshū

NAN SHAN

Qingdao

East China Sea

KYŪSHŪ

N SHAN

Lanzhou

Yellow Huang

Zhengzhou

Shanghai

RYUKYU ISLANDS

Xi'an

C H I N A

Wuhan

Minya Konka
▲ 7556

Chongqing

T'aipei

TAIWAN

hasa

hmaputra

Kanton

Kunming

Macau

HONGKONG

haka

BURMA

3L

VIETNAM

Chittagong

LAOS

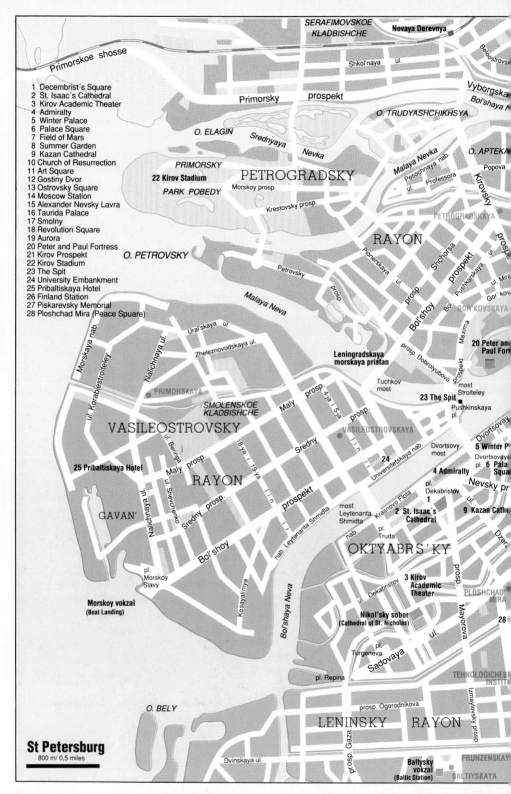

St Petersburg

1 Decembrist´s Square
2 St. Isaac´s Cathedral
3 Kirov Academic Theater
4 Admiralty
5 Winter Palace
6 Palace Square
7 Field of Mars
8 Summer Garden
9 Kazan Cathedral
10 Church of Resurrection
11 Art Square
12 Gostiny Dvor
13 Ostrovsky Square
14 Moscow Station
15 Alexander Nevsky Lavra
16 Taurida Palace
17 Smolny
18 Revolution Square
19 Aurora
20 Peter and Paul Fortress
21 Kirov Prospekt
22 Kirov Stadium
23 The Spit
24 University Embankment
25 Pribaltiskaya Hotel
26 Finland Station
27 Piskarevsky Memorial
28 Ploshchad Mira (Peace Spuare)

800 m/0,5 miles

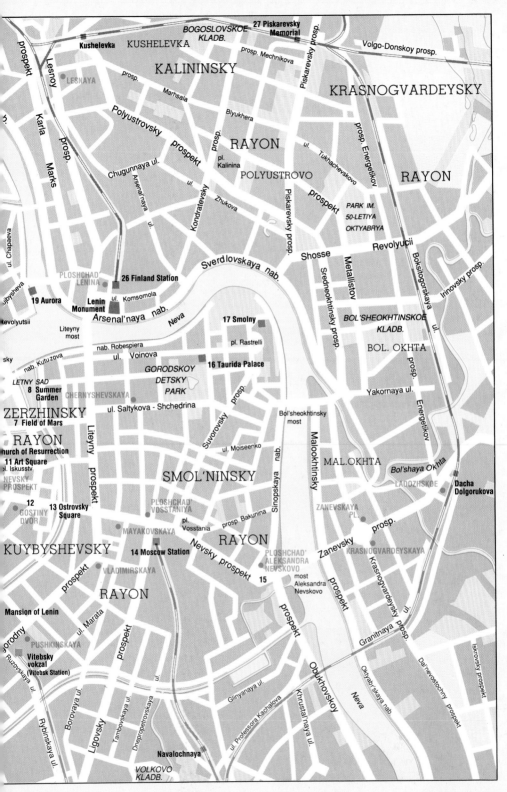

prospekt

Kushelevka KUSHELEVKA

BOGOSLOVSKOE
KLADB.

27 Piskarevsky
Memorial

Volgo-Donskoy prosp.

Lesnoy

LESNAYA

prosp.

Marhsala

Piskarevsky prosp.

prosp. Mechnikova

KALININSKY

KRASNOGVARDEYSKY

Karla

Blyukhera

Polyustrovsky

prospekt

prosp.

RAYON

prosp. Energetikov

Marks

Prosp.

Chugunnaya ul.

Arsenal'naya ul.

Kondratevsky

Zhukova

pl.
Kalinina

ul.

POLYUSTROVO

ul. Tukhachevskovo

RAYON

Piskarevsky prosp.

prospekt

PARK IM.
50-LETIYA
OKTYABRYA

Revolyucii

ul. Chapaeva

ul.

Sverdlovskaya nab.

Shosse

Sredneokhtinsky prosp.

Metallistov

Boksitogorskaya

Irinovsky prosp.

ul.

PLOSHCHAD
LENINA

26 Finland Station

Neva

17 Smolny

BOL'SHEOKHTINSKOE
KLADB.

ubysheva

ul. Komsomola

BOL. OKHTA

19 Aurora

Lenin
Monument

Arsenal'naya nab.

pl. Rastrelli

prosp.

Yakornaya ul.

Revolyutsii

Liteyny
most

nab. Robespiera

16 Taurida Palace

sky

nab. Kutuzova

ul. Voinova

GORODSKOY
DETSKY
PARK

Suvorovsky

Bol'sheokhtinsky
most

Energetikov

LETNY SAD
8 Summer
Garden

CHERNYSHEVSKAYA

ul. Saltykova - Shchedrina

ul. Moiseenko

Malookhtinsky

MAL.OKHTA

Bol'shaya Okhta

ZERZHINSKY

7 Field of Mars

Liteyny

prospekt

SMOL'NINSKY

Sinopskaya

nab.

MAL.OKHTA

LADOZHSKOE

Dacha
Dolgorukova

RAYON

hurch of Resurrection

11 Art Square

pl. Iskusstv

NEVSKY
PROSPEKT

PLOSHCHAD'
VOSSTANIYA

Zanevskaya

ZANEVSKAYA
PL.

prosp.

12

GOSTINY
DVOR

13 Ostrovsky
Square

pl.
Vosstania

prosp. Bakunina

Zanevsky

KRASNOGVARDEYSKAYA

MAYAKOVSKAYA

RAYON

PLOSHCHAD'
ALEKSANDRA
NEVSKOVO

prospekt

KUYBYSHEVSKY

14 Moscow Station

Nevsky prospekt

15

most
Aleksandra
Nevskovo

Krasnogvardeysky plosp.

VLADIMIRSKAYA

Granitnaya

Iskrovsky prospekt

RAYON

Mansion of Lenin

prospekt

Oktyabr'skaya nab.

Dal'nevostochny prospekt

orodny

ul. Marata

Ruzovskaya ul.

PUSHKINSKAYA

Vitebsky
vokzal
(Vitebsk Station)

prospekt

Obukhovskoy

Neva

Khrustal'naya ul.

Borovaya ul.

Tambovskaya ul.

Dnepropetrovskaya

Glinyanaya ul.

ul. Professora Kachalova

prospekt

Ligovsky

Rybinskaya ul.

Navalochnaya

VOLKOVO
KLADB.

FINDING YOUR WAY

None of the great 19th-century imperial powers could boast that its capital stood on 42 islands and isles – that is, except for St Petersburg, the capital of the Russian Empire. As the years went by, St Petersburg first surrendered its status as a capital to Moscow, then it even lost its name. But it has never lost its fame as the Venice of the North. That is what Leningrad is often called with good reason: Nevsky Prospekt, Leningrad's main avenue, passes over as many as four islands. Walking along Nevsky it is difficult to realise this fact – somehow, the **Moika**, the **Fontanka** and the **Griboyedov** canals, all of which are crossed by Nevsky, do not look as if they separate one island from another.

The place where the island nature of the city does dawn on you is on the tip of Vasilievsky Island. If you stand on what is universally known as the **Spit**, between the two huge red **Rostral Columns**, with your back to the Stock Exchange (today, the **Central Naval Museum**), you have the feeling that the city is built right into the water.

The islands on which downtown Leningrad stands are united into a series of large groups by the capricious bends of the Neva. The central group, which is also the largest, with Nevsky and nearly all of the main highlights of the town, is to your right, across the Neva. It consists of **Admiralteisky (Admiralty) Island**, where the Winter Palace ensemble, the Admiralty itself and St Isaac's, are situated, and the adjacent **Novoadmiralteisky (New Admiralty) Island**. **Novaya Gollandia (New Holland)**, **Kolomensky**, **Matisov**, **Kazansky**, **Pokrovsky** and **Spassky** islands, all lie to the west, where they are embraced by Leningrad's largest island, called **Bezymianny (Nameless)**. This downtown group also includes the isles on which the Summer Garden, the Field of Mars and the Alexander Nevsky Monastery, at the eastern end of Nevsky Prospekt, are built.

The second group of islands, to your left, is called the **Petrograd Side**. The eye is immediately caught by **Zayachi (Hare) Island**, where the majestic Peter and Paul Fortress stands. The other islands on that side are **Petrovsky**, **Krestovsky**, **Aptekarsky**, **Yelagin** and **Trudiaschikhsya**. Kirov Park stands on Yelagin Island. Trudiaschikhsya (Worker's) Island, formerly known as Stone Island, is where all the *dachas* of the Leningrad *nomenklatura* are.

Standing at the Spit, you are on **Vasilievsky Island**. This is part of the Baltic shoreline. You'll find the Sea Terminal and one of the town's best hotels, the Pribaltiskaya, on that part of the island called **Cavan** (Harbour).

Below and above water: Owing to the fact that the upper layers of the city are unstable (Peter built St Petersburg on bogs and marshlands), it was decided that a deep subway would be both cheaper and easier to build than a more shallow one. Construction started in 1940, but the war froze the project, and the first line did not come into operation until 1955. Today, four lines cover some 150 km (93 miles). On the map each subway line seems to cross the Neva but, in fact, the river passes quite a way above. Locals are used to this, but it may be a new experience to some visitors to think that boats and barges are floating somewhere overhead.

Besides going under the river, you can, naturally, also go on the river – there is certainly water enough. Summertime traffic on the water is heavy. Unfortunately, most of the city's rivers and canals are too narrow for river-going passenger transport, but they are just right for small powerboats, which will take you on an exciting water-tour of this Northern Venice. You only have to strike a bargain with one of the numerous boatman along the quay in front of the Winter Palace.

Official routes run along the **Neva**, the **Bolshaya (Greater)**, **Malaya (Little)** and **Srednyaya (Middle) Nevka** to **Krestovsky Island** and into the centre of Leningrad's city archipelago. Should you want to go on a longer trip, you can take the hydrofoil to **Petrodvorets** (Peterhof).

In addition, Leningrad has buses and trams. Minibus taxis with fixed routes take 10 passengers and offer better service than the city bus lines. They can be stopped anywhere along the route and the fare is only 15 kopecks. Then there are taxis, with or without meters. The latter are both more numerous and, alas, more expensive. Electric suburban trains will take you to any of Leningrad's satellite towns.

Cheer up, lovers of the horse-drawn carriage! One is still waiting in **Dvortsovaya Square**. The cabby, complete with old-fashioned uniform, will happily show you around old Leningrad.

The main streets: Nevsky Prospekt is the main artery or, rather, the backbone of downtown Leningrad. It starts at **Dvortsovy (Palace) Bridge** which links Vasilievsky and Admiralteisky Islands, runs across **Vosstania (Uprising) Square**, and ends in **Alexander Nevsky Square**. To one side of the square is the entrance to the Alexander Nevsky Monastery; the other side is occupied by the Moskva Hotel. The section of Nevsky between Dvortsovaya Square and Vosstania Square (where the Moscow Railway Station is situated) forms a perfectly straight line.

The largest avenues act as the city's "ribs" to Nevsky's "spine". Running at right angles to Dvortsovy Bridge and Nevsky are two embankments, **Dvortsovaya** and **Krasnogo Flota** (Red Fleet). In the place where Nevsky crosses **Sadovaya Street**, you will find, in a large old rectangular two-storey house, the Gostiny Dvor Department Store.

Further on, **Liteiny** and **Vladimirsky Avenues**, **Marata Street** and **Mayakovsky Street** branch off to the left and right from Nevsky. After that, Nevsky continues until it ends at the **Ligovsky Prospekt** intersection.

Aristocratic mansions on the Fontanka.

132

From Alexander Nevsky Square, two streets start out in opposite directions along the Neva embankment – **Sinop Embankment** and **Obukhovskoi Oborony Prospekt**. On the far side of the Neva, **Zanevsky Prospekt** continues where Nevsky leaves off; the street that crosses it at right angles and runs along the bank is called **Malookhotinsky Prospekt**.

Further to the south, **Komsomolskaya Square** is the starting point for two other thoroughfares – **Marshal Zhukov Prospekt**, which leads to the **Tallinn Highway**, and **Krasnoputilovskaya Street**, which leads to the **Moscow Highway** via **Pobedy Square**. **Prospekt Stachek** itself leads to the **Peterhof Highway**, the road to Petrodvorets.

From the Petrograd and Vyborg sides several important transport arteries stretch out to the north. Near the Field of Mars, **Kirov Bridge** links **Dvortsovaya Embankment** to the starting point of **Kirov Prospekt**, the main artery of the Petrograd Side.

Marx Prospekt, which starts at **Lenin Square**, close to the Finland Station on Vyborg side, continues as **Engels Prospekt** and brings you to the **Vyborg Highway**. From the city centre Marx Prospekt can also be reached via **Liteiny Prospekt** over **Liteiny Bridge** crossing the Vyborg Embankment. **Suzdalsky Prospekt** and **Rustaveli Street** form a semi-circle to the northeast of the city.

The original layout: St Petersburg started with Petropavlovskaya (Peter and Paul) Fortress on Zayachy Island. The first houses were built near the fortress, on the Neva shoreline of what was later named the Petrograd Side. Admiralty House was then built on the left bank of the Neva. In the early 18th century, three avenues fanned out from that spot – Nevsky Prospekt, Voznesensky (now Mayorov) Prospekt, and Gorokhovaya (now Dzerzhinskogo) Street.

The architects of the first master layout of 1737, Pyotr Yeropkin, Mikhail Zemtsov and Ivan Korobov, figured that the trident formed by these three av-

Aristocratic mansions on the Moika.

enues would be the backbone of future construction. Their plan was to build separate areas for the "noble" and the "base" classes. The plan also envisaged further construction of administrative buildings on Vasilievsky Island.

The next master plan was prepared by a group of architects led by Alexei Kvasov (1763–69). This time, emphasis was laid on regulated patterns. The plan was approved and became the basic grid for further construction.

Architectural wonders: If urban development can be compared to the stages of human life, then the time of youth and bloom for St Petersburg was the second half of the 18th and the first half of the 19th centuries. It was then that the city's main architectural wonders were built – **Dvortsovaya Square** with the **Alexander Column** and the **Winter Palace**, the **Kazan Cathedral**, the square known today as **Ostrovsky Square**, the **Alexander Nevsky Monastery** and the **Smolny ensemble**.

The middle of the 19th century is associated by local people with three major projects: **Blagoveschensky Bridge**, **St Isaac's Cathedral** and the **Petersburg Railway.** All three, St Isaac's in particular, took forever to complete. Sceptics called the bridge project a swindle and prophesied that it would collapse immediately after its opening. Public opinion on the subject was reflected by the wits of the day, who said, "We'll see the bridge over the Neva, but our children won't. The railroad, our children will see, but we won't. And neither we nor our children will see St Isaac's completed."

The second half of the 19th century brought an incredible boom in speculative housing and amusement establishments, along with numerous banks and industrial enterprises.

Returning to our human-life analogy, the city of the late 19th century was the young and energetic *bon vivant*, who had just developed a taste for entrepreneurial activity and had suddenly started earning good money.

The builders of today's – still growing – Leningrad continue their predecessors' task. Day by day they spin the web of streets, tie the knots of squares, thread the beads of buildings. All this, however, takes place in the suburbs – almost nothing new is being built in the centre these days. But a lot of work, which is probably more difficult, goes on in the central part of town, which has to be restored.

In the late 1980s, Leningrad had over 1,800 avenues, boulevards, streets, side streets and quays with the net length of over 2,000 km (1,200 miles). The longest streets in the city are the Obukhovskoi Oborony Prospekt and the Moscow and Lenin Prospekt, each of which is roughly 10 km (6 miles) long.

In Peter's time, over 40 large and small rivers threaded the city, serving as thoroughfares. But even such an impressive number of waterways could not satisfy all the city's transport needs. Hence the 20-odd man-made canals and ditches, which we regard today as souvenirs of the past epoch.

A city of bridges: Peter prohibited the construction of bridges for fear of hampering navigation on the Neva. In 1727 the Czar died, and the first bridge across the Neva was built. It stood on floats and could be moved to make way for shipping. By the time it finally became clear that the first solid bridge, the **Blagoveschensky** *most* (bridge), would not collapse after all, the floating bridge lost its importance. It was still used until 1916, when it burned to the ground (or, rather, to the water) after a spark flew out of the funnel of a passing tug.

Today, the number of bridges in Leningrad – over 100 – far exceeds the number of rivers and canals. The bridges on the Neva can be raised to let the larger vessels through. As for the hydrofoils that cruise the Neva, they have no reason to fear the bridges, since they sit low in the water.

In fact, Leningrad itself is like a raised bridge between the glittering days of the empire and its current lacklustre situation as a regional centre lost in the endless Russian Soviet Federative Socialist Republic.

The districts: Although they may appear to be a bureaucratic formality at first sight, administrative districts (*rayon*) with their characteristic names (and the principles in accordance with which their borders are established) have a tell-tale significance – they reflect the history of the nation and help the visitor to understand the soul of a Soviet city.

For instance, there are several compulsory, "ritual" titles. Every Soviet city has to have an **October District** and a **Lenin District** in commemoration of the Revolution. Some titles are connected with geography: the district located nearest to the capital city is usually called **Moskovsky**. Many are named after assorted revolutionaries and party figures. Here, too, there are clear leaders – **Kalinin**, **Dzerzhinsky** and **Kirov** are names encountered everywhere.

In St Petersburg, the process of division was marked by considerable re-straint of the bureaucratic flight of fantasy. Unlike other cities, the chief architect of this town has been the Neva. Hence, when it came to dividing the city into districts, the Neva acted as the chief bureaucrat (together with its executive apparatus – its tributaries). The only thing left for the bureaucrats to do was to find suitable names for the pieces of land that were neatly cut up by the waterways.

In the ensuing decades, however, the municipal authorities got their chance to get in on the act, for new districts appeared – beyond the river's reach. And, as the ever-growing town perimeter moves further and further away from the banks of the river that gave it life, new names have to be thought up for the up-and-coming suburbs.

Leningrad also has numerous lesser administrative units called *massivy* (communities). Their names, it is pleasing to report, have survived all renaming campaigns, mostly owing to their historical origins.

The former Stock Exchange on the Spit.

DOWNTOWN

Leningrad's imperial heritage is best seen along the quays of the Neva's left bank. It is customary to start a visit to the city with the **statue of Peter the Great** in the **Decembrists' Square** {*map reference* 1} – it was, after all, Peter who gave life to the city. The *Bronze Horseman* is the square's visual centre; he was at the centre of events of 14 December 1825 – the date of the Decembrists' abortive Revolution.

In the Soviet era, most of the old names gave way to new ones that were, directly or indirectly, connected with the Revolution and the post-revolutionary era. It would only be just to say that even the conservative czarist system had trouble finding an appropriate name for the square. Its original name was Senatskaya (the Senate was the highest state body in czarist Russia). Next to the Senate, there was the Synod – the highest authority in the Russian Orthodox Church from Peter's day up to the 1917 Revolution. When the monument to Peter was opened in 1782, the square was renamed Petrovskaya. But, somehow, the name did not stick, and the square was rechristened. In 1825 it was once more called Senatskaya.

The Decembrists' rebellion: On 19 November 1825, Emperor Alexander I died suddenly. By 14 December, a group of progressively minded officers of the Imperial Guard decided to seize their opportunity to take power. The rebels assembled the troops under their command in Senate Square, and deployed them in square formation around the statue of the *Bronze Horseman*.

Then the unexpected happened. The senators, who had been warned about the coming rebellion, hurriedly swore allegiance to the new Emperor, Nicholas I, and left the building. The initiative had been taken from the rebels' hands. Nicholas ordered the troops loyal to him to attack. By six o'clock that evening, the insurrection was over. The surviving rebels filled the dungeons of the Peter and Paul Fortress that very night. Five of them were later sentenced to death and more than 500 to hard labour. The Decembrists, as the rebels came to be known, were later seen as early revolutionaries, hence the eventual renaming of the square after them.

But let us return to the monument. Sculptor Etienne Falconet started working on it in 1768. In compliance with the desire of Empress Catherine II (who is mentioned in the inscription in Russian and Latin, *Petro Primo Catherina Secunda,* on two sides of the pedestal), he aimed to personify enlightened absolutism in his statue of the monarch leading the country along the road of progress. Catherine, as historians will confirm, aspired to this image herself, and corresponded with progressive French writers, such as Voltaire.

Falconet became totally absorbed in his task. To give him an insight into the dynamics of movement, accomplished horsemen reared their mounts, the prize stallions of the royal stables, *Diamond* and *Caprice,* in full gallop. When Falconet drew his sketches, he made the grooms hold the horses motionless on a specially made platform. An illustrious cavalry general, who resembled Peter in body and build, endlessly posed for Falconet until the sculptor finally decided how to cast his statue.

To the right of the monument stands the yellow edifice that was once the home of the **Senate** and the **Synod**. In 1829–34, Carlo Rossi redesigned the entire complex, his last large project. Architect Staubert managed the actual building. The new project reflected the tastes of the Czar and the Synod. The buildings were united by a baroque, statue-decorated arch. Colonnades were erected, and statues of Justice, Piety and other allegorical figures appeared on the facade as symbols of the united might of secular and clerical power.

In 1955 the buildings got their "historical content" back. They were turned over to the Central State Historical Archive of the USSR, which is responsible for millions of documents pertaining to the activities of central state authorities since the early 18th century.

Deeper into the square, two columns mark the beginning of what was once a canal. Later it was filled in and named, of all things, Trade Union Boulevard.

Naked pagans: The building with the eight-column portico alongside the Senate used to be an arena for horse races. It was built by **Giacomo Quarenghi** between 1804 and 1807. The architect skilfully tied the edifice into the general square ensemble. In 1817, the statues of Castor and Pollux (cast by Paulo Trickorni), were installed on the facade (they are miniature copies of the statues in front of the Quirinal Palace in Rome). They did not stay for long – naked young men of dubious pagan ancestry were not wanted as neighbours by St Isaac's, nearby, and the Synod had them removed in 1840.

After 1917, the revolutionary authorities closed St Isaac's, but the moment of triumph for the mythological heroes came only in 1954, when they were reinstalled in their old places. In 1977 the building was handed over to the Artists' Union, and there is an exhibition gallery there now. The Moscow horse arena, or *manège,* suffered a similar fate: it too is now a gallery where works of art are on display. The racing arena was not always used in accordance with its original purpose even in pre-revolutionary St Petersburg. On one occasion it housed an exhibition of agricultural machinery, and later served as a concert hall. Johann Strauss conducted a performance of his music there.

Before we continue our walk along the quay to the Admiralty and the Winter Palace, we will make a side tour that brings us to St Isaac's Cathedral to the south of the Decembrists' Square and to the Kirov Academic Theatre of Opera and Ballet.

St Isaac's Cathedral {2}, today shining with its golden dome (it took

Peter I on Decembrists' Square.

146

100 kg/220 lbs of the precious metal to cover it), is the fourth – and final – version of the **Church of Isaac Dalmatiisky**, Peter the Great's patron saint. St Isaac lived in the 4th century and was punished for his Christian faith by the heretic Emperor Valens but was later set free by Emperor Theodosius.

The construction of the cathedral was started in 1818 and completed 30 years later. The interior is decorated with malachite, lapis lazuli, porphyry and other costly materials. Its walls are in some places up to 5 metres (16 ft) thick. The building has a length of 111 metres (366 ft), a width of 98 metres (320 ft) and a height of 102 metres (333 ft). Its construction cost 10 times more than the Winter Palace. Up to 14,000 visitors can be accommodated in the cathedral at the same time.

Legend has it that the constant repair work, that started immediately after construction was completed, had to do with the belief (widespread in quarters close to the royal family) that the dynasty would fall should repairs be terminated. It is difficult to say who is to blame, but repairs must have stopped in 1917! In the Soviet era, repairs have been an on-and-off affair. If we stick to the legend, the last time they must have been stopped was when the Soviet "Czar of Leningrad" (who had the same last name as the royal family, Romanov), a corrupt and arbitrary creature of the Brezhnev era, finally stepped down.

The high reliefs in the cathedral are of exceptional beauty. On the southern pediment we find the *The Adoration of the Magi* by Ivan Vitali, where Mary and the child are surrounded by the kings of Mesopotamia and Ethiopia. The relief above the western portico, *The Meeting of St Isaac of Dalmatia with the Emperor Theodosius*, is by the same sculptor (Theodosius and his wife have the features of Alexander I and his spouse). In the corner of the relief there is a semi-naked man with a model of the cathedral in his hands; it depicts Auguste Montferrand, the architect of the edi-

The pedestal of Nicholas I's equestrian monument.

fice. The reliefs on the eastern and the northern pediments depict *The Meeting of St Isaac with the Emperor Valens* and *The Resurrection of Christ* respectively.

In the centre of St Isaac's Square, in front of the cathedral, there is an **equestrian monument to Nicholas I** (1859, by Klodt and Montferrand). The wily Klodt paid lip-service to the wife and daughters of the late emperor who wanted to perpetuate an idealised image of Nicholas, though he actually created a mercilessly realistic portrait of the clever yet ruthless and cold man that the people called Nikolai Palkin ("Nicholas of the Stick").

Where serfs were traded: Between the monument and the **Mariinsky Palace** (1839–44, by Andrei Stakenschneider), built for Nicholas I's daughter, Maria, and now occupied by the Executive Council of the Leningrad City Soviet, lies the **Siny (Blue) Bridge**. Unlike other bridges in the city, which are usually continuations of streets or roads, this bridge is a continuation of a square. Its width (100 metres/328 ft) makes it difficult to guess that you are standing on a bridge with the Moika flowing underneath. The bridge owes its name to the underside, which was painted blue. Siny Bridge is a place of sad fame: serfs were bought, sold and exchanged here from the 18th century until serfdom was abolished in 1861.

Memorable hotels: To the left of the cathedral, on the other side of **Mayorov Prospekt**, stands the **Astoria Hotel** (1910–12). More accurately, that is where it once stood: the Astoria was razed to the ground in 1988 following an irresponsible ruling by the Leningrad Executive Council. Even round-the-clock pickets organised by people who wanted to save the Astoria proved futile. The hotel was demolished and rebuilt from scratch by foreign companies. It is now a very comfortable hotel – but the death of the old Astoria continues to evoke public wrath.

The Astoria was the best hotel in town before 1917. It was patronized by army top brass. After the Revolution, it was the turn of the party top brass. Lenin and the delegates of the Second Communist International stayed here, as did the writer H. G. Wells in 1934.

Another fashionable old hotel, the **Angleterre**, formed a part of the Astoria. It was in one of the Angleterre's rooms that the famous Russian poet, Sergei Yesenin, committed suicide on 27 December 1925.

Truda (Labour) Square faces the quay of the canal that separates Admiralty Island from New Holland Island. New Holland was an ideal place for storing flammable shipbuilding materials (rope, wood, etc.) – it was close to the Admiralty and safely surrounded by water. Savva Chevakinsky, the architect who presided over the construction on the island, stacked the timber that was stored there vertically rather than horizontally. The length of the timbers used by the shipbuilders varied, so he built several warehouses of several different heights.

Truda (Labour) Street leads to Potseluyev Bridge. Nearby, on the bank of the Moika, is a yellow palace (by Vallin de la Mothe and Andrei Mikhailov Junior). Before the Revolution, the palace was owned by one of the wealthiest men in the country, Count Felix Yusupov, who was said to be as rich as the Czar himself. In his palace one of the most ghostly episodes of the czarist era took place.

The Siberian Demon: In 1907, the Rector of the St Petersburg Spiritual Academy introduced Grigory Rasputin to the court. Under the guise of a *starets* (holy man), who posed as a faith healer, Rasputin was a dyed-in-the-wool conman, devoid of any trace of decency. He used his not inconsiderable powers of hypnotism to put the royal family under his power. He established a particularly strong hold over the Empress, who blindly believed that only the prayers of the "holy man" could save the life of her haemophiliac son, Prince Alexei, and help her husband with affairs of state.

The ignorant Rasputin was soon enmeshed in the dirty dealings of the various political forces around the throne, and he served to destabilise further the already rocky boat of Russian politics. For a fee Rasputin could get rid of ministers, including cabinet members, organize deals and distribute state orders. Rasputin's wild orgies were even talked about abroad. His imagination knew no bounds where sex was concerned. The least of his "innocent pranks" was to arrange several naked girls on the floor in the form of a cross.

In an attempt to save the crumbling monarchy and lead the country away from disaster, several influential people, including Felix Yusupov, State Duma Deputy Vladimir Purishkevich and the Czar's relative, Grand Prince Dmitry Pavlovich, decided to rid the nation of Rasputin. In the small hours of 17 December 1916, the holy man was lured to Yusupov's palace and given cakes laced with poison. Some time passed, but the Siberian demon exhibited no inclination to leave this world. Shaken, the conspirators must have explained this as the intervention of the Devil himself, for they could not have known then that sugar weakened or neutralised the poison's toxic effects.

They were, nevertheless, sober-minded people, and they decided to shoot Rasputin. He was aware, by this time, that something was afoot and tried to get away from the palace. They shot him several times, tied the body with a rope, and dropped the bundle into the Moika. When the body was found later, it turned out that even that had not been enough for Grigory – dropped into the icy water, he had nearly managed to extricate himself from the knots that held him. Yusupov had to flee the country after the plot was uncovered.

Birth of the Bolshoi: From New Holland and the Yusupov Palace, our route leads over Potseluyev Bridge into **Teatralnaya (Theatre) Square**. The square derives its name from the artistic establishments that are situated there – the **Kirov Academic Theatre of Opera and Ballet**, {3} and the **Rimsky-Korsakov Conservatoire**.

The square's theatrical history dates to the middle of the 18th century. In 1782 a stone structure was built in place of the old wooden theatre. In 1783 Catherine the Great said that the theatre was "intended not only for comedy and tragedy, but for opera as well", and it was named the **Bolshoi Theatre**.

In 1803 the opera and ballet troupes were separated off from the drama group. For nearly a third of a century after that the opera troupe was headed by the Italian conductor and composer, Caterino Cavos. The ballet troupe was managed until 1829 by the French ballet master, Charles Didelot. The ballet stars of the early 19th century were Yevgenia Kolosova, an accomplished performer of folk dances, and Avdotia Istomina, to whom Pushkin dedicated a few lines of poetry and who willingly performed in ballets written in accordance with plots the poet supplied. In 1836, when Mikhail

Leningrad's Kirov ballet is world-famous.

Glinka's *Ivan Susanin* ("Life for the Czar") was produced on the Bolshoi's stage, the theatre ushered in the new age of Russian classical opera.

The Conservatoire was founded in 1862 by the composer Anton Rubinstein and renamed after Rimsky-Korsakov in 1944. It became the first establishment for higher musical education in Russia. The Conservatoire building was restructured and the St Petersburg Bolshoi ceased to exist. The list of the school's graduates is adorned with the names of Tchaikovsky and Shostakovich, among other famed composers.

Meanwhile, an enormous new theatre was built in Moscow in 1825, also called the Bolshoi. The Moscow Bolshoi produced operas and ballets by Russian and foreign authors and featured renowned masters of the stage, but St Petersburg was not about to be outdone. It needed a new opera, and one that could rival Moscow's Bolshoi. The right building was found in front of the Conservatoire. Albert Cavos helped restore the burned-down building in 1859, redecorated it, and the **Mariinsky Theatre** (named in honour of Alexander II's wife Maria) was born the following year.

The theatre proved a formidable rival for the Bolshoi. At the end of the 19th and the beginning of the 20th century, its stage saw performances by the Russian ballet stars Anna Pavlova, Matilda Kseshinskaya, Vatslav Nijinsky and Tamara Karsavina, the sister of Lev Karsavin, the religious philosopher. Tamara Karsavina was vice-president of the Royal Dance Academy in London between 1930 and 1955. Fyodor Shaliapin and Leonid Sobinov performed on the Mariinsky stage. Marius Petipas and Lev Ivanov were directors here and the Konstantin Korovin/Alexander Golovin team painted the sets.

After the Revolution the theatre went through hard times, since many members of the troupe emigrated. Then things took a turn for the better. In the Soviet era it gained new popularity thanks to Prokofiev and Khachaturian, the ballet

The Kirov, an old-world theatre.

stars Galina Ulanova and Vakhtang Chabukiani and the conductors Yevgeny Mravinsky and Vladimir Dranishnikov. Today, buying tickets to the Kirov with Soviet currency is not unlike solving a system of differential equations with a multitude of unknowns.

Symbol of maritime might: Returning to the Decembrists' Square, we continue our walk along the quay. **The Admiralty {4},** on the other side of the square, is connected with the armed forces – not to the cavalry this time but, as the name implies, to the navy. Its form resembles the doubled Cyrillic letter "P". It is a mighty building that stretches along **Admiralty Embankment** for 407 metres (1,300 ft); each of its two wings is 163 metres (535 ft) long.

At the time when it was built it was considered a major architectural accomplishment. Today this opinion is shared by the international community: the Admiralty is now on the UNESCO list of masterpieces of world architecture.

Pointed like a needle, the Admiralty's spire is crowned by a frigate-shaped weathervane. This frigate has now become the city's emblem. There is one drawback to the Admiralty building: there is no spot left today from which the entire building can be observed in its full splendour. According to the rules of fortification (the Admiralty was originally planned as part of the city's defences), it was prohibited to build houses in the immediate vicinity so as to make it impossible for an enemy to approach the fort under cover. The rules were observed but the open space around the building gradually filled with trees; these now make up **Gorky Park** and effectively block the view of the Admiralty from Dvortsovaya Square.

The view from the opposite bank of the Neva was spoiled in the late 19th century by the Minister of the Navy who sold, "with criminal unconcern", as the papers complained at the time, the land between the wings of the Admiralty into private hands. The empty space quickly filled with profitable houses.

Inside the Kirov Theatre.

The history of the Admiralty dates to the early days of the city, when Peter ordered the construction of a fortress on the side of the former Admiralty yard in 1707. In 1738, the Admiralty was redesigned under the guidance of Ivan Korobov, who preserved the layout but reinforced the structures of the building and made the spire taller. The significance and central situation of the Admiralty cried out for a more formidable structure, so Andrean Zakharov prepared a reconstruction plan in 1801. The architect struck the best possible proportions in order to play down the monotony of the facade and make it attractive to the eye.

The new Admiralty was to symbolise the maritime might of the Russian empire, as the numerous sculptures on the facade show. The arch is crowned by the statue of Victory with flags. Somewhat higher, in the centre of the bas-relief entitled *Virgin of the Russian Fleet*, Peter the Great accepts Neptune's trident as a symbol of supremacy on the high seas. The corners of the cube-shaped tower carry sculptures of the great military leaders of antiquity – Achilles, Ajax, Pyrrhus and Alexander of Macedonia. In all, there are 56 large sculptures and 11 bas-reliefs. The Admiralty is still connected with the navy. The Higher Naval School (named after Felix Dzerzhinsky) has owned the building since 1925.

Along Palace Quay: Moving from Decembrists' Square along Admiralty Embankment, we soon reach **Dvorsovy (Palace) Bridge**. Beyond the bridge lies the building that was once the sanctuary of supreme power and the coordinating centre of the vast Russian Empire for two centuries. There, stretched out along **Dvortsovaya (Palace) Embankment**, is the front of the luxurious residence of the czars – the **Winter Palace {5}**.

If we leave the quay, we can walk along the street between the wing of the Admiralty and the side facade of the Winter Palace. Up ahead, we shall see **Dvortsovaya (Palace) Square {6}** with the **Alexander Column** against the background of the gigantic inverted half-circle of the **General Staff Building**.

The huge Palace Square – which became the arena for the events of 25 October 1917 (7 November according to the new calendar), events which influenced the destinies of both Russia and the world at large – has an area of 59,964 sq. metres (645,000 sq. ft).

On the night of 25 October the battleship *Aurora* fired a signal charge, the cue for troops loyal to the Military-Revolutionary Committee of Petrograd to cross the square and arrest the Provisional Government inside the Winter Palace. Previously the Provisional Government had ignored the Committee's ultimatum to surrender its authority. The operation was nearly bloodless (6 killed, 50 wounded). The Government was arrested and power was now held by the Bolsheviks. A new epoch had begun in the land of Russia.

One account says that when the main forces of the operation stormed the palace they found a unit of revolutionary seamen already there; the sailors had infiltrated the building through the drainage ditch. Some wits use this story to claim that "the Revolution was ushered in through a sewer". Whether this account is accurate or not, it points to the conclusion that historic events can begin in the most unlikely places, even in sewerage pipes.

Commemorating Napoleon's defeat: But let us now leap back another century in the square's history, to 1812. Russian troops drove Napoleon's army from their native country and defeated Bonapartism in the course of a military expedition into Europe. Something grandiose had to be erected to commemorate their historic victory. In September 1812 it was decided to set up a triumphal column in the middle of the square.

The design that won the contest belonged to architect Auguste Montferrand. Work on the **Alexander Column** started only in 1830 and took four years. For three years, the granite

Right, the Admiralty forms the architectural centre of the city.

152

monolith weighing some 700 tons was being cut out of a rock face on the Karelia Isthmus and transported to Dvortsovaya Square. In 1832, under the guidance of the craftsmen who had also installed the columns of St Isaac's, over 2,000 volunteers (participants in the war against Napoleon) and 400 builders raised the column on the pedestal with the help of an intricate system of ropes and pulleys. The installation took all of 100 minutes, even though preparations had taken much longer. The column is not attached to the pedestal in any way; to this day, it stands in place under its own weight, which was reduced to 650 tons after smoothing and polishing.

The figure of an angel was mounted on top of the column. The statue was created by Boris Orlovsky to symbolise the peace that had come to Europe after the victory over Napoleon's armies. In 1834 work was completed and the opening ceremony was finally held.

The column got heavy press coverage in the early 1830s. The way the granite monolith was erected inspired many artists and nearly every museum specialising in the early 19th century has drawings depicting the moment of its final installation.

The column rises 47.5 metres (156 ft) above the ground, outscoring its rivals in other capitals, including the 44.5-metre (146-ft) Trajan Column in Rome and the 46-metre (151-ft) Vendome Column in Paris.

The base is decorated with bas-reliefs by P. Svintsov and I. Leppe (they used drawings by Giovanni Scotti). The bas-reliefs depict the rivers that the Russian troops had to cross in pursuit of Napoleon and allegories of Wisdom, Plenty, Victory, Peace and Justice.

The column is the knot that holds together the architectural ensemble of the square. The square means a lot to the people of Leningrad and is much favoured by tourists. People come here to celebrate – or to protest. In the tragic days of December 1989, when the country and the world lost one of the greatest

The Alexander Column and the Winter Palace.

humanists of our time, Andrei Sakharov, hundreds of people came here to mourn him. In the evening, in accordance with Christian tradition, scores of candles were lit around the column.

The Empire's spirit in stone: The impetuosity of line and the imposing dimensions of the **General Staff Building**, which formed the background for the Alexander Column when we looked at it from the Winter Palace and the Admiralty, fills one with a sense of the spirit of the empire. Once again, that spirit found expression in stone under the hands of a famous Italian.

In 1819, Carlo Rossi set out to transform the Dvortsovaya Square ensemble into a showcase for the monarch to rest his eye upon if he chanced to look out of a window in the Winter Palace. At that time, the Alexander Column was still part of a mountain somewhere in Karelia. Ever the master of extra-large architecture, Rossi got down to his task. He redesigned the facades, whose overall length totalled 2 km (1¼ miles). The inverted half-circle was 580 metres (1,900 ft) long. He designed a triumphal arch in honour of the victory over Napoleon, which blended both buildings into a single whole. They were supposed to house the Ministries of Foreign Affairs and Finance and the General Staff.

An impressive 10-metre (33-ft) tall sculpture, the chariot of winged Glory drawn by six horses, was installed on top of the arch. The sculptures were created by Stepan Pimenov and Vasily Demut-Malinovsky.

The sceptical and the envious said that the arch would collapse under the weight of the bronze statues on top. But Rossi, who had no reason to doubt the accuracy of his calculations, assured Emperor Nicholas I that if the arch went he would go with it. They say that on the day the arch finally stood without supports, the architect climbed to the top of the structure to show everyone its sturdiness. Today you can see for yourself who was right. Note that the arch is actually made up of two arches, which

The raising of the Alexander Column in 1832.

run at an angle to each other – yet the structure does not appear incongruous.

Before we turn our gaze towards the Winter Palace, let us examine another building, the one between the Hermitage and the General Staff Building on the other side of the square. The building is the **Headquarters of the Guard Corps**, built in 1837–43 by Alexander Bryullov. Its greatest merit is its modesty and total harmony with the rest of the ensemble. It is just what it should be, the connecting link between the square's two masterpieces – the Winter Palace and the General Staff Building.

From here Lenin headed the Bolshevik effort to stop advancing counter-revolutionary troops in October 1917. Until recently on revolutionary festivals and other formal occasions the building was adorned with portraits of "the three beards" – Marx, Engels and Lenin. Not any more: in the new political climate the facade is unobscured and the square is often full of banner-carrying democratic-front supporters.

The Winter Palace: Construction of the Winter Palace was started in 1754 during the reign of Peter's daughter, Elizabeth, who wanted the residence to demonstrate Russia's growing might. It was completed in 1762, in the reign of Catherine the Great, who ascended the throne after the death of her husband, Peter III, himself assassinated (with the blessing of his tender and loving wife) after 12 months in power.

The Winter Palace, that yardstick of the Russian baroque, was built by the famous Italian architect Bartholomeo Rastrelli. He made a point of writing later that the palace "had been built exclusively to the greater glory of Russia." The tell-tale signs of the Russian baroque include the alternately projecting and sunken elements of the facade, curves, abundant sculpture and decoration and the invariable two-colour painting pattern. In 1838–39 the palace was restored by architects Vasily Stasov and Alexander Bryullov in the wake of the 1837 fire.

The archway of the General Staff Building.

In order to give off a sense of power, a building must be large. And large it appears today, even in the age of skyscrapers and concrete highrises. This is what the figures say: length – roughly 200 metres (656 ft); width – 160 metres (450 ft); length of the perimeter cornice – 2 km (1¼ miles); height – 22 metres (72 ft). The palace has 1,057 rooms with a net area of 46,516 sq. metres (500,000 sq. ft), 117 staircases, 1,786 doorways and 1,945 windows. The interior is decorated with polished marble, lapis lazuli, malachite, porphyry, jasper and other semiprecious stones. Other materials used in the interior decoration include bronze, crystal, gilt, valuable woods and tapestries.

Catherine, as well as all of her successors, preferred the Winter Palace as her residence. Pavel I was the only exception: haunted by fears of assassination, he moved from the Winter Palace to the Mikhailovsky Castle (which he had built as a safer place) – and was killed there.

In the last quarter of the 19th century, when the revolutionary movement was dominated by terrorist acts, the Czar almost met his end in the Winter Palace. Stepan Khalturin, a young carpenter on the palace staff (the street between the palace and the Guard headquarters now bears his name) smuggled small amounts of dynamite into the palace on orders from the terrorist Norodnaya Volya (Freedom for the People) group until eventually enough was accumulated for his purpose.

The bomb worked: the only thing that saved Alexander II's life was that he was not there when it exploded. The terrorists finally killed him in 1881. Ignaty Grinetsky threw a bomb at him as he stepped out of his carriage, mortally wounding the Czar and killing himself in the process.

Lenin, and some of the other members of the revolutionary cabinet thought it important to preserve the historico-cultural legacy of past ages. The Winter Palace was put on the list of state-protected monuments.

Leningraders love to stroll through their city.

A palace dedicated to the arts: The restoration of the lost beauty of the Winter Palace began when the building was turned over to the **Hermitage Museum of Fine Arts**. Today, the museum also occupies several other buildings which face Khalturina Street and Dvortsovaya Embankment: the **Hermitage Theatre** (built 1787, by Giacomo Quarenghi), formerly Catherine's personal theatre, now the museum's lecture hall; the **Old Hermitage** (1775–84, by Yury Felten) and the **New Hermitage** (1839–1952, built by Nikolai Yefimof and Vasily Stasov in accordance with Leo von Klenze's designs).

The New Hermitage was built as Russia's first public art gallery. The museum dates to 1764, when special rooms in the Winter Palace were assigned for works of art that were purchased abroad. As far as public access of the collection was concerned, Catherine declared that only she and the palace mice could admire the pictures freely. Later the collection was made accessible to the

cream of the nobility who were presented with special tickets that allowed them to come and go whenever they chose to do so.

Today, the Hermitage is a universal museum. It is one of the world's largest and richest. Its collection includes pieces from many historical periods. To visit every one of its rooms would involve an excursion of nearly 20 km (12 miles).

The **Oriental Wing** displays works of art from ancient Egypt, India, the Arab countries, China and the Caucasus. A separate exhibit displays the material culture of the ancient Slavs – archaeological finds from Kiev, Novgorod and Pskov. The **Western Wing** is not exactly poor, either, with its hundreds of unique paintings, including works by Leonardo, Titian, Rubens, Raphael, Van Dyck, Rembrandt, Poussin, Murillo, Watteau, Picasso, Matisse, Modigliani, Michelangelo, Canova, Falconet and Rodin.

Jewellery is exhibited in a special section of the Hermitage, a vault which is carefully guarded. Admittance to the vault is limited. The average Soviet museum-goer will more likely be impressed by the well-preserved mummy from the **Egyptian Room** or the armed militiamen at the entrance to the vault than the jewels themselves – there are so many, and they are so valuable that, given the average Soviet wage of between 2,000 and 3,000 roubles (US$100–200) at the current rate per year, the worth of the collection is so hopelessly beyond their imagination that it is simply regarded with indifference.

The Hermitage is more than the place where the "wide popular masses meet with world culture" (thousands crowd near the entrance, forming lengthy queues in the summer season); it is a unique educational aid for professionals. Hundreds of art critics and students of art and architecture flock to the museum where they have the opportunity to be under the same roof with thousands of world-famous masterpieces.

It is impossible to get anything even **Medal mania.**

remotely approaching a comprehensive notion of the Hermitage in a single day. In order to find your way around the museum, you should seek professional guidance from museum staff or come several times, "diluting" the collection with other Leningrad highlights.

Home of the God of War: A 15-minute walk along the quay separates the Hermitage and the place whose name asserts that it belongs to Mars, the Roman god of war. When the city was founded, this marshy piece of land located between the source of the Moika and the Neva was ignored by the builders. Then, in 1710, when the Summer Garden was founded, the marshes were drained, yielding a flat field where nothing ever seemed to grow. It was, in fact, so out of favour with vegetation that it was dubbed the Sahara of St Petersburg. As we look at the prolific hedges and manicured lawns of the **Field of Mars {7}** today, it isn't easy to imagine what the place used to look like.

The war god's name was given to the area at the end of the 18th century, when Pavel I started to use it as a drilling ground for his troops, as the ancient Romans did in their Field of Mars.

On 23 March 1917 (4 April by the modern calendar), a crowd set out for the Field of Mars to mourn those who had fallen in skirmishes with troops loyal to the deposed Czar. To the accompaniment of a burial march and 180 rifle salvos, the remains of 180 revolutionaries were buried there. The next day, the first stone was laid in the foundation of the future memorial. Architect Lev Rudnev completed it in the summer of 1920.

In 1957, a **memorial (eternal) flame** was lit in the centre of the monument in honour of the Revolution's 40th anniversary. All the other flames that burn at memorial complexes throughout the Soviet Union have been lit on this spot.

On Khalturina Street, we find the **Mramorny (Marble) Palace**, built in 1768–85 by Antonio Rinaldi. The palace was intended for the illustrious

aristocrat and statesman of the 19th century, one of Catherine the Great's favourites, Grigory Orlov. In terms of architectural style, the palace is a mixture of classicist and baroque styles. The materials used more than make up for the relative modesty of its facade and consist of natural marble and granite (unlike most of the other building in St Petersburg).

In the early 1930s one of the party chieftains must have asked himself why such a splendid building as this was totally left out of the campaign to promote the ideas of the Revolution. The situation was soon remedied, and an affiliate of the **Central Lenin Museum** (in Moscow) was opened here after several changes in the interior layout.

Amid the more than 10,000 objects exhibited – photographs, newspapers, magazines, manuscripts, household items and all the other things one finds in all museums dedicated to a celebrated individual – it is rather a shock to see an armoured car, complete with machine-gun turret and the inscription *Enemy of Capital*. Lenin made a speech standing on that car on 3 April 1917.

At the beginning of Kirovsky Bridge stands the 7.9-metre (26-ft) tall **statue of Alexander Suvorov**, the famous 18th-century general. The granite pedestal, created by Andrei Voronikhin, bears, under the figures of Glory and Peace, the inscription *Prince of Italy, Count Suvorov-Rymniksky, 1801*. The sculptor who worked on the statue, Mikhail Kozlovsky, didn't pay much attention to likeness in his desire to show Suvorov as the ideal warrior. It is difficult to appreciate when one looks at the monument, that Suvorov was a master of the unpredictable manoeuvre and an advocate of the simple lifestyle (he shared the same scanty food as his soldiers on the march).

Regicide: Close to the spot where the Moika joins Lebyazhya (Swan) Ditch, we see, behind the trees, the building which to this day retains a patina of notoriety – the place where Pavel I was assassinated: **Mikhailovsky Castle**. Pavel hated his mother Catherine so much that when he succeeded her to the throne, he embarked on a policy that was in every way opposite to the one his mother had pursued. He liberated those Catherine had imprisoned and filled his suite with those who had been out of royal favour in the preceding reign.

In doing so, he displeased too many, for Catherine had had many more admirers and supporters than she did enemies. In fact, even those whom Pavel thought were close to him believed his policies erroneous and felt no gratitude to him at all. The officers of the guard, too, were angered over the Prussian-style discipline that Pavel set out to enforce in the army.

The Czar sensed that conspiracy was afoot, and was terrified for his life. He was afraid of the Winter Palace with its endless rooms, all of which were ideal for regicide; in addition, the palace reminded him of Catherine. In 1797, Pavel ordered the Mikhailovsky Castle to be built on the southeast edge of the Field of Mars. The project was drafted by Vasily Bazhenov and work was supervised by Vincenzo Brenna.

The castle was planned as an impenetrable fortress. Pavel believed that the water-filled moats, the dirt walls, the drawbridges and the secret passageway into the castle could protect him from the conspirators. Since the castle had the protection of a natural waterway only on the north side (the Moika) and the east side (the Fontanka), canals were dug along its south and west facades (they were later filled up).

Early in 1801 the castle was ready. Pavel immediately moved in and recovered from his previous paranoia, apparently thinking that he was safe at last. But, as fate would have it, he was destined to live in the castle for a mere 40 days. On 11 March he was strangled in his bedchamber by soldiers of his own household guard. Alexander I was appointed his successor.

In the ensuing years, none of the Russian emperors exhibited any inclination to set up residence in Mikhailovsky Castle. A charity home for widows opened in the castle after the Czar's death. Soon after that it was turned over to the Military Engineer's College. The preparations for this takeover lasted for several years and when they were completed the building received the name by which it is known today – **Inzhenerny (Engineer's) Castle**.

In the 1830s, 16-year-old Fyodor Dostoyevsky, soon to become a world-renowned writer, was a cadet at the college. But the Engineer's College did not only train masters of the classic novel; many famous engineers graduated from its walls, among them Pavel Yablochkov, the inventor of the arc lamp. Today the castle houses the library of the Leningrad Scientific-Technological Information Centre. It is currently under restoration and will become part of the Russian Museum.

Children love ribbons.

The Summer Garden (8): Ever dreamed of seeing Truth, Plenty and Justice with your own eyes? Don't let the chance slip away – take a walk through the Summer Garden. Let's enter, but not from the Neva side, as most other guidebooks usually recommend, but from the Mikhailovsky Castle side.

Even though we won't see the famous ornamental grille that separates the garden from Kutuzov Embankment, we will at least have saved ourselves from committing the same error as a British traveller and patron of the arts. The story goes that he came up the Neva in his ship and cast anchor directly opposite the Summer Garden. The traveller then gazed at its grille through his telescope for some time before giving the order to raise anchor and head for Britain. When he was asked why he hadn't set foot ashore, he replied that it had not been necessary, for his goal – to marvel at the exquisite iron lattice-work – had been attained. The gentleman made, however, precisely the mistake that we shall avoid – he missed half of the grille's beauty, because he didn't look at it from

under the trees against the background of the St Petersburg sky.

The south entrance has a charm of its own. For instance, there is the nearly 5-metre (16-ft) tall **porphyry vase**, the work of Aldvalen masters, which was presented to Nicholas I by Karl Johann, the King of Sweden, and installed in the garden in 1839.

The Summer Garden is well advanced in years. Besides being the oldest part of the city it is also one of those places where the city originated and, as such, shows some of the creative drive of Peter the Great's efforts. The garden is only a year younger than the city of St Petersburg itself.

Where ideas took shape: The garden was planned for the summer residence of the royal family, and Peter took a most active part in its construction. The trees and hedges were kept trimmed. The park abounded in sculptures, summer houses, fountains and pavilions. The pond at the south end had symmetrical outlines. Symmetry and geometric forms were a bold innovation in 18th-century park construction. The people who created the Summer Garden were not afraid of new modes.

By the middle of the 18th century the Summer Garden was no longer considered fit for the residence of the czars. It became a resting place for aristocrats – and immediately started to change. Symmetry and geometry gave way to naturalistic landscapes.

In the middle of the 19th century, Nicholas I issued a special decree that regulated admission to the Summer Garden. The Czar allowed all army officers and decently dressed people to walk there. The lower classes were not permitted to go in. But if the lower classes dressed in the proper way, that rule could be bent. In the middle of the 19th century, for instance, Taras Shevchenko, the Ukrainian poet and artist who was born into a family of serfs, often came here to work. The garden was generally favoured by writers and artists. Its shady paths attracted and inspired writers like Alexander Pushkin, Vasily Zhukovsky, Ivan Krylov, Nikolai Gogol, Alexander Blok, and the future Nobel Prize winner in literature Ivan Bunin, as well as the musicians Fyodor Shaliapin, Peter Tchaikovsky and Modest Musorgsky.

One of them, the fable-writer Krylov, was even honoured with a bronze monument. This creation by Pyotr Klodt was installed in the Summer Garden in 1855. Among the sculptures of the garden, note the 17th-century group entitled *Cupid and Psyche*. The sculptor depicted Psyche at that moment when she is illuminating the face of her sleeping lover. There are also sculptures of the Roman emperor Claudius, his wife Agrippina and Nero.

Finally, we come to the ultimate human values, portrayed in material form: Beauty, Truth, Nobility, Glory and even Victory – the garden overflows with allegorical figures, reflecting fully the eclectic spirit and classical aspirations of the 18th century.

A view from the Hermitage.

To the right of the central avenue, as you move towards the Neva, several buildings remain intact. The first is the **Coffee House**, built by Carlo Rossi in 1826 in place of the grotto that had existed in Peter's time but was later destroyed by a flood. Rossi strove to recreate the outlines of the old grotto in his design. Next comes the **Tea House** (1827) by Louis Charlemagne.

One of the oldest: Then comes the structure that still remembers the town's first days. It stands behind the Tea House and is one of St Petersburg's first stone edifices. The building we are talking about is Peter's two-storey **Summer Palace**. It was built in 1712 by Domenico Trezzini. Peter moved in before the decorators had finished working on the place and spent all his summers there until the day of his death in 1725. Today the Summer Palace is a museum.

The palace has a simple layout. The rooms on both floors are positioned almost identically: each floor has six halls, a kitchen, a corridor and servants' quarters. The first floor of the palace was intended for Peter's wife, Catherine, who reigned as Catherine I for two years after his death.

From the palace, whose northern entranceway is decorated with an allegorical sculpture depicting Russia's victory in the Northern War, the road takes us to the ornamental grille that runs along Kutuzov Embankment. The grille was made in 1784 by Yuri Felten and P. Yegorov. The influence of its ornamental pattern is felt whenever one looks at other Leningrad ironwork. Consider, for instance, the fence around the church in the Peter and Paul Fortress, or the one near the former Bank of Issue (Nos. 30–32 Griboyedov Canal). It is said that immediately after the October uprising, when the country was racked by famine and economic dislocation, an opportunistic Western businessmen offered to trade several locomotives for the grille. Even though the Bolsheviks desperately needed locomotives to get the country's transport

mess straightened out, the businessman's offer was declined and the grille stayed in place.

The Summer Garden was very nearly destroyed, a short time ago, when archaeologists who were searching for the original, early 18th-century appearance of the park stumbled across artillery shells late in 1989. The shells had been fired by the Germans during the Leningrad blockade but, for some unknown reason, did not explode.

The anchorman of Leningrad's most popular TV news programme, *600 Seconds* (who later became the victim of a mafia assault), appealed to the people of Leningrad with a request that they bring old blankets, jackets and rags to cover and protect the sculptures in the event of an explosion. Fortunately all turned out well – the shells were safely removed and the unanimous response evoked by the TV appeal once again underscored the sincere respect felt by the people of Leningrad for the cultural legacy of their city.

A sculpture with a raincoat in the Summer Garden.

NEVSKY PROSPEKT

Nevsky Prospekt begins in the heart of the town, at **Dvortsovaya Square**. The Prospekt may appear grey and monotonous in bad weather owing to its ironed-out skyline, for which Nicholas I bears responsibility by issuing a decree forbidding the construction of houses that are taller than the Winter Palace. But there is a silver streak to that particular cloud: the height limit must have spurred the architects' ingenuity when they worked on facades and interiors, most of which are unique examples of creative vision.

Nevsky, as Leningradians call the Prospekt, can only be understood by walking its entire length. If you are not in the mood to cover the 4.5 km (2¾ miles) to the **Alexander Nevsky Monastery**, try at least to walk at least the 2 km (1¼ miles) to **Anichkov Bridge** over the Fontanka. Then take a bus to **Vosstania Square** and walk around it before moving on to the Alexander Nevsky Monastery.

The Great Perspective Road: To answer the question how Nevsky came to be where it is now, we must go back several hundred years to the times when the marshy territories of the Neva estuary, the cradle of the future city, were part of the Novgorod Principate. To the east of the estuary a road led from the capital city of the principate, Novgorod, to the provinces. The Novgorod Road ran along today's Ligovsky Prospekt.

When the Admiralty Yard was built it needed wood, metal, fabrics and other useful things. Yet there was no route worth speaking of linking the Yard to the Novgorod "highway". In 1709–10, the Great Perspective Road was built through the forests, running from the Novgorod Road to the Admiralty. In 1738 it was renamed Nevskaya Road, since the Admiralty was situated on the bank of the Neva. In fact, all roads in St Petersburg lead to the Neva, just as all the roads in Italy lead to Rome. In 1783 the road became an avenue.

Before the revolution, Nevsky Prospekt and the neighbouring streets were called the City of St Petersburg. Between the Admiralty and Anichkov Bridge, 28 of Russia's largest banks and insurance companies had their offices. No. 9 was a bank, too. Now it is an airline ticket office; the shuttle bus to Pulkovo Airport leaves from nearby. Architect Marian Peretiatkovich, who built the bank in 1911–12, fashioned it after the Palace of the Doges in Venice. It is this similarity that makes the house unlike any other structure in town.

The first street that crosses Nevsky is **Gogol Street** (formerly Malaya Morskaya). Here at No. 17, Nikolai Gogol, the prominent writer, lived between 1833 and 1836 in a modest three-room apartment. In this house he wrote his play *The Government Inspector*, his famous novel about the Cossacks *Taras Bulba*, and the early chapters of the prose-poem *Dead Souls*.

Preceding pages: pedestrians crossing Nevsky; the Prospekt is always crowded. **Left**, taking a rest outside the Kasan Cathedral. **Right**, the Singer symbol above Dom Knigi.

Lovers of paintings should cross the street to No. 8, where there is a permanent exhibition and sale of works by contemporary Leningrad artists. Nos. 8 and 10 (1768–80) are the oldest of these that mark the beginning of the avenue.

Beware of shells: The sign near No. 14 which reads "This side most dangerous during shelling" is not there to scare pedestrians. It is a reminder of World War II. Since reconnaissance reported that the heavy German artillery that shelled Leningrad during the blockade was deployed in a forest to the southeast of the city such signs were put up on northwest sides of all streets to prevent unnecessary casualties.

The short section of **Herzen Street**, to the left of Nevsky's No. 16, was planned by Carlo Rossi to run exactly along the Pulkovo Meridian. On a sunny day, you know when it is noon since the houses have no shadows.

No. 15, on the opposite side, is known as the "house with columns". It was built in 1760 for the St Petersburg Chief of Police. In 1858 it was purchased by the wealthy Yeliseev family, who redecorated it and slightly altered the initial harmony of its facade in the process. Today it houses the **Barrikada Movie Theatre**. No. 17 is half-brother to the Winter Palace and was built by Bartholomeo Rastrelli. The famous Italian built the house in 1753–54 for Count Stroganoff, whose coat of arms is still visible over the gates.

Unorthodox churches: There were many Christians in St Petersburg who did not belong to the Orthodox church. They too needed to address God and required churches. For this reason, the 18th and the early 19th centuries were marked by the construction of so-called heterodox, i.e. non-Orthodox Christian churches. No. 20 used to house a Dutch church (1837, by Paul Jaquot); today it is home to the district's public library, named after Alexander Blok. Nearby (Nos. 22 and 24), is a Lutheran church – **St Peter's** (1832–38, architect Alexander Bryullov).

Nevsky Prospekt is Leningrad's main avenue.

Let us cross the street to get a better view of one of St Petersburg's architectural masterpieces – the **Kazan Cathedral**, {*map reference* **9**} built in 1801–11 by Andrei Voronikhin. A total of 96 columns, 13 metres (42 ft) high, make up the frontal Corinthian colonnade and produce one of the best sights in the city. Huge, 15-metre (29-ft) long bas-reliefs at both ends of the building depict biblical themes, sculpted by Ivan Martos and Ivan Prokofiev.

The statues of generals on each side of the portico were installed to commemorate the 25th anniversary of the victory over Napoleon. One depicts Field Marshal Kutuzov, his sword pointing towards the imaginary enemy, and the other pensive figure is Barklai-de-Tolli (sculptor Boris Orlovsky). Kutuzov, the commander of the Russian forces that opposed Napoleon, is buried here in a vault in the northern chapel. The Kazan Cathedral (which currently houses a museum) presents its side wall to Nevsky, rather than its fa-

Queueing for food on Nevsky.

cade, because the altar in Orthodox churches is positioned near the eastern wall – and Nevsky runs along the northern side of the cathedral.

Living democracy: Silent for many years, the square in front of the cathedral got a new lease of life recently as a public meeting place. The sudden upsurge in the activity of various political forces – assorted democrats, anarcho-syndicalists, "informals" and yes, even representatives of today's party elite, meet here and demonstrate that the democratic tradition was not uprooted during the many years of suppression when dissent was prohibited. Heated debates that, as a rule, take place in an atmosphere of unrestrained pre-election campaigning, are today the characteristic traits of a city that jealously nurtures its revolutionary traditions.

It seems that the nonsensical **Museum of the History of Religion and Atheism**, which has occupied the cathedral for decades, will soon surrender its rights to the Orthodox Church. At

least that's what the town's Orthodox community is fighting for. Let us hope that this, until recently an uphill fight, will end in their victory. At present the museum holds approximately 150,000 items from ancient Egyptian mummies to paintings of modern art that are intended to demonstrate the power of religion over people.

On the other side of the street, the house with a globe on the corner tower once belonged to the Singer sewing machine company. Now it is the largest bookstore in Leningrad, the **Dom Knigi.** Here you can find books in various languages on different branches of knowledge, along with books about art, educational literature and fiction. Several Leningrad publishing houses have their offices in the building.

On the left-hand side of Griboyedov Canal is the exquisite **Church of the Resurrection,** {10} reminiscent of the Pokrovsky Cathedral in Moscow. The church is also known as the Saviour on Blood. The reference to blood is a re-

minder that Alexander II was mortally wounded on that spot in a terrorist attack. On 1 March 1881 he was assassinated by members of the revolutionary Narodnaya Volya organisation.

The artistic centre: Inzhenernaya Street leads to the **Square of the Arts {11}.** The centre of the architectural ensemble is the yellow **Mikhailovsky Palace**, home to the world-famous **State Russian Museum.** It was built by Rossi for Nicholas I's brother, Mikhail, in 1819–25. At the end of 19th century, the palace was redecorated and rebuilt. Fortunately the entrance stairway and the white column hall managed to escape this sad fate. In 1898, under Nicholas II, the palace, by then the Imperial Russian Museum, was opened to the public.

In 1910–12, two huge edifices were built alongside the palace. The right wing houses Western paintings from the Russian Museum, and the left acted originally as the ethnography section. In 1934 this section gained independence and became the **Museum of Ethnography of the Peoples of the USSR.** The museum has over 450,000 pieces in its collection, which pertain to the customs, rituals, languages and religion of practically every nation in the Soviet Union. The collection includes Ukrainian and Byelorussian embroideries, Turkmenian carpets, amber from the Baltic republics, Vologda lace and many, many more items.

Directly in front of the museum is Mikhail Anikushin's **Monument to Alexander Pushkin** (1957). The house where the Assembly of the Gentry used to meet is now home to the **Leningrad State Philharmonic.** Nearby are the **Theatre of Musical Comedy** and the **Komissarzhevskaya Drama Theatre.**

But let us return to Nevsky. The house at No. 30 is another of Rastrelli's great creations. The building, one of the oldest in town, is also owned by the Philharmonic. The next house is another heterodox church – a Roman Catholic one, built by Jean Baptiste Vallin de

Rossi Street and the Pushkin Theatre.

la Mothe in 1763–83. It was dedicated to **St Catherine**. The houses around the church are even older.

The last king of Poland, Stanislaw August Poniatowski, who lived out his days in St Petersburg, is buried here. To the right of the entrance is the tomb of Marshal Maureau, who emigrated from France after Napoleon seized power. Maureau fought in the Russian army against Napoleon. He lost a leg in the Battle of Dresden in August 1813 and died the next day. His ashes were then buried, with honours, in the grounds of St Catherine's Church.

Beyond the Catholic church is the **Yevropeiskaya Hotel**, recently restored by a Finnish company. In front of it is the "building of the silver rows" and the former **Town Duma** (municipal council, 1799–1804), crowned with a pentagonal turret. In its day the turret was used as a fire-tower, from where firemen sounded the alarm in the event of fire or to warn of flood or a particularly vicious frost.

Between the Duma and the Gostiny Dvor building is the small portico of Feather Lane – once a long row of stalls that were demolished to give way to the Metro. The portico, built in 1802–06 by Luigi Ruska, was restored in 1972 in accordance with the original architectural blueprints and now houses the theatre ticket-office.

Leningrad's consumer temple: In former times, travelling merchants stayed at special hotels, where they were given room, board and an opportunity to ply their trade. Such a hotel was called a **Gostiny Dvor {12}** (merchants' yard). The new Gostiny Dvor in the capital of the Russian Empire was built by Vallin de la Mothe in 1761–85. The length of its facades combined totals nearly 1,000 metres (3,280 ft). The rectangular building had such a felicitous design that it was copied when similar establishments were built in other cities. The place retains its trading function to this day – it is now one of Leningrad's largest department stores. The truth is,

On the Moika.

however, that the old rooms of the building are too small for our chaotic age. They do little for the needs of the contemporary shopper.

A book the size of a stamp: The Temple of Mercury (Gostiny Dvor) faces the Temple of Minerva – the **State Public Library** (which bears the name of Saltykov-Schedrin), whose main facade looks over the nearby **Ostrovsky Square {13}** (1828–32, by Carlo Rossi). This library, the second largest in the USSR after Moscow's Lenin Library, was opened in 1814. It served as the working place for St Petersburg writers, scientists, composers, architects and revolutionaries, Vladimir Lenin among them.

Among its treasured possessions is the oldest surviving handwritten book in Russian, the 11th-century Ostromirov Gospel, Voltaire's library (6,814 volumes), and the world's smallest printed volume, the size of a postage stamp, containing Krylov's fables. The print on the pages of the book is so clear that it can be read with the naked eye. The oldest manuscripts in the library's possession date to the 3rd century BC.

In the centre of Ostrovsky Square stands the **Monument to Catherine the Great** (1873). The great Empress is surrounded by her faithful supporters and favourites – Prince Potyomkin-Tavrichesky, with a Turkish turban underfoot; Generalissimo Alexander Suvorov; Field Marshal Pyotr Rumiantsev; Princess Catherina Dashkova; the President of the Russian Academy of Sciences, book in hand; the poet and statesman Gavriil Derzhavin; Admiral Chichagov and other policymakers of 18th-century Russia.

Behind the monument, if we look from Nevsky, is the **Pushkin Academic Drama Theatre** (or the Bolshoi Drama Theatre – BDT as it is known here), built in 1823 by Carlo Rossi. On the other side of the theatre is Rossi Street. The first of its buildings is the **State Choreography School** (named after Vaganova); it was founded in

One of Klodt's horses on the Anichkov Bridge.

174

1738. Its neighbour is the **Museum of Theatrical Art**.

Further along the right-hand side of Nevsky, deep in the overflowing greenery of the square, stands **Anichkov Palace** (now the Pioneer Palace). Its construction was started in 1741 for Count Razumovsky. After the Revolution, it was turned over to children's circles, clubs and hobby groups. Until recently, the palace bore the name of one of Stalin's henchmen, the former secretary of the Regional Party Committee of Leningrad, Andrei Zhdanov.

On the opposite side is the **Puppet Theatre**, which is much favoured by locals under 12. It dates to 1918 and is Russia's oldest. The hearts of local adults belong, however, to the **Comedy Theatre** on Malaya Sadovaya Street. On the floor below is the city's largest supermarket, formerly owned by the Yeliseevs. The luxurious decor of its main salon is in sharp contrast to the squalor on its shelves.

The next building faces the Fontanka.

Looking good.

It is the **House of Friendship**, the Dom Drushba, where representatives of Soviet friendship societies meet with guests from foreign countries.

Klodt's horses: Crossing the Fontanka is **Anichkov Bridge**. Both the bridge and the palace are named after Anichkov, the engineer who supervised the construction of the first wooden bridge over the Fontanka in 1715. Today's stone bridge is 54.6 metres (179 ft) long and 37 metres (121 ft) wide. It was built by Alexander Bryullov and engineer Andrei Gotman in 1839–41.

The Anichkov bridge is known far and wide for its sculptures. When Pyotr Klodt first cast the statues, Emperor Nicholas I impulsively gave them to the Prussian king. In Prussia, the statues were installed near the Great Palace in Berlin and Klodt was made honorary member first of the Berlin, and then of the Rome and Paris Academies of the Arts. Meanwhile, plaster-cast statues were installed on Anichkov Bridge. Klodt replaced them with bronze ones, but not for long: Nicholas once more decided to give them as a present, this time to the King of Naples.

Klodt was told to make bronze copies from the old moulds, but he thought that the central bridge of the capital deserved better. In 1850, a new set of statues was installed on the bridge, and remained there until World War II. During the blockade, Klodt's horses were buried underground in the garden near Anichkov Palace, in order to protect them from the shells.

Saigon coffee: A bus ride from here to Vosstania Square passes seven cinemas along the way and several cafés and restaurants. The café on the corner of Nevsky and Vladimirsky Prospekt, dubbed the "Saigon" by its regulars, used to be in favour with the "hopeless" youth of Leningrad.

Saigon was known far beyond the city limits. Its cheap coffee attracted hippies, punks, heavy-metal freaks and other young rebels who, until recently, triggered an "arresting" reflex in policemen and cardiac arrest in old veterans and party functionaries, who believed that youth is the time for crewcuts and white shirts with pioneer ties and *komsomol* (communist youth league) buttons. On the right-hand side of Nevsky, near the crossing with Marata Street is a **Museum of the Arctic and the Antarctic**.

In **Vosstania (Uprising) Square**, the eye is drawn towards Moscow Station. Lovers of paintings and crafts may find it interesting to visit the **Nasledie (Heritage) Shop** on the left corner, the one that juts out into the square; music buffs will be attracted to the **Oktyabrsky Concert Hall** (No. 6 Ligovsky Prospekt).

From **Moscow Station {14}** nearly 100 daily long-distance trains connect the city with the rest of the country. The station was built in 1851 when the first trains ran from St Petersburg to Moscow but was then rebuilt 100 years later, preserving, however, the outside appearance. The station and its environs have become a notorious meeting place for diverse "night people". A small garden in the centre of the square opens up to a splendid view along the lower part of the Prospekt all the way to the Admiralty.

Our trip along Nevsky ends at the **Alexander Nevsky Lavra {15}**. *Lavras* were the highest-ranking monasteries. Before the revolution, Russia, which abounded in monasteries, had only four *lavras*: Kievo-Pecherskaya, Troitse-Sergieva (in Moscow), Pochayevskaya and the Alexander Nevsky.

The monastery ensemble includes the **Troitsky (Trinity) Cathedral** (1778–90, by Ivan Starov) and the two-storey house to the left of the entrance (by Starov and Trezzini). This building houses two chapels – the **Alexander Nevsky Chapel** above and the **Chapel of the Annunciation** below. Military commander Suvorov is buried there; it is said that the laconic inscription on his tomb – *Here lies Suvorov* – was of the generalissimo's own composition.

Walking though the park near the monastery, you will see a large yellow building behind a fence. This is the **Leningrad Orthodox Spiritual Academy and Seminary**, where both clergymen and regents of the church choir (excellent specialists in religious music) are trained.

Last resting place of genius: The **necropolis** of the monastery includes those graves that lie inside the churches as well as several large cemeteries – Tikhvinskoye, Lazarevskoye, Nikolskoye (outside the monastery's limits) and the small cemetery near the entrance to Troitsky Cathedral. **Lazarevskoye Cemetery** is the oldest in town. It was "founded" in 1716, when Peter the Great buried his sister, Natalia Alekseevna here. Here, also, are the graves of Mikhail Lomonosov, the architects Andrei Voronikhin, Andreyan Zakharov, Carlo Rossi and Giacomo Quarenghi and the builder of the lavra, Ivan Starov.

In front of the cemetery is the **Tikhvinskoye Cemetery**, where the remains of several artistic geniuses lie: the composers Peter Tchaikovsky, Modest Mussorgsky and Nikolai Rimsky-Korsakov, the actress Vera Komissarzhevskaya, the writers Fyodor Dostoyevsky and Ivan Krylov, and the sculptor Pyotr Klodt.

To the southwest of the monastery at No. 30 Rastannaya Street is another necropolis – the **Literatorskiye Mostki** (Volkovo Cemetery). This is the last resting place of the writers and literary critics Ivan Turgenev, Mikhail Saltykov-Schedrin and Vissarion Belinsky, the chemist Dmitry Mendeleev (the father of the Periodic Table), the physiologist Pavlov and members of Lenin's family (his mother, sister and brother-in-law).

Behind Nevsky, where the Neva flows around **Bezymianny Island**, are **Smolny** and the **Taurida (Tavrichesky) Palace {16}**. The trolley bus No. 16 from Alexander Nevsky Square goes to Smolny. The Taurida Palace stands not far away, where Voinova Street crosses Tavricheskaya Street.

Potyomkin's villages: The Taurida palace was built by Catherine II for her favourite, Count Grigory Potyomkin. Potyomkin was a man of formidable talent. He commanded military expeditions into the Crimea, and finally attached the peninsula to Russia (winning the title *Tavrichesky* in the process).

His greatest talent, however, was in his ability to pull the wool over the eyes of his beloved mistress – and get away with it. When Catherine set out to inspect the Crimea – the newly added pearl in Russia's crown – the solicitous count decided that the unpleasantness of everyday existence which Catherine was certain to encounter on the road would disappoint Her Majesty.

So Potyomkin thought and thought and finally found an answer. He arranged for the old huts to be substituted with freshly whitewashed cottage facades along the entire route of the imperial journey (most of which lay through his vast estates). Peasants were dressed up in pretty clothes and ordered to smile, sing songs and generally act in the pastoral manner as soon as they saw Catherine's carriage. Meanwhile, 10 steps away from the road, their dirty shacks remained as before. Catherine was pleased, and Potyomkin rejoiced.

Potyomkin lives: Potyomkin's fiction was elevated to new soaring heights during the seven decades of Soviet power by party bosses and administrators, some of whom still fill their posts to this day. Instead of villages, the bureaucrats, egged on (or simply forced) by their superiors, prepared all-is-well reports, and made no bones about increasing industrial output indices on paper: mountains of cotton were created, and whole herds of cattle and pigs were born with the stroke of a pen. Prior to the visit of party oligarchs to provincial towns, it was customary for the local chiefs to "polish things up". The streets were washed, the buildings and fences were given new coats of paint,

Inside Alexander Nevsky Monastery.

and unheard-of foods suddenly appeared in all the stores.

After Catherine died, Potyomkin's fame dwindled. Pavel I, seeking revenge against the late favourite of his late mother, ordered stables to be set up in the grand halls of the palace. When the Czar died, the stables were removed. The palace was redecorated, and once again became fit to be the residence of the royal family. Alexander I lived here for a time in the first third of the 19th century, and he was followed by the heir to the Persian throne. The palace then stood empty until 1906, when the State Duma (Russian Parliament) took it over. Today, it belongs to the Higher Party School.

In the south end of the **Taurida Garden**, which is now a children's park, where Saltykov-Schedrin Street crosses Tavricheskaya Street, is the **Alexander Suvorov Museum**. Suvorov (1729–1800) was Russia's greatest military leader; he never suffered a defeat. The museum will acquaint you with his life and achievements.

Noble maids and Bolsheviks: One of Leningrad's most interesting historical ensembles is found not too far away on Rastrelli Square: **the Smolny {17}**. The building gets its name from the fact that the site was once occupied by the Smolyanoi (Tar) Yard, where tar was prepared for the shipyards. The yard was later moved to another location, and Peter's daughter Elizabeth decided to found a monastery on the spot.

The first houses were built by Rastrelli in 1764. Then, in 1832–35, architect Stasov added several new structures. Catherine II ordered the facilities of the monastery to be turned over to Russia's first educational establishment for women – the **Institute of Noble Maids**. But the Noble Maids found the monastic cells too small, and in 1806–08 a separate building was erected in the monastery grounds designed by Giacomo Quarenghi; it took the form of a classical palace.

The institute existed until August, 1917, when the Noble Maids were forced to give way to the Bolsheviks. Smolny then became the headquarters of the Military-Revolutionary Committee, the conspiratorial centre where the revolt was prepared and carried out in October 1917.

Two symmetrical pavilions serve as the entrance to the park in front of the Institute. One of them bears an inscription from the Communist Manifesto: *Workers of the world, unite!* In the park there are bronze busts of Karl Marx and Friedrich Engels and the 6-metre (20-ft) high statue of Lenin by S. Yevesev that has become one of the symbols of Leningrad.

The former **Smolny Cathedral** today houses the permanent exhibition "Leningrad Today and Tomorrow". It might very well be that "tomorrow" the cathedral will again be used for its original purpose. For the time being, the former convent is still occupied by the Bolsheviks, housing the regional and municipal committees of the CPSU.

Left, a symbol of the Orthodox church. Right, the Smolny Monastery seen from the Neva.

THE PETROGRAD SIDE

Time is merciless to things that human hands create. Frequently, the human yearning for change and innovation acts as time's ally, rendering the original outlines of streets and squares totally unrecognisable. Today's **Revolution Square** {*map reference* 18} is a case in point: looking at it now, who could tell that it was here, under the protection of the Peter and Paul Fortress, that the capital's first houses appeared in the early 18th century? Along the northern side of the square stood the first Gostiny Dvor (merchant's hotel) along its eastern side the Senate Building. In the centre, there was a church whose spire rivalled the masts of the ships that gathered in the port. The other two original buildings in the square were a printing shop and the customs house.

The houses overlooking the quay belonged to powerful officials of the day – Gagarin, Zotov, Shafirov, Golovkin, Bruce (the scientist) and Siniavin, the director of the town chancellery. Until 1728, before it moved to Vasilievsky Island, the Academy of Sciences had its headquarters in the houses of Shafirov and Golovkin. The palace, deep in the square, belonged to Peter's closest friend and aide-de-camp, Alexander Menshikov. Menshikov presided over magnificent diplomatic receptions, which is why it was known as Posolsky (Ambassador's) House.

The cottage of Peter the Great: In May 1703, not far from the future Troitskaya Square, local carpenters built the **Primary Palace** in just three days. It was here where the Czar, who supervised the construction of the Peter and Paul Fortress, spent the summer. The palace is not large: 12 by 5.5 by 2.5 metres (39 by 18 by 8 ft). In Peter's time the rooms – study, dining room and bedroom – had had neither stoves nor fireplaces, nor even a stone foundation. The stone house was a much later project – it was

built by architect Kuznetsov in 1846.

As soon as the palace in the Summer Garden was completed, Peter moved there, leaving the original house empty and neglected. Somehow it never disintegrated entirely and was fully restored to its original form in the 1920s. Since 1930 it has been a museum.

Not far from this house on the bank of the Neva there are two curious **sculptures of Shi Chze.** These mythological creatures guarded the entrances to Buddhist temples and crypts in Mongolia, China, and Southeast Asia. Somehow, the winds of history brought these fairy-tale animals all the way to the northern capital of Russia in 1907.

Gunshot of a new era: On the spot where the Bolshaya (Greater) Nevka parts with the Neva, the battleship *Aurora* {19} cast anchor for the last time in 1948. One of the ship's legendary guns fired the historic shot (9.40 p.m. on 25 October 1917) at the Winter Palace, giving the signal for the government headquarters to be stormed. There are

two versions concerning the ammunition that was used: some say that it was a blank and others insist that it was a non-exploding shell.

The cruiser's history began in 1903. It was named after the frigate *Aurora*, whose crew fought bravely in the 1853–56 Crimean War. The *Aurora* was christened by fire in the Tsushima Battle during the Russian-Japanese war (1904–05).

Its crew were the first in the Baltic Fleet to take the Bolsheviks' side. When the ministers of the Provisional Government were safely locked away in the Peter and Paul Fortress, the cruiser broadcast Lenin's address *To the Citizens of Russia!* proclaiming the victory of the proletarian revolution. The *Aurora* then became a training ship. In the years of World War II the battleship's guns were deployed near the front line. In 1956 the ship was repaired and turned over to the Central Naval Museum.

There is a joke concerning the ship's role in the Revolution. A Czech tourist saw the *Aurora* and, remembering an aircraft carrier he'd seen once (the Czechs are well-known "experts" on naval matters, since Czechoslovakia is landlocked) exclaimed: "Why, it's such a little boat! I was expecting something much bigger!" The other Czech replied: "Little or not, this boat has made more trouble for the whole world than any other boat yet."

On the corner of Kuibyshev Street and Maxim Gorky Prospekt there is a pretty mansion in Modern style. It belonged to **Matilda Kshesinskaya**, the prima ballerina favoured by Czar Nicholas II. As the "ballet expert" Maxim Gorky remarked, the ballerina earned her house "with leg-shaking and arm-swinging."

As with most houses in Leningrad, this mansion was also connected with the Revolution and Lenin. It housed, from March to July 1917, the Central and Petrograd City Committees of the Bolsheviks. On the night of 4 April, Lenin came here after his boisterous

The Peter and Paul fortress.

arrival at Finland Station. In the following weeks he visited the mansion almost daily to write articles and proclamations, address the crowd from the balcony and to preside over meetings and party conferences. Lenin's wife, Krupskaya, helped him with his work.

The origins of St Petersburg: The fortress whose foundation in the summer of 1703 started the clock of history ticking for St Petersburg had a rather strange fate. Built with every innovation known to the fort engineers of the time, this powerful defensive stronghold was never once attacked by an enemy; moreover, it has yet to fire a shot at an enemy soldier. The place cried out for a purpose until it finally became a political prison, a function it fulfilled for two centuries.

Peter had been in a hurry to build the fortress because the Northern War was in full swing and the danger of an enemy attack was real. The prototype of modern fortresses, Fort St Petersburg, (or **Peter and Paul Fortress {20}**) was built in record time and was completed in the spring of 1704.

It was originally built of wood and clay, materials which offended Peter's love of thoroughness. Consequently Domenico Trezzini started to substitute wood with stone in 1706. Construction proceeded on a section-by-section basis in order not to weaken the military might of the stronghold.

In 1740 the entire fortress was finally dressed in stone; it was then that it assumed its present complex geometrical form with forward-thrusting bastions that are named after the potentates who had personally managed their construction. Clockwise, from the main gates, they are the Gosudarev, Naryshkin, Trubetskoi, Zotov, Golovkin and Menshikov Bastions. The Ioannovsky and Alekseevsky Ravelins were added later, in 1730, and were then separated from the fortress with water-filled moats.

From Revolution Square, you can get to the fortress via **Ioannovsky (John's)**

Her cannons initiated an era: the *Aurora*.

Bridge over the Kronverksky Strait, crossing from Zayachy to Petrograd Island. Ioannovsky Bridge is the oldest in the city, though today's ironwork and lamps date to 1953.

The bridge leads to the main entrance – the **Ioannovsky (St John's) Gate** (1740). Passing through, we find ourselves in front of the **Petrovskiye (St Peter's) Gate**. Trezzini built them in 1718 in place of the old wooden ones. Petrovskiye Gate is the only triumphal structure of those times to survive in its original form. Conrad Osner's bas-relief, *Apostle Peter Overthrowing Simon the Magus,* is an allegory of Russia's victory in the Northern War. In 1722, the coat of arms of the Russian Empire was installed beneath the bas-relief.

Emblem of the Third Rome: Russia's state emblem – the two-headed eagle and the horseman slaying the dragon – dates to the late 15th century. It emulated the emblem of the Roman Empire, where the eagle's two heads symbolised the empire's two capitals – Rome and Constantinople. When Constantinople fell to the Turks in 1453, Moscow became the "Third Rome", and this was expressed in the new emblem. Later, the two heads of the eagle were interpreted as the union between Christianity and Monarchy – the foundation of the Russian Empire. Historical documents say that the horseman slaying the dragon was referred to as St George for the first time during the reign of Peter the Great's wife Catherine I.

The gate is decorated with sculptures. In the right-hand niche is a statue of Bellona, the Roman goddess of war, and in the left stands Minerva, the goddess of wisdom, arts and crafts.

The central passage leads from St Peter's Gate to the **Peter and Paul Cathedral**. The silhouette of the cathedral, just like the frigate on the Admiralty spire, is a symbol of the city.

The stone cathedral was founded in 1712 in place of the wooden Peter and Paul Church that was built in 1703. In the year the cathedral was founded, the capital of the empire was moved from Moscow to the new city, which was then less than a decade old.

Construction lasted until 1773 under Domenico Trezzini's supervision. Peter the Great wanted the cathedral to be built section by section. The first structure to be completed was the belfry and the rest of the cathedral followed (the belfry was so heavy that if the entire church had been be built at the same time, the added weight of the other structures would have caused the unstable ground to sink).

The silhouette of the belfry bears a likeness to St Peter's in Riga and the Menshikov Tower in Moscow. Trezzini managed, however, to communicate a measure of originality to his creation by building in Petersburg-baroque style. The first wooden spire was crowned, just as the one you see today, with a statue of an angel carrying a cross.

An unforgettable feat: In 1830 the spire was struck by lightning. The angel, whose wingspan totals 3.8 metres (12½ ft), slumped to one side and threatened to fall. A roof-maker by the name of Pyotr Telushkin offered his services to set things right. Knowing nothing of mountain climbing, he climbed the spire, secured a rope ladder to its summit, and used it several times before completing his mission. You have to see the structure to understand his boldness. His daring and quick thinking earned Telushkin a great deal of money.

In 1858 the wooden spire was replaced by with a metal one (under engineer Zhuravsky's guidance). With its height of 122.5 metres (402 ft), the Peter and Paul Cathedral remains Leningrad's tallest building (excluding the TV tower).

Resting place of the Romanovs: The richly decorated main hall of the cathedral, which looks more like a gala ballroom, is dominated by its baroque iconostasis. The cathedral owes its fame to its tombs. All the Russian Emperors, from Peter the Great to Alexander III, lie here. Particular splendour distinguishes the tombstones over the remains of Alexander II, who was killed by terrorists, and his wife Maria. The tomb is made from 5 tons of Altai jasper and 6.5 tons of rodonite from the Urals. The stones were hand polished at the Peterhof Lapidary Works for all of 16 years, between 1890 and 1906.

A special passage leads from the cathedral to the crypt of the Grand Princes, where close relatives of the Czars used to be buried. Today there is an exhibition in the crypt, which explains the constructional history of the fortress.

On the eastern side of the cathedral is a cemetery where fortress commandants are buried. To the left of the main entrance is the elegant **Boat House** (1762–66, by Vist), which was originally intended for the *Grandfather of the Russian Fleet*, Peter's first sailboat. Today, the boat is in the Central Naval Museum on Vasilievsky Island.

In front of the Boat House, not far from the cathedral, in the former Commandant's Residence, there is a perma-nent exhibition entitled "History of St Petersburg/Petrograd 1703–1917". To the left of Petrovskiye Gate, in the **Engineer's House**, is another permanent exhibition: "Architecture of St Petersburg/Petrograd in the 18th–Early 20th Centuries". The third exhibition explaining the history of Soviet spaceship development is to be found in the St John's Ravelin.

Behind the Commandant's Residence is the huge **Naryshkin Bastion**, which points its signal cannon at the Neva. According to the old Petersburg custom (which was reinstated in 1957), the gun is fired daily at noon.

Floods: Walking back a little from the Naryshkin Bastion, along the wall towards Petrovskiye Gate, is **Nevskiye (Neva) Gate**, which leads to the Komendantsky Moorage. Under the arch of the gate is a list of "catastrophic floods", the scourge of St Petersburg. It is difficult to solve the problem of floods even with today's technology since the reasons lie deep in the Baltic,

A wide square in the fortress.

into which huge quantities of water pour every spring.

Let us now return to the main entrance of the Peter and Paul Fortress. The building opposite the cathedral is one of the city's oldest enterprises – the **Mint**. Until Antonio Porto built an edifice specifically designed for the Mint (1798–1806) it was housed in the Naryshkin and Trubetskoi Bastions. Here, gold, silver and copper coins, along with orders and medals, were minted. Today it is the only mint in the USSR producing metal coins.

Political prisoners: The dark pages of the fort's history – its "criminal past" – are first and foremost connected with **Trubetskoi Bastion** and **Alekseevsky Ravelin**; the latter was constructed off the western wall in the reign of Empress Anna Ioannovna.

The first political prisoner to be held in the Trubetskoi Bastion was Czarevich Aleksei, Peter the Great's son. He took part in a Boyar conspiracy against Peter's reforms. Disregarding the fact that he was his own son, Peter dealt with him as harshly as he did with all the other conspirators.

The statesman Artemy Volynsky was imprisoned there for taking part in the conspiracy against Duke Biron, the all-powerful minister of Anna Ioannovna. The cells also remember Princess Tarakanova, the adventuress whose gamble to ascend the throne of Russia backfired, as well as many courtiers who fell victim to palace intrigues.

In 1790, the fortress received Alexander Radischev, the author of *Voyage from St Petersburg to Moscow*, a critique of monarchy from a position of enlightenment. In 1826, the economist and publicist Ivan Pososhkov, the author of *The Book of Scarcity and Wealth*, died in the fortress.

The fortress also held the participants of the December 1825 rebellion in Senatskaya Square. The most important fo these were kept in a maximum-security dungeon, the so-called "Secret House" of the Alekseevsky Ravelin.

The bridges have an old-world charm.

Here, the defendants were condemned to *katorga* (labour camps) and exile. The five leaders of the revolt were sentenced to death and hanged.

Writers' second home: The prison was particularly "hospitable" to men of letters. In the middle of the 19th century, the fortress was "visited" by Fyodor Dostoyevsky. It very nearly became the home of Vissarion Belinsky, the revolutionary democrat and literary critic. The commandant of the fortress used to approach Belinsky in the street and enquire "What's taking you so long? We've got a nice warm cell ready and waiting for you." But the humour was probably lost on Belinsky – only his early death in 1848 saved him from the dungeons of the Peter and Paul Fortress.

Another revolutionary democrat – critic, publicist and philosopher Nikolai Chernyshevsky – succeeded where Belinsky failed. Chernyshevsky, goodness knows how, managed to write a novel in his cell. The book, *What Is To Be Done?*, was even published in the 1860s through the negligence of some government official or another.

The final chord of the prison symphony sounded in 1917, when the fortress received the ministers of the deposed Provisional Government. The Bolsheviks then transformed the prison into a museum. Other places were found for the enemies – real and imaginary – of the new regime (the notorious Kresty Prison, for instance).

In Stalin's day, when there were more political prisoners than ever there were in the times of all the Russian Czars put together, there were never enough jails. Hence the network of concentration camps – Trotsky's brainchild.

To the north, the ensemble of the Peter and Paul Fortress adjoins a horse-shoe-shaped building, which stands on Kronverksky (Kronwerk) Island. This is the **Artillery Museum** which displays nearly every kind of weapon system, from ancient swords and muskets to the latest ballistic missiles.

On the opposite shore of the Kron-

Sightseeing along the canals.

versky Strait is an obelisk that marks the place were the leading Decembrists were executed. It bears a poem by Alexander Pushkin that he wrote to a friend who served a term of hard labour in Siberia:

Dear friend, have faith:
The wakeful skies presage a dawn of wonder,
Russia shall from her age-old sleep arise,
And despotism shall be crushed;
Upon its ruins our names incise.

A meeting with the stars: If you want to relax after visiting the prison and the military museum, take it easy in the floating **Petropavlovsky Restaurant**, which is anchored in the Kronverksky Strait near Petrograd Island opposite the western tip of Zayachy Island. Or take a walk through **Lenin Park**. The park, dating to 1845, is very popular. In 1959 a planetarium for children was opened here so they could get acquainted with the basics of astronomy. The inverted cupola is used to display maps of the stars and imitates the movements of the constellations and the rising and setting of the sun.

Perestroika has boosted attendance at the planetarium. Not that our children suddenly developed a love of astronomy – it is the adults, particularly the women. The fact is that the planetarium today is host to assorted experts on contacts with extraterrestrial civilisations, UFOs and astrology. Many Leningrad ladies, hitherto kept in the dark about the existence of the exciting sphere of paranormal phenomena by our pitiless propaganda, now take enormous pleasure in accounts of the influence of various constellations on human destiny and of mysterious flying-saucer kidnappings.

Lenin Park is semi-circled by **Maxim Gorky Prospekt**. The writer lived here in No. 23 between 1914 and 1921, when he left for Capri. Rising over the tree-tops en route for Revolution Square is the dome of a **Muslim mosque** and two minarets decorated with blue majolica

(1914 by Vasiliev). The mosque resembles the Tamerlain Mausoleum (Gur Emir) in Samarkand (15th-century).

To honour a Party secretary: We continue our tour along **Kirov(sky) Prospekt**, {21} which leads through Petrograd to Aptekarsky Island. Kirov Prospekt is the central avenue of the Petrograd Side. It took some time for it to gain its modern appearance. In accordance with the urban construction plan of 1831, several adjacent streets between Kronwerk and Kamenny Island were turned into an avenue, which was named Kamenoostrovsky Prospekt. Then came the housing boom of the early 20th century, following the completion of the **Troitsky (now Kirov) Bridge** across the Neva. The Modern-style houses that were built on the avenue were let and sold to amusement establishments.

With the Revolution came the frenzy of renaming. In 1918, Kamenoostrovsky was changed to the Street of Red Dawns. The name survived until 1934 when Kirov, the Leningrad party secretary, was assassinated – after which the name was inevitably changed to Kirov Prospekt. It was then, with the consent of Stalin (who was very pleased to see a dangerous competitor eliminated), that several places in Leningrad got Kirov's name – the above-mentioned avenue, a group of islands, a theatre, a stadium and many enterprises.

On the corner of Kirov and Gorky avenues, near the apartment building with a semi-circular front, a **monument to Gorky** (by Vera Isayeva) was opened in 1968. The house on the opposite side (Nos. 1–3), decorated with original animal sculptures, is an interesting specimen of the northern version of the Modernist style that flourished at the beginning of the century (1899–1904, by Fyodor Lindval).

The cradle of Russian film: In 1896, a cinema film was shown for the first time in Russia. Nos. 10 and 12 are connected with the industry, too. Since 1924, they have belonged to the **Lenfilm Studios**

(founded in 1918). This company developed the technology for recording sound onto camera film in the late 1920s, opening the era of soundtrack films in the USSR. The studio produced such world greats as *Chapayev*, *Deputy of the Baltic* and *Peter the Great*.

The street that joins Kirov Prospekt was named after the Vasiliev brothers who directed *Chapayev*. In this street, at No. 14, lived the composer Dmitry Shostakovich. Shostakovich cooperated with Lenfilm – among other things, he wrote the music for *Hamlet* and *King Lear*. Kirov Prospekt and the nearby streets have several well-known research centres. The first of them is the **Pasteur Institute of Epidemiology and Microbiology** (No. 14 Mira Street). True to the name of Roentgen Street, which crosses Kirov Prospekt, there is the **Radium Institute**, which is a centre for radiochemistry, nuclear physics and radiogeochemistry.

Russia's poets and thinkers: No. 21, which hides behind the trees, was origi-nally designed for the Aleksandrovsky Orphanage. In 1844, the house was turned over to the **Tsarskoye Selo Lyceum** (whose graduates included Pushkin and his Decembrist friends, Wilhelm Kuhelbeker and Ivan Puschin, and other famous figures of culture, science, diplomacy and politics). In the spring of 1844, the list of famous graduates expanded to include the satirical poet Saltykov-Schedrin. The Lyceum building is the oldest on the avenue.

Sergei Kirov lived in apartment 20 of Nos. 26–28 between 1926 and 1934. In 1938 Shostakovich moved there. In 1957 the **Kirov Memorial Museum** was moved to apartment 20 from the Kshesinskaya Mansion. The secretary lived in what was then considered a luxurious apartment (although it appears modest today), which included a dining room, a library (over 20,000 volumes), a study and a guest-room. The museum displays Kirov's personal effects, the telephone he used as a hotline connection to the Kremlin, documents

A backyard facade on Kirov Prospekt.

and important historical photographs.

Kirov was a talented organiser and orator. Sharing every delusion of his time, he remained a dyed-in-the-wool Bolshevik until his final breath. His speeches contained as many resolute demands to "make short work of the enemies" as Stalin's own. Once Kirov was out of the way, Stalin and his henchmen, who rid themselves of an important political adversary, were free to proceed with their campaign of mass terror against alleged enemies (who, it was claimed, had assassinated Kirov and were planning innumerable other atrocities), a campaign that rapidly grew into outright genocide.

Leo Tolstoy Square is dominated by the building known by locals as the "tower house" (1913–16, by Belogrud). Leo Tolstoy Street, which starts at the "tower house", contains another research centre – the **First Medical College** (named after Pavlov). The Medical College employed the virtuoso surgeon Nikolai Pirogov (in the 1840s), scien-

tists Vladimir Bekhterev, Leon Orbeli, and Georgy Lang (late 19th and early 20th centuries).

The vestibule of the Petrogradskaya Metro Station incorporates the first floor of the **House of Fashions** (No. 37). It is even possible to have a decent suit made there. The **Concert Hall** with the giant glass portal (No. 42, 1934, by Levinson and Munts) rents out its stage to visiting theatrical companies from out-of-town. But even its 4,500 seats are not enough when the most famous troupes are in town. That same building houses a number of clubs and hobby groups – amateur cinematographers, tourists, radio buffs, aviation model-builders and choreographers.

A world of islands: Pioneer's Bridge (1936) over the quiet and winding Karpovka River leads to **Aptekarsky Island**. The strange name ("Apothecary's") comes from the Apothecary's Kitchen Garden on the Karpovka, where medicinal herbs were grown in 1713. In 1823 the "kitchen garden" be-

Young Pushkin at the Lyceum.

came the Botanical Garden. In 1931, the **Komarov Botanical Institute** was founded on the garden's premises. Today, the Institute's garden has over 700 kinds of plants; there are an additional 3,500 in the hothouses, whose main pride has, for over 100 years, been the Korolev Night Cactus, whose flowers open on warm summer nights and close at dawn.

The herbarium of the institute's **Botanical Museum** has approximately 5 million samples of plants collected from all over the world. The museum is one of the largest in Europe. There you will find out what dinosaurs had for dinner, see medieval treatises on medicine and learn how to make potions from the medicine-man's handbook. A special exhibition is devoted to the extremely diverse flora of the USSR and to environmental protection.

Dynamic news coverage: The **Leningrad TV Centre** is situated on the right-hand side of Kirov Prospekt, on Chapygin Street. The TV tower was built between 1956 and 1962. In 1986 it was given a new antenna and, as a result, lost 6 metres (19½ ft) from its former 316 metres (1,036 ft). This, however, in no way affects the tower's status as the tallest structure in the city (it is 9 metres/ 29½ ft taller than the Eiffel Tower in Paris, which is, by the way, eight times heavier). On a windy day, the antenna's sway approaches 2 metres (6½ ft).

Since the late 1980s, Leningrad television has gained popularity far beyond the borders of the town, owing largely to its dynamic and to-the-point news coverage. The programme *600 Seconds*, which covers current Leningrad events, is also a hit in Moscow and all the other places where it can be received. The programme is one of the most critical and popular in the country. It features heated debates between scientists, politicians, writers and assorted other interesting people touching every taboo, of which there are plenty. In doing so it exposes and annoys both politicians and the Soviet mafia.

Kirov Prospekt in 1937.

Beyond Chapygin Street, at No. 2b Gorky Street, lived the "great reformer of Russian opera", Shaliapin, between 1915 and 1922. To this day, lovers of chamber music are drawn to concerts performed in the hall of his house. The place also houses an exhibition entitled the "History of Russian Opera".

Not far from the end of the avenue, at the **Institute of Experimental Medicine** (12 Academician Pavlov Street), Ivan Pavlov (1890–1936) worked for almost five decades.

After the revolution, Pavlov's research – surprisingly – was not banned; Lenin considered his theory of reflexes and higher nervous activity an important contribution to materialist philosophy. The government turned a blind eye to Pavlov's religious activities as an elder of one of Leningrad's Orthodox Churches, which would ordinarily have branded him an ignorant and backward enemy of materialism (the official attitude to all believers). In 1935 Pavlov had a statue of a dog installed in the institute's forecourt as a symbol of human gratitude.

An archipelago within the city: Kirov Prospekt ends at the wide Stone Bridge over the Malaya (Little) Nevka. Here, north of the Petrograd Side, lie the **Kirov Isles**, a picturesque archipelago with parks and old mansions. Originally, this piece of land, lying between the Bolshaya Nevka and the Malaya Nevka, was owned by Peter the Great's comrade-in-arms, Chancellor Gavriil Golovkin.

Ownership then passed to Chancellor Aleksei Bestuzhev-Riumin, who brought thousands of serfs over from his Ukrainian estates. Today the new residential areas built on the site of their settlements preserve the original names – Old Village and New Village.

In the 18th century, canals were dug to guard against "catastrophic floods". At the same time the construction of luxurious mansions and a park was started. The island was becoming the summer *dacha* area of the Petersburg

The logo of the famous news telecast "Wremya".

nobility. Walking along the island's lime-tree alley to the eastern section we reach **Stone Island Palace**. This was built between 1776 and 1781 for the son of Catherine the Great, the future emperor Pavel. Today, the **Large Hall** with caryatids and the **Blue and Crimson Guest rooms** are occupied by a sanatorium.

The domed building on Malaya Nevka Embankment (No. 11) was built between 1831 and 1833 by Smaragd Shustov for the wealthy Dolgorukiy family. Cast-iron sphinxes, made by sculptor Soloviev in 1824, sit on the granite mooring of the Malaya Nevka.

A memorial to the beginnings of the city is the oak tree that Peter I planted in 1714 on the Krestovka River. The oak has braved all the hardships of the Petersburg climate and has managed to survive to this day.

The *dacha* where Pushkin spent the last summer of his life in 1836 has not survived. On its site the neoclassical out-of-town residence of Senator

A typical Leningrad couple.

Polovtsev (1911–16, by Ivan Fomin) has been built. The Senator liked his rooms to be decorated with marble, Italian silks and gilt. From behind the stern classicism of the palace, the mellow traits of the Empire style, which was popular in the 1900s, shine through.

The island across the Srednaya (Middle) Nevka belonged originally to Pyotr Shafirov, a diplomat from Peter's retinue. Then it came into the hands of the wealthy aristocrat Yelagin, who gave his name to the island. Yelagin's serfs irrigated the island and built a dam to guard against flood.

Soon afterwards **Yelagin Island** was made the summer residence of the czars. In 1818–22 Alexander I commissioned Rossi to build a house there. The facades of the palace have different "tempers" – the one facing the river is somewhat sterner than the one overlooking the park. Both facades are decorated with white marble vases with tritons, which were sculpted according to Rossi's sketches. Opposite the palace is the two-storey semicircle of the kitchens. In order to save the inhabitants of the palace from kitchen odours, Rossi designed a windowless facade for the building. Those windows that it does have face the inner courtyard.

Today **Yelagin Palace** is an exhibition and lecture hall. The park on the island has been turned into the traditional site of the White Nights Leningrad Festival of Art.

Before the Revolution the largest of the Kirov Isles – **Krestovsky Island** – was never as popular among the nobility as Kammeny Island and Yelagin Island. This is probably explained by the greater danger of flooding (Krestovsky Island juts out farther into the Baltic) and, of course, by the distasteful proximity of the worker's quarters on Petrograd and Petrovsky Islands. One of the few surviving 19th-century establishments on the island is the **Yacht Club**, founded in 1860.

A stadium made of mud: The island was developed in the Soviet era. The **Dy-**

namo Stadium was built in 1925 and the **Kirov Stadium {22}** followed, in 1950, on the western part of the island. The remarkable thing about the Dynamo stadium is that its foundations incorporate neither stone nor concrete. Instead it was built on mud. Mud was piped from the bottom of the Gulf of Finland. The millions of cubic metres that were raised formed a kind of low volcano with a very wide crater. It is in the crater that the stands and the stadium itself are located; it seats 75,000.

Across the Greater Neva to the **Novaya Derevny (New Village District)** are two other places of interest. The **Buddhist Temple** at No. 91 Primorsky (Maritime) Prospekt and the **site of Pushkin's duel**.

Architect Gavriil Baranovsky, who was commissioned to build a Buddhist temple early in this century, consulted Lama Agvan-Khamba, who arrived from Lhasa just for this purpose. The temple was built because St Petersburg developed a Buddhist community ow-ing to the interest in non-traditional religions that arose in the late 19th and early 20th centuries.

In those days the city both thrived on the existing philosophical doctrines of the Orient and became a breeding-ground for new synthetic ones, such as the theosophic school of Yelena Blavatskaya or the Georgiy Gurdzhiev theory. Gurdzhiev's lectures and seminars were quite popular among the nobility in early in the 20th century.

Pushkin's death: The site of Pushkin's duel lies along the **Chernaya Rechka (Black River)**. The prelude of Pushkin's duel with D'Anthes, the adopted son of Heeckeren, the Dutch Ambassador, was quite ordinary for the life of high society in the beginning of the 19th century. Pushkin's young wife, Natalia, was beautiful, courteous and clever. Her popularity equalled the popularity of her husband.

D'Anthes, the dashing officer and wit who was a sought-after guest in St Petersburg salons, fell in love with her. His insistent attentions placed Pushkin in a singularly uncomfortable position. As rumours were whispered from ear to ear, a hate letter was disseminated among the poet's circle of acquaintances, which pronounced Pushkin the historiographer of the Order of Horn-Bearers – a cuckold.

Yet Natalia remained faithful to her husband. She informed her husband about D'Anthes' attempts to seduce her, and about the dubious role of Heeckeren in the affair. Pushkin concluded that the hate letter was written by the old Ambassador, who was quite capable of "helping" his adopted son with his love life. On the other hand, the tongue-waggers spoke about the homosexual nature of D'Anthes' adoption by the old lecher – which made the young officer's chasing after women undesirable in Heeckeren's eyes.

Meanwhile, D'Anthes grew more and more insistent. He never missed an opportunity to express his admiration to Natalia Pushkina. Finally, Pushkin

The reason of Pushkin's fatal duel: Natalia Pushkina.

could bear it no longer and, following the tradition of the times, challenged D'Anthes to a duel. On this occasion the challenge was not taken up but trouble continued to simmer under the surface.

The affair was finally settled with great difficulty. D'Anthes married Catherine, Natalia's sister. Unfortunately, he persisted with his attentions towards Pushkin's wife, this time trying to achieve success as a "member of the family". Driven to the breaking point by jealousy and suspicion, Pushkin mailed a letter full of insults to old Heeckeren. He wanted a duel and the insults were too serious to be avoided this time. D'Anthes challenged Pushkin.

The duel took place on 27 January 1837. Pushkin was mortally wounded on the bank of Chernaya Rechka, and D'Anthes received a bullet in his arm.

Pushkin was brought to his apartment. His friends and the best doctors in town remained at his side. From time to time short bulletins about his condition were hung on the front door: crowds of people came to ask about the poet's health, because news of the outcome of the duel had spread through St Petersburg like wildfire.

Vladimir Dal, the medic and philologist who was Pushkin's friend, remained with him to the last breath. This is what he wrote: "He seemed to awake, suddenly, with a start. Eyes opened wide, face bright, he said, 'Life is over.' I did not hear, and asked, 'What is over?' 'Life is over!' he said distinctly and positively. 'Can't breathe, something's choking' were his last words... a ghost of a breath – and an impassable, immeasurable chasm separated the living from the dead!"

The pines which witnessed the duel have given way to willows and poplars. One hundred years after the event, in what was, for Russia, the far more tragic year of 1937, a 19-metre (62-ft) high stone of pink granite with a bas-relief was installed at the site of the duel where Russia's greatest poet met his untimely end.

There are many peaceful spots around the Kirov Isles.

VASILIEVSKY ISLAND

Neither country nor graveyard I want to choose,
'Tis Vasilievsky Island on which I'll come to die.

Thus wrote **Iosif Brodsky**, the winner of the 1987 Nobel Prize for literature. Living abroad, the Russian poet still feels the link with the places in his homeland that he loves most.

For a long time Vasilievsky Island had trouble finding a purpose, even though the powers-that-be groomed it to play the leading role in the city. Recognising the value of the island's position (with its long stretch of Baltic coast), Peter the Great was determined to found the administrative centre of the city there. Much effort went to make his vision come true. Peter ordered all newcomers to the city to settle on Vasilievsky Island.

Plans were made to improve the transport system on the island with numerous man-made canals and to provide a comprehensive irrigation system. Meanwhile, the absence of permanent bridges across the Neva and over to the Petrograd Side stalled Peter's project.

Geometrical proportions: In 1722, supervised by Domenico Trezzini, work began on the construction of 12 colleges on the island. These colleges were the equivalents of today's ministries; united, they formed the highest government authority – the Senate. But Peter's time was running out fast. When the great reformer died in 1725, the island's administrative significance dwindled.

The 12 colleges still stand as a monument to Peter's intentions, along with the strict geometrical division of the island into 34 avenues. Roads known as lines, also survive and these correspond to the banks of the filled-in canals, each forming a 90-degree angle to the three main avenues of Vasilievsky Island – **Bolshoi**, **Sredny** and **Maly Prospekts**.

All in all, there are 29 lines (each street comprises two lines), and the street that crosses Bolshoi Prospekt at a sharp angle is known as the slanting line.

It is customary to start an acquaintance with Vasilievsky Island on its **Spit** {*map reference* **23**}, also called the **Strelka**, which divides the mighty Neva in two. We shall observe this custom. Of all of Peter's schemes, the Spit is the one that came closest to realisation. It became an important centre, though a commercial one rather than the political centre that Peter had in mind, and long retained that role.

In 1733, the seaport was relocated to the Spit, and remained there until 1855. Throughout this period, the area we know today as **Pushkin Square** remained (as with any other port area in the world) the most lively and troublesome place in town. Bonded warehouses and the customs house were relocated near the port. At first these agencies found whatever shelter they could; later they built impressive headquarters for themselves. That grandiose barometer, the weather indicator in the ocean of business, the **Stock Exchange** also sprang up here.

The Stock Exchange Building, which resembles an ancient temple, was finished in 1810. It was designed by Thomas de Thomon, with the assistance of Andreyan Zakharov. Its entire interior is taken up by the exchange hall (900 sq. metres/9,700 sq. ft). The stairs leading to the building are so wide that they were used as a stage for 2,000 actors in the Soviet era, when mass performances were fashionable.

On the main facade is the figure of Neptune gliding through the waves in his chariot in the company of two rivers – the Neva and the Volkhov. The other statues are of the Goddess of Navigation and of Mercury, the god of trade. Inside, near the entrance, there are allegorical sculptures of Time, Plenty and Justice on one side and Commerce and Navigation on the other.

When the port went the Exchange

Preceding pages: the Strelka. **Left**, detail of one of the Rostral Columns.

went with it, leaving behind this luxurious Greek temple that could not keep up with the speed and scale of commercial operations in the last third of the 19th century. In 1940 the Exchange was turned over to the **Central Naval Museum**, which was founded in 1805. The collection of the museum includes over 650,000 items. Among its better-known properties are model ships, Peter's boat, the personal effects of Admiral Pavel Nakhimov, weapons, flags and shipyard blueprints. There is also a salvaged oak boat from the bottom of the Yuzhny Bug River, which experts date to the first millennium BC.

The Exchange's construction gave the Spit its present-day appearance. The shores were dressed in granite; stairways led down to the Neva, where huge stone spheres were installed on pedestals close to the water. The granite-lined paths descending to the Neva were not so much designed for promenading as for loading and unloading ships.

In the wintertime, if you are willing to brave the vicious wind and go down to the water's edge, you'll marvel at the numerous champagne bottles whose pieces are frozen in place among the stillness of the ice-covered waves. All the bottles derive from a local custom – it is traditional for newlyweds to come to the Spit on Vasilievsky Island and break a bottle for good luck and future happiness.

The glory of the Russian fleet: The crews of every ship that dropped anchor off the Spit could marvel at the two curious structures on either side of it – the **Rostral Columns**. The 32-metre (105-ft) high columns were built between 1805 and 1810 by de Thomon. Their name is derived from the Latin *rostrum* which means the prow of a ship. The Romans decorated their triumphal columns with trophies of war, which included the sawn-off prows of Carthaginian ships, and these columns have a similar purpose. They are symbols of the glory of the Russian fleet. The columns were badly damaged in

A view across the Neva towards Vasilievsky Island.

the blockade, and the *rostra* we see today are of quite recent origin.

The sculptures at the foot of the columns depict the rivers of Russia, which serve as major transport arteries. From left to right (seen from the Exchange), they are the Dnieper, the Volga, the Volkhov and the Neva. There are spiral staircases inside the columns that lead to metal basins on their tops. In the past they were used to light beacon fires. Today there are gas pipes in the basins, and 7-metre (23-ft) tall gas torches flame over the columns on holidays.

The ensemble on the Spit also includes the **South** and the **North Bonded Warehouses** on either side of the Exchange and the **Customs House**. The modest grey-green of their facades creates the required atmosphere of seriousness and serves as the background for the Exchange. The southern building has housed the **Zoological Museum** since 1900, and the northern one the **Dokuchayev Soil Museum**.

The Zoological Museum has over 40,000 animal species from all over the globe. Its collections consist of over 10 million specimens of insects, 185,000 specimens of fish, and 88,000 mammals. It even has a stuffed mammoth, which was found in 1961 in the permafrost near Berezovo and is 44,000 years old as well as a baby mammoth found in 1977 near Magadan. The museum has a special **Hall of Mammoths** to accommodate these rarities.

The soil museum is based on the unique collection of one of the fathers of modern agronomy, Vasily Dokuchayev. It has no parallel anywhere in the world. Dokuchayev's collections fully reflect the diversity of soils found in the USSR. There is abundant information about soil quality, ways of improving fertility and the history of soil sciences. Samples of various soils are supplied with diagrams, soil maps and photos.

The next building along Makarova Embankment behind the North Warehouse is the former Customs House. Constructed in 1829–82, it is the young-

In front of the Naval Museum.

est building here. The portico is decorated with the bronze statues of Mercury, Neptune, and Ceres.

The turret was used for observation and for making signals to ships arriving in port. Today, the house belongs to the **Institute of Russian Literature of the USSR Academy of Sciences** and is also known as **Pushkin House**.

The institute continued, in Soviet times, a collection that was started in 1905 as the Literary Museum. Today it is one of the foremost authorities on Russian literature. Over the years, it has gathered manuscripts, archives and first editions of the best-known works of Russian literature, plus collections of pre-revolutionary newspapers. There are also the personal libraries of several writers. In 1905, Pushkin's library became the museum's first acquisition.

One section of the museum contains old handwritten and printed books, most of which were found as a result of book-finding expeditions. They are mainly holy books, written by hand and used for religious purposes by the peasants. Their abundance dispels the myth that the *raskolniki* (Orthodox Protestants) had no culture of their own, a belief that was widely endorsed in scientific quarters. The museum also has the manuscript of Archpriest Avvakum (17th-century); this Magna Carta of the rebels against church reform is today cherished as a holy relic by all the *raskolniki* in the world.

In the past few years, the staff of the museum have been working on documents which date to the 20th century. They are gathering what promises to become a unique collection of letters from the Gulag camps.

Famous scholars have worked at Pushkin House. Today, one of its departments is headed by Dmitry Likhachev, Member of the Academy of Sciences, President of the Culture Fund, and one of the most popular people in the USSR (who also contributed the essay, *City on the Neva*, to this book). Early in 1990 Likhachev took a bold

There are still many coaches driving through Leningrad.

204

step. He threatened to leave the Academy if Leningrad's party bosses did not authorise the long-promised work to conserve the Institute's manuscripts and rare books. Likhachev emphasised the urgent nature of the project, because of a series of catastrophes that took place in Leningrad between 1988 and 1990: fire in the library of the Academy of Sciences and the disastrous flooding in the Main Public Library. Each time, unique documents and books were either destroyed or endangered.

The centre of academic life: From the Spit, let us head along **University Embankment {24}** and marvel at its jewels. On the opposite side of the Neva you can see the side wings of the Admiralty and the Decembrists' Square.

The first scientific establishment we encounter is the baroque house with the turret (No.3). It was built between 1718 and 1734 for Russia's first **museum of natural science** and enjoyed the protection of Peter the Great himself. It also contained Russia's first public library

Peter I's best friend: Alexander Menshikov.

and astronomical observatory. To create the museum, Peter issued a decree ordering all unusual, curious and freakish creations of nature (the only requirement was for them to be out of the ordinary, things that people did not see around them in everyday life) to be brought to the capital. Soon the Czar had quite a collection of curiosities. But the house where the collection was kept, and to which everyone was soon freely admitted, fell into decay.

Peter ordered a new building, which is known today as the **Kunstkammer** (from the German *kunst*, "art", and *kammer*, "chamber"). The upper part of the building, the turret, was destroyed by fire in 1742; two centuries later, in 1948–49, the turret was restored to its original form in accordance with the initial drawings.

Mikhail Lomonosov, the famous Russian scientist, worked in the building in 1741–65. Here this extraordinary polymath, born of peasant stock, conducted experiments in chemistry and physics, observed the stars, wrote verse, codified the rules of Russian grammar and studied minerals. Here, too, the Russian Academy of Sciences started its work. The hall where its members (Lomonosov was the first Russian in the academy) used to meet, has survived in its original form.

Today, there are three scientific establishments under one roof in the Kunstkammer: the **Museum of Anthropology and Ethnography**, which continues where the Kunstkammer left off, the **Mikluho-Maklai Ethnography Institute**, and the **Lomonosov Museum**.

The museum of anthropology offers one of the largest exhibitions in the world. It is divided into subject collections which describe, in the utmost detail, life on the Volga, the Americas, Siberia and the Far East, Africa and Oceania. The collection includes costumes, house utensils, coins, weapons, tools and other objects used by various peoples in their everyday life.

Monster collections: The greatest interest is invariably provoked by the round hall in the eastern gallery of the building. Here the anatomical specimens made by the famous Dutch pathologist, Frederik Ruysch, are on display. They include the so-called "monsters" – human and animal anomalies. There are Siamese twins, a two-faced man, a two-headed calf and enough assorted specimens to inspire many a horror film. Certain objects from the collection caused such unhealthy interest that they were removed from display and transferred to the museum's storerooms several years ago. This fate befell the unusually long penis, which belonged to a guard who lived in Peter's day, and several similar items.

Our age has almost made a contribution of its own to the collection of monsters. According to not very reliable sources, the territory of Zhitomir in the Ukraine, which was showered with radioactive rain after the Chernobyl disaster, has produced several animal monsters – a colt with all its legs fused together, a piglet with two heads, and so on. All these died or were stillborn.

There is a different mood in the **Lomonosov Museum**, where they'll tell you in the dull manner usual for such places about the life of the scientist who founded Russia's first university (and who was, as the poet put it, "a university unto himself") a man who made considerable contributions to physics, chemistry, astronomy, geography, history, poetics, linguistics, medicine, economics and technology.

At the end of the 18th century, the needs of the Academy of Sciences outgrew the close confines of the Kunstkammer. Hence the new academy building was erected between 1783 and 1788 next door. It was designed by Giacomo Quarenghi. The central staircase of the academy is decorated by Lomonosov's mosaic panel, *The Battle of Poltava*. In 1934 the administrative bodies of the academy moved to Moscow, but the scientists got to keep the

Peaceful evening hours on the banks of the Neva.

building, which now belongs to the Leningrad Branch of the Academy.

Turning right here, along **Mendeleev's Line**, we come to the large grey building of the **Library of the USSR Academy of Sciences** (1 Birzhevaya Linia). Today, the library has approximately 9 million volumes (12 million if the collections of affiliates are added to the grand total).

The library owns *The Apostol*, Russia's first printed book, which was published by Ivan Fyodorov in 1564, books from Peter the Great's personal library and the textbooks that Lomonosov used as a student. Peter ordered the library to purchase copies of all books published in Russia. Fortunately, none of these rare editions were damaged in the fire that recently ravaged the building.

Also in Mendeleev's Line are the 12 Colleges, where the University opened its doors in 1819. The complex of interconnected buildings was built in 1722–42. The main facade of the Collegia is over 400 metres (1,300 ft) long and runs at a 90° angle to the Neva. These buildings did not look as they did back in the early 18th century. There was no grille, and each college had a separate entrance with an arcade, according to Peter's instructions. The isolation of the buildings symbolised the independence of the colleges which were granted a considerable degree of autonomy.

Even so, all the buildings were arranged in a single row, indicating that they were expected to pull one oar within the unified system of state administration. Peter's 12 Colleges were set up to replace Russia's numerous administrative bodies, known as *prikazy*. In their turn, the Colleges gave way to ministries at the beginning of the 19th century. The reform of the administrative apparatus took place in the new building in Senate Square, for the old Collegia building was already turning out future Russian intellectuals and dangerous free-thinkers.

Famous graduates: The university's research workers have glorified their alma mater by their world-famous work. One of the graduates was Alexander Popov (1859–1906), who performed all the relevant experiments, assembled the first radio and transmitted the first radio signal consisting of two words, "Heinrich Hertz", in the university labs.

Another graduate was Dmitry Mendeleev (1834–1907) who lived and worked at the university between 1866 and 1890. Mendeleev discovered the periodic law of chemical elements and elaborated the periodic system known to anyone who takes even a passing interest in chemistry.

There is a museum in Mendeleev's apartment now, which tells of his childhood and youth, about the way the periodic table came to the scientist in his sleep after a long and fruitless struggle to find the correct element order. Mendeleev was aided, in the final stages of work on his system, by his love for the game of patience. The museum has the scientist's personal effects and the

Women from the Leningrad region are known for their beauty.

chemical devices that he designed – the scale for weighing liquid and gaseous substances, for example. Mendeleev's beautiful daughter, by the way, married the grandson of the university rector, the Symbolist poet Alexander Blok.

The university has also seen Pavlov and Sechenov, Alexander Butlerov (the chemist), Pafnuty Chebyshev (the mathematician), natural scientists Vasily Dokuchayev and Kliment Timiryazev. The place was also crawling with revolutionaries. Mikhail Butashevich-Petrashevsky, Nikolai Chernyshevsky, Dmitry Pisarev, Alexander Ulianov (sentenced to death for plotting a terrorist attack against Alexander III) and his younger brother Vladimir Ulianov (who took his graduation exams here and graduated *magna cum lauda,* with honours); Ulianov is better known today by one of his party pseudonyms – Lenin.

Today, the University of Leningrad is one of the largest educational centres of the nation. It can no longer fit into the Collegia, and occupies several other buildings not far away. There are over 20,000 students. Some 10 percent of the faculty are Doctors of Science. Courses at all of its 16 faculties are free, and most students receive a small state scholarship of 50 to 100 roubles a month.

Until recently, the university has born the name of one of Stalin's henchmen, former party secretary of the Leningrad Committee, Andrei Zhdanov. Remembering their revolutionary traditions, the students protested against the executioner and enemy of science and the arts. Zhdanov was one of the organisers of the notorious party decree concerning the *Zvezda* and *Leningrad* magazines (1948). He slandered the satirical writer Mikhail Zoschenko and the poetess Anna Akhmatova, who was later elected Honorary Doctor of Oxford University. The students found many supporters in Leningrad and Zhdanov's name was finally removed from the university. Various new names have been proposed including those of Peter the Great and Academician Sakharov.

The Czar's best friend: Two buildings away from the Collegia, at No. 15 University Embankment, there is another house that dates to the earliest days of the city. It is the palace of the "almost-monarch", as Pushkin called him, the Czar's closest friend and advisor, and St Petersburg's first governor, Alexander Menshikov (1673–1729).

In 1707 Peter presented the entire Vasilievsky Island to his favourite as a gift. However, in 1714, when the Czar set out to create his administrative centre on the island, he took the island back. Menshikov nevertheless managed to build a palace for himself on the island between 1710 and 1714 (architects Giovanni Fontana and Gottfried Schädel), which was the most luxurious building in St Petersburg in its time and then the only stone building in the whole town.

When Peter died in 1725 Menshikov fell into disfavour and was exiled. The Menshikov Palace was turned over to a

A gift from the Nile.

military school – the First Cadet Corps. In the Soviet era, the building was given to the Hermitage to house an exhibition entitled "Russian Culture in the First Third of the 18th Century". In the 1970s, the decision was taken to restore the palace. After a prolonged study of its structure, including the examination of the remaining blueprints, restoration was finally started, and will probably continue for some time.

Much of the palace, however, is now back to its original form. There are Roman and Greek statues in the niches of the main entranceway (Menshikov imported them from Europe in his desire to emulate Peter). The stairway grille bears the intertwined monograms of Menshikov and Peter. Then follows the secretary's quarters, decorated with Dutch landscapes and astronomical instruments. Beyond, there are the palace halls, of which the first is decorated with Dutch tiles. Of the 25,000 tiles that had originally been used in the decoration of the palace, 1,500 have been restored by

The red Rostral Columns are like a gate to Vasilievsky Island.

specialists who first had to discover the lost secrets of the Dutch masters.

Then comes the bed chamber, Varvara's room (where the sister of Menshikov's wife lived), and the governor's favourite Walnut Study. The windows of the study face the Neva. The restorers were in for a surprise when they got to that room – they discovered a full-sized portrait of Peter in military uniform.

On the wall of the study hangs Peter's mirror. Mirrors were a bold innovation in the 18th century. Before Peter's time everyday life in Russia was governed by the code known as *Domostroi*, which expressly forbade people to look at themselves. It was therefore considered the height of bad manners to keep mirrors in the house.

The palace from which Menshikov was chased out after Peter's death soon became too small for the cadets, so another long building was added behind it in 1758–60. The building assumed its present form in 1938. Between 3 and 24 June 1917, the First Russian Congress of Soviets took place here; the event was commemorated by the renaming of the former Kadetskaya Line as the Sjezdovskaya (Congress) Line.

In the park beyond the Menshikov Palace and further down University Embankment, there is an obelisk commemorating the victory over the Turks in 1774. In 1779, architect Vikentiy Brenna installed it on the Field of Mars, but in 1818 Rossi recommended that it be relocated to its present position. Rossi made some alterations when he installed the monument. The site near the Cadet Corps was chosen because the Russian army that won the 1768–74 war was headed by Marshal Rumiantsev, a graduate of the school.

The Most Noble Arts: Behind the park is the former Academy of Fine Arts. Now the building houses another establishment which revels in being "the largest" – in this case the world's largest art school, the **Repin Institute of Painting, Sculpture and Architecture**.

The house was built in 1764–88 by Alexander Kornilov and Jean Baptist de la Mothe for the Academy of Art. It is a typical specimen of Russian classicism. The portico above the entrance is decorated with sculptures depicting Hercules and Flora.

"The Academy of the Three Most Noble Arts" was founded in 1757. The "Most Noble" implied painting, sculpture and architecture. One of the building's architects was rewarded for his efforts – he went on to become a professor and later the rector of the Academy.

Graduates of the Academy include Pyotr Klodt, Fyodor Shubin, Mark Antokolsky, architects Andrei Voronikhin, Andreyan Zakharov, Ivan Starov, Vasily Bazhenov, the painters Dmitry Levitsky (who became famous by his portraits of aristocrats in the second half of the 18th and the early 19th centuries), Ilya Repin (whose most famous picture depicts Cossacks writing a letter to the Turkish Sultan), and Karl Bryullov, the painter of Italian scenes.

The Ukrainian poet and artist Taras Shevchenko spent the last years of his life (1858–61) at the Academy. Much tied him to the Academy: he studied here after Bryullov's masterpiece *The Last Day of Pompeii* (which depicts the eruption of Mount Vesuvius and the imminent destruction of the ancient city) had been auctioned off to buy him, a serf, freedom from his master. A museum-studio of Taras Shevchenko's work was opened here in 1964.

In 1947, the Academy moved to Moscow. The **Repin Institute** and the **Research Museum of the Academy** stayed on. The museum displays graduation works collected over the years. It also has a collection of copies of the world's great masterpieces, made directly from the originals by artists who were masters in their own right. This unique educational aid was collected in the late 18th and early 19th centuries.

From the Nile to Peter: Of the three moorings on the quay, the most remarkable one is near the Academy. In 1834,

The Spit during the 18th century.

the ornamental girandoles and griffons were installed. At the turn of the century, the griffons disappeared under mysterious circumstances. Copies were restored to the mooring in 1959 made in accordance with surviving sketches.

Fame was brought to the place by its two **Egyptian sphinxes** of pink granite (from the famous Aswan Quarries). The sphinxes probably date to the era of the Pharaoh Amenhotep III (1417–1379 BC). The hieroglyphic inscription on one of the sphinxes says: "Son of Ra, Builder of Monuments, Who Rises to the Sky As the Four Pillars Which Hold the Vault of the Skies." The sculptor gave the sphinxes the face of the Pharaoh Amenhotep.

The sculptures were buried by silt after a Nile flood and only re-emerged in 1820. Russia bought them from Egypt in 1831. It took a year for the 23-ton sculptures to travel to the city up the Neva. The time of their arrival in the capital is recorded in a Russian inscription that reads: "This sphinx from an-cient Thebes in Egypt was delivered to the City of St Peter in 1832."

The sphinxes are separated from **Lieutenant Schmidt Embankment** by a bridge that also bears his name. He stood at the head of the mutiny on the battleship *Ochakov* of the Black Sea Fleet during the 1905–07 Revolution in Russia. Schmidt had been a graduate of the Petersburg Naval College.

The bridge was built in 1842–50. It was the first stationary bridge to connect Vasilievsky Island with the central part of the town. First called Blagoveschensky, it was later renamed **Nikolayevsky**. In 1937–38 the bridge was widened by 4 metres (13 ft) and restructured once more in 1975–76.

On Lieutenant Schmidt Embankment the "academic relay" of the University Embankment continues. House No.1 (1750, by Savva Chevakinsky) has 26 memorial tablets. Eighty academy members lived here during the 250 years of St Petersburg's history. There is a museum in the former apartment of

The Zoology Museum and the Kunstkammer.

scientist and Nobel Laureate Ivan Pavlov (1890–1936).

Further down the quay are the buildings of the **Naval Cadet Corps** (1796–98, by Fyodor Volkov), which are presently occupied by the **Higher Naval School** (named after Frunze), Russia's first naval school. The college trained Admiral Fyodor Ushakov, the father of the Russian school of navy tactics, Admiral Pavel Nakhimov, the hero of Sevastopol in the Crimean war of 1854–55, and Admiral Mikhail Lazarev, who accompanied Faddei Bellingshausen on his 1820 Antarctic expedition.

The college, like just about every other place in the city, bears the traces of Lenin's energetic drive. In May, 1917, he spoke here before an audience made up of members of the Petrograd Bolshevik Organisation and gave a public lecture entitled *War and Revolution.*

Another of the famed graduates of the college was Admiral Ivan Krusenstern (1770–1846), whose monument stands in front of the building on the Neva bank

(1873, by Ivan Shreder). Krusenstern was later appointed director of the Cadet Corps. He commanded the first Russian round-the-world voyage in 1803–06. Krusenstern's observations during the voyage were an outstanding contribution to science, recognised by the several academic establishments in Russia, Germany, France and England who elected him an honorary member. The 5.6-metre (18-ft) tall monument is inscribed: "To the first Russian to sail around the world, Admiral Ivan Fedorovich Krusenstern".

Treasures of the earth: Between Lines 21 and 23, not far from Lieutenant Schmidt Embankment, is a building with a majestic 12-column portico (1801–11, by Andrei Voronikhin). It is the building of the **Mining Institute**, which was founded in 1773 and became the world's second establishment of its kind. The entrance is adorned with sculptures which reflect the purpose of the college. To the left is Cerberus, the three-headed dog, who guards the underworld, lying placidly near the feet of Pluto, the master of the dead. To the right is Hercules with Antaeus, the son of the Earth, symbolising the victory of reason over the chaotic forces of nature. It also contains mythological scenes symbolising the penetration of the secrets guarded by the bowels of the Earth and the use of their riches for the benefit of humanity.

In 1956, the Mining Institute was given the name of its former student Georgiy Plekhanov (1856–1918), one of Russia's first Marxists. Plekhanov was a supporter of Lenin in the social democratic movement, but became his irreconcilable adversary and a Menshevik leader after the revolutionary movement split into the Bolsheviks and the Mensheviks.

The **Mining Museum** is as old as the Institute. Its collections offer a fascinating insight into the treasures of the Earth. There are thousands of minerals from 60 or so countries. Its unique items include a chunk of Ukrainian malachite **The Baltic Yacht Club.**

weighing 1,054 kg (2,323 lbs), a Kazakhstani nugget of copper weighing 842 kg (1,855 lbs), a Ukrainian quartz crystal weighing 800 kg (1,763 lbs), an iron meteorite of 450 kg (990 lbs), and a palm tree that blacksmith Alexander Mertsalov fashioned from a strip of iron.

To the sea: This book's tour of the quays ends here near the Mining Institute. To discover the sea gateway to the city you can take any tram to **Bolshoi Prospekt** and **Morskoi Slavy Square**, from where there is view of the activity in the harbour.

Morskoi Slavy (Naval Glory) Square is dominated by the **Sea Terminal** (1977–82). The metal panels lining the facade resemble wind-filled sails. The 78-metre (226-ft) spire of the terminal is crowned with a caravelle, which reminds one of the Admiralty. The 270-metre (885-ft) long granite quay makes it possible for two ocean-going passenger ships to moor here at the same time.

On the opposite side of the bay there are two turrets with flagpoles (*kronspitses*) which mark the entrance to **Galernaya Bay**. In 1720, Domenico Trezzini fashioned this as a hiding place for the galleys of Peter's fleet. In 1754, architect Bashmakov changed the wooden towers for stone ones.

On the shore of the Baltic (14 Korablestroitelei Street), is the **Pribaltiskaya Hotel {25}** (1976–78), which was built by Swedish construction companies. The hotel has an H-shaped layout; it is open towards the sea and towards the city and stands in the middle of a large residential area. The hotel was opened for the 1980 Olympics and, though standards of service are not quite what you may be used to, it has some superb suites with windows that look out across the Bay of Finland – perfectly positioned for a view of the dramatic sunsets characteristic of the "white nights" of midsummer. A 6-km (3½-mile) embankment is under construction on the sea coast. It will become the sea facade for the entire city.

Modern living quarters.

THE VYBORG SIDE

The Vyborg Side is the name given to the mainland area to the northeast of the Bolshaya (Greater) Nevka. Traditionally this was where the ordinary people of St Petersburg built their settlements. Subsequent generations of settlers built further away from the river and along the road to Vyborg. The road was divided into three sections in the old days (today they are all within the city limits and known as **Karl Marx Prospekt**, **Engels Prospekt**, and **Vyborg Highway**). Somewhat later, the nobility started to build summer houses there, followed by less noble but still rich people who built *dachas*.

Fertile ground for Revolution: Industrialists were attracted to the area by its considerable manpower resources. The Vyborg Side was turning into the district with the highest concentration of industrial production in the city, a major centre of metallurgy, machine-building and textile production.

Miserly wages and miserable working and living conditions fuelled discontent and made the working classes easy prey for Bolshevik agitators. Revolutionary groups and circles cropped up here and there among the workers who studied Marxism and propagated its ideas. The workers were told that they were the "leading class", and, as such, deserved a better life (which was, of course, quite true). The hitch was that this better life, they were told, had to be wrested by force from the hands of the bourgeoisie.

In the days of the 1917 coup, and in the subsequent effort to defend the new regime, the workers of the Vyborg Side were the trump card of the Bolsheviks. Attempts to restore and improve the workers' quarter were made in the early 1920s; the party had to show how much it cared about the life of ordinary people. In the end the project fizzled out. Only since the last war did large-scale construction of quality housing begin in the district. The area became fashionable in the 1960s, when local residents began to take pride in the fact that they lived in the centre of Leningrad.

The areas to the north and to the east of the Neva were the focus of development. Many apartment blocks, shops, industrial enterprises and schools were built. Today, several major enterprises are located here: they include the Leningrad Optico-Mechanical Association, the Leningrad Metal Works which produces turbines, the Plastopolimer Corporation and the Svetlana Electronic Instrument Building Corporation. There are also large academic institutions such as the Forestry Academy and the Polytechnic Institute.

Lenin's triumphant return: The most rewarding areas of the Vyborg Side are the square in front of Finland Station, a part of Karl Marx Prospekt and the adjacent areas. The square in front of the station is a wonderful example of how even the most insignificant places could

Preceding pages: waiting for the next train. **Left,** Lenin arrived at Finland Station and the Revolution caught momentum. **Right,** Lenin's armoured *Enemy of Capital*.

be made holy by the priests of the new religion – Communism. The reason is that the square was fortunate enough to see Lenin's arrival from exile abroad.

Having learned about Nicholas II's renunciation of the throne and the fall of the monarchy, Lenin decided to return immediately to Russia. Experiencing all the discomforts of wartime travel (World War I was in progress), Lenin finally made it to Petrograd in the small hours of 3 April 1917. Bolsheviks, their sympathisers from among the workers, soldiers and sailors and simple idlers formed a welcoming crowd several thousand strong.

The new and charismatic leader received a reception equal to that of a Czar in the old days. Soldiers fired into the sky and everyone cheered. Lenin scrambled onto an armoured vehicle bearing the inscription *Enemy of Capital*, which was used as a podium by assorted left-wing leaders who wished to air their views. Lenin gave a short and fiery speech: he congratulated the audience for having accomplished the fall of the monarchy which, he said, opened the way for the Revolution.

Father of all Lenin monuments: When Lenin died in 1924, the nation plunged into a frenzy, giving his name to everything that could have one. The city on the Neva became one of the epidemic's first victims. It was followed by the square in front of the Finland Station.

In April, 1924, the government decided to make sure that Lenin's speech would be remembered by everyone, not just those who had actually heard it. The lucrative order for a monument went to sculptor Sergei Yevesev and two architects – Vladimir Schuko and Vladimir Gelfreikh, whose model won the contest. The dark-grey granite for the pedestal was delivered from the Onega Quarries. The statue was then cast at the Krasny Vyborzhets Works. The monument was initiated on 7 November 1926 and became the prototype for hundreds of thousands of similar statues and busts of Lenin which started to cover the USSR and many other countries.

To begin with, the overall shape of the square provided an awkward backdrop to the freshly installed monument. Some areas were outright slums of the kind typically found near railway stations in those days. Gradually, however, the slums disappeared.

Today the focus of the square is **Finland Station** {*map reference* **26**}, which was redesigned in 1955. It is second only to Moscow's busy Yaroslavl Station. The central part of the old station was preserved for the sake of ritual and incorporated into one of the new buildings. Near the boarding platform, under a glass cover, is another relic of the revolution: **locomotive No. 293**. Hugo Jalava (a Finn) brought Lenin (dressed as a coal hand) back into Russia on board the engine in October 1917; Lenin had fled the country, using the same locomotive, in August 1917. The historic locomotive that played an important part in the revolution was presented to Russia by Finland in 1957.

There's a lot of industry on Vyborg side.

Centre of medical research: Representatives of the medical profession occupy Academician Lebedeva Street (named for Sergei Lebedev, who was a chemist) and the right-hand side of Karl Marx Prospekt. Here stands the **Military Medical Academy**. The main hall of the academy (Lebedeva Street No. 6) was built in 1798, in the same year the academy was founded simultaneously in St Petersburg and Moscow. It was originally called the Medico-Surgical Academy and was later given its present name. The Academy is proud of its staff, whose members have included physiologists Pavlov and Sechenov, chemists Lebedev and Zenin and Sklifosovsky, the surgeon.

Between 1841 and 1856, the academy's department of hospital surgery (one of the first in the world) was headed by Nikolai Pirogov who pioneered numerous medical innovations; he was one of the first to use ether for sedation during surgery and hypothesised about the existence of wound-infecting microbes. Pirogov's body, embalmed by his students, is in excellent condition to this day. The sarcophagus with the surgeon's body lies in his former estate of Vishnya (now the village of Pirogovo near Vinnitsa in the Ukraine). There is only one other embalmed body of Russian origin in the USSR – that of Lenin in Moscow's Red Square (it is not in such good condition as the surgeon's).

Karl Marx (Marksa) Prospekt: This avenue links Lenin Square with the Vyborg Embankment. The old buildings of the Academy are flanked by the modern complex of the **Leningrad Hotel**, its facade turned to face the Neva. On the even-numbered side of Karl Marx Prospekt there are examples of the Constructivist style: No. 14 was built in 1933 by Bartuchev and No. 16, an electric-power substation, was built in 1927 by Schuko and Gelfreikh. On the other side of the avenue, the Academy is flanked by the **Surgical Clinic** (1865–73, by Soklov). In the garden

Local transport with post-war charm.

behind the central wing is a monument to a past President of the Medico-Surgical Academy, "Leib-Surgeon" Jacob Wylie (by sculptor Jensen and architect Stakenschneider, 1859). Wylie, who was of Scottish origin, built the clinic with his own money. In the garden on Botkin Street is another monument – to Hygeia, the goddess of health (1871, by Jensen) – and a fountain.

Downtown Vyborg ends here. Up ahead is the industrial area, the sugar factory (No. 24) and the Russian Diesel Factory, built by the Swedish immigrant Emmanuel Nobel in 1824 to produce naval mines. His son, Ludwig, organised the production of pig iron there in 1862. At the far end of the avenue is the silhouette of the **Sampsonievsky Cathedral belfry**.

Memorial of woe and suffering: Since we are already on the Vyborg Side, we should proceed to one of Leningrad's most important sites: **the Piskarevsky (Piskaryovskoye) Memorial {27}**. To reach it we will have to drive along Piskarevsky and Nepokoryonnykh Prospekts. This memorial to the Leningrad blockade was created between 1955 and 1960 and is an embodiment of all the woe and suffering that remains an important part of the city's memory to this day. It was designed by Vasiliev and Levinson.

The **Motherland Sculpture** is the work of Isayeva and Taurit. The overall area of the cemetery is 26 hectares/64 acres. The length of the memorial wall is 150-metres/492-ft and the height is 4.5 metres/15 ft. The **Motherland figure** is 12 metres/39 ft tall. The touching poetry on the monument is by Olga Bergholts, who lived through the blockade herself.

Buried in the long lines of graves are the many victims of the blockade: some 640,000 people starved to death and more than 17,000 were killed by shells and air-raids.

At the entrance to the cemetery is a museum devoted to the **Siege of Leningrad** displaying documentary photographs and personal momentoes. One of the most sorrowful documents there is the diary of Tanya Savicheva, a schoolgirl, who recorded, in her childish scribble, the deaths of every member of her family. Tanya herself was evacuated but she too died soon afterwards. The museum also documents the "life line" over the frozen Lake Ladoga and the occasion when more than 1,000 vehicles and their drivers were lost while attempting to supply the starving city in the winter of 1941–42.

The cemetery was opened on 9 May 1960 and an eternal flame, lit from the flame on the Field of Mars, has continued burning ever in the vicinity of the graves of the fighters for the revolution.

Part of Olga Bergholts' long and sad stone-hewn poem reads:

So many beneath the eternal protection
Of granite here lie, But you, who hearken to these stones, should know
No one is forgotten, nothing is forgotten…

Below, Tanya's diary at the Piskarevsky Memorial. Right, cemetery of the victims of the blockade.

SOUTHERN SUBURBS

Early in the 18th century, who could have imagined that the stretches of forest beyond the canal that served as the town's southern border, would give way to huge residential areas? The area did, however, have the right credentials for development since the highways – vital for the town's budding economy – that linked St Petersburg with Narva, Moscow and Arkhangelsk – passed through it. Originating along these routes, settlements started to grow outwards until the forests that once encircled St Petersburg on the south totally surrendered to apartment blocks in the second half of the 20th century.

For some time the area, populated mainly by the working classes, was refused municipal status – the workers' barracks were cordoned off behind the Narva, Moscow and Nevsky Gates. Pickets of soldiers checked the credentials of everyone coming into or leaving the town.

While nearly every tour in downtown Leningrad could be easily made on foot, some transport is necessary to get to the southern environs. So let us first take the subway to **Narva (Narvskaya) Station** and then continue on foot along Stachek Prospekt (Strike Avenue) – a section of the old highway to Narva.

Leningrad's Arc de Triomphe: In front of the elegant Metro station stands the only old building in the square – the **Narva Triumphal Gate**. Erected in 1814 to celebrate the arrival of the Russian Guards from defeated France, the original gates were made of wood (architect Quarenghi). Alexander I loved the gate the moment he first laid eyes on it. He was very generous to the architect, bestowing an order and the title of honorary citizen on Quarenghi.

Quarenghi, by the way, was particularly proud of this ultimate honour – and for good reason. In 1811, when Napoleon was preparing to invade Russia, he

drafted Italians into his service. Napoleon's ally, the viceroy of Italy, ordered all Italians who were working in Russia back to Italy. Quarenghi refused – and was sentenced to death in his absence. Hence the pleasure with which the architect worked on the Triumphal Gate.

Ten years after the victorious return of the Russian army, the notorious climate all but destroyed the monument. The wooden gate was torn down and gave way to a stone structure (1817–34, by Vasily Stasov), which bore little resemblance to Quarenghi's original (the great Italian died in 1817).

Victory's chariot, which crowns the arch, was cast by Klodt and Pimenov. The statues on either side of the arch depict old Russian folk heroes with laurels. In our day another of Stasov's original intentions was realised – a small museum will soon open its doors in the upper part of the arch. Its displays will be dedicated to the 1812 war.

On one side of the arch is the **Gorky Community Centre**. The Constructivist structure was built in 1927. Its opening was timed to coincide with the 10th anniversary of the October coup. The hall of the centre, which seats 1,900, is a favourite place for amateur and professional troupes. A little later (1931), the **Kirov Department Store**, opposite the centre, was opened.

Next door to the department store is one of the many freakish additions that the Soviet era has made to the Russian language – something called a "factory kitchen". Hundreds of these strange establishments cover the land these days – yet it is difficult to say how they differ from ordinary cafés. On the right-hand side is another memorial to the October coup – **the 10th Anniversary of the October Revolution School**. It would have been just another school if it were not for the hammer-and-sickle shape of the building (supposed to represent the union of workers and peasants).

It was probably because of the shape that the school was awarded the status of a "pace-setter" (another Soviet term denoting an establishment recognised as a leader within its field and required to demonstrate its methods and achievements to similar, less efficient establishments). This status guaranteed better financing and educational methods – and never-ending visits by top party bosses and foreign VIPs. The distinguished-visitor book contains entries signed by Commissar of Culture Anatoly Lunacharsky, Henri Barbusse, Maxim Gorky, the founder of "socialist realism", and the like.

Walking further along Stachek Prospekt we come to **Kirov Square**, with its 50-metre (164-ft) high building, home to the **District Soviet of People's Deputies.** In the foreground we find the 15-metre/50-ft **Monument to Sergei Kirov** (the statue itself is 8-metres/25-ft tall), erected in 1938. In 1927, the statue adorned the entrance to the Soviet pavilion at the Paris World Exhibition. Its forcefulness and the fortunate way in which the artist grasped the energetic, wilful nature of the up-and-coming party bureaucrat earned it the honour of a silver medal.

The best place to end our tour of the area is in the park named after 9 January. Here, to the south of what is now the District Soviet building, the downtrodden inhabitants of the worker's quarter gathered on 9 January 1905 ("Bloody Sunday") to march towards the Winter Palace. The demonstration was met by army units near Narva Gate and in Dvortsovaya Square.

The sophisticated beauty of the ironwork grille surrounding the park also merited the highest award at the 1901 Paris World Exhibition, after which it was promptly dismantled and removed to the park near the Winter Palace. Yet it blocked the view of the palace front and generally disagreed with the ensemble of the square. In 1919, it was once again removed to the position where we see it now.

Moscow Prospekt: To reach Moscow Prospekt we shall again take the Metro to **Ploshchad Mira (Peace Square)**

{*map reference* **28**} where the 11-km (7-mile) road starts. It runs straight as an arrow along the Pulkovo Meridian.

The avenue branches out when it reaches Victory Square and continues straight to the south as Pulkovo (Pulkovskoye) Highway; this leads to the observatory and on to the Kiev Highway. Moscow Highway (Moskovskye Shosse) runs to the southeast, through the town of Pushkin (formerly Tsarskoye Selo). The avenue was designed in the 18th century as the road to Tsarskoye Selo and appropriately christened Tsarskoselsky Prospekt.

Not far from Peace Square along Moscow Prospekt, on the left-hand side of the street, just beyond the bridge over the Fontanka, is one of the few shops in Leningrad where you can frequently find vodka (since the crackdown on alcohol, it is not so easy to find vodka). On the side of the square opposite the beginning of the avenue is the former **Sentry House** (Vikenti Bereti, 1818–20), where military patrols were quar-

The Moscow Triumphal Gate.

226

tered. Today long-distance coaches leave from this elegant building with its Doric porticos.

For those who want to check the accuracy of their watch, there is an interesting place on the opposite side of the street; No. 19 houses the **Meteorological Institute** (founded by Dmitry Mendeleev). The tower over the building has the largest – and most accurate – clock in town.

On the same side as the vodka shop, a little further on, is the imposing bulk of the **Technological Institute** with a statue of Georgi Plekhanov in front.

Commemorating another victory: Taking the subway again at the Tekhnologichesky Institute Station, skip a stop and disembark at the Moskovskiye Vorota, (Moscow Triumphal Gate) Station.

The **Moscow Triumphal Gate** was built by Vasily Stasov in 1834–38 to commemorate Russia's victory in the Turkish War of 1828–29. The monument is decorated with statues of Plenty, Glory and Victory (by Boris Orlovsky). Parts of the gate are made of cast iron. A century after they were installed these parts suddenly found their way to the field of battle – they were used as tank traps at the southern approaches to the city in 1941. In 1958–60 the gate was restored; the missing parts were newly cast at the Elektrosila Works.

Walking from the gate towards the centre, we find the **Palace of Furs** (No. 98), where international fur auctions are held three times a year. Agents of the world's major fur-buying companies flock to these auctions. Behind the Palace of Furs, away from the avenue, is the former **Novodevichy (New Maiden) Convent**.

We will now continue by subway from Moscow Gate, skip the Elektrosila Station and disembark at Moskovsky Park Pobedy (Moscow Victory Park). Behind us, on both sides of the avenue, there is the **Kirov Elektrosila Association of Industrial Enterprises**. In 1911 Siemens-Halske built a factory

Vintage cars Russia style.

assembling small electrical appliances here. Nationalised after the revolution, the factory was assigned an important role in the GOELRO Project (the electrification of Russia).

Disbelief in the project prompted a sceptical H.G. Wells to call Lenin "the Kremlin dreamer". Unlike the Revolution's promise of universal equality and prosperity, the electrification project was actually achieved. The factory was given the task of building the extensive network of electric power plants and stations that were planned for Russia; for this purpose, its capacity was augmented to a considerable degree.

Leaving the subway we find ourselves in **Victory Park**, founded by survivors to commemorate the end of World War II, which caused such terrible damage to the city. The layout of the park combines elements of what the Soviets, with their love for "isms", call "landscapism" and "geometricalism".

The central avenues are unerringly straight; the lesser paths wind underneath the trees. In the **Avenue of Heroes** are the bronze bust-size sculptures of those Leningraders who have been awarded the Gold Star (Heroes of the Soviet Union or of Socialist Labour).

Here we find the monument to Brezhnev's prime minister, Alexei Kossygin (who worked as director of a Leningrad factory during the war). On the bank of one of the park's ponds is a monument to Raymond Dieu, who lay down on the railway tracks to stop a trainload of tanks on its way to Indochina on 23 February 1950.

The fountain at the entrance has a pool diameter of 25 metres/82 ft, and a spring height 12 metres/39 ft; it is considered Leningrad's largest.

From the western edge of the park there is a view of the sports complex at its eastern end. The arena, which is the second largest in Europe, was built in 1980. People flock here not only for sports events: the place is a favourite venue for concerts by Soviet and foreign rock groups. It also hosts large conferences, congresses and festivals.

Church turns to war: Walking along the avenue towards Pushkin, we find, on the left-hand side, the **Chesma Palace and Church** (1770, by Yury Felten). The palace was built as a stopover where the road-weary Catherine II could rest on her way between St Petersburg and her out-of-town residence. The palace got its name from a victorious naval battle fought against the Turks in the Aegean Chesma Bay.

The green frog on the palace's coat of arms refers to the site (known as Frog Swamp) where the palace, fashioned after a medieval castle with its turrets, moat and drawbridges, was built. For major receptions, the Green Frog – a set of china – was ordered from the Wedgwood porcelain company. The 592 pieces of the set offer 1,244 landscape scenes of England. Naturally, each piece also bears the symbol of the palace – the green frog.

The Chesma Church, one of the few neo-Gothic buildings in the city, was built between 1777 and 1780, also by Felten. Exactly two centuries after work on the church was started, the building was converted into the **Chesma Museum**, which displays old naval maps and devices, documents, weapons, portraits of admirals, medals and Russian and Turkish flags. A museum of war in what once was a church seems awkward, and with the wind of change blowing in the USSR, it might well be reconverted into its original use.

Square of socialist pomp: Further along to the south on the avenue, not far away from the palace, is **Moscow (Moskovskaya) Square**. Here the eye is immediately caught by the 220-metre/720-ft bulk of the **House of Soviets** and the usual statue of Lenin in the centre of the square. The House of Soviets was built by a group of architects headed by Noah Trotsky in 1936–41. It was designed with as much pomp as was humanly possible, following the architectural preferences of party bureaucrats.

The **Monument to Lenin** (sculptor

Mikhail Anikushin, architect Valentin Kamensky) was erected on the occasion of his 100th anniversary, as the inscription on the pedestal attests. The charismatic leader, with either a cap or a copy of *Pravda* (it is hard to say which) in hand, is depicted delivering one of his innumerable speeches.

Further to the south comes **Victory Square** with its grandiose monument to the heroic defenders of Leningrad (opened on 9 May 1975, the 30th anniversary of the victory against the Nazis). A 48-metre (157-ft) obelisk stands at the centre of the broken circle that symbolises deliverance from the blockade. Several groups of sculptures depict sailors, partisans, soldiers and volunteers. In the memorial hall under the monument, Shostakovich's 7th Symphony sounds to the accompaniment of a metronome. In the centre of the memorial hall is the **Bronze Book of Memory**, a chronicle of the blockade. The hall displays moving reminders of the privations suffered during the 900-day siege, as well as having screens which continuously show contemporary film footage, vividly recreating the appearance and atmosphere of the city at the time.

On the west side of the square you'll find the nine-storey **Pulkovskaya Hotel** built by the Polar Company of Finland. A capsule with Soviet and Finnish newspapers, coins and a memorial message, which describes the hotel as a token of Soviet-Finnish friendship, was sealed into the foundation.

Still further along the Pulkovo Highway there are several other structures of interest. To the right, on Pulkovo Hill, is a pavilion which is open on four sides. The granite pool inside is guarded by four sphinxes, which gave the place its name – the **Four Witches**. The **Pulkovo Observatory** which we see on the right is the country's astronomical centre. In the world at large, the observatory is acclaimed for its pioneering experiments with computer-controlled telescopes.

Families come to mourn for fallen heroes at the Victory monument.

PARKS AND PALACES IN THE SUBURBS

One of the shrewdest commentators to travel through Russia, the French Marquis de Custine, noted as early as 1839 that the Empire-style architecture of St Petersburg was similar to that of Athens or Rome, but that the buildings were arranged in a completely different manner: you couldn't look up at them from below because they seemed to be sunk into the marsh. He also realised that Leningrad was a city of facades, that buildings with antique porticos or churches might not be what they seemed from the exterior – behind a Greek temple you might easily find a Stock Exchange (Custine was talking about the main building of the Strelka ensemble on Vasilievsky Island).

So it has always been, but that grandiose experiment known as the Revolution made the city even worse: our city is almost the only place on earth where every name, and correspondingly every meaning, has been misplaced. Not one building in the city is used for the purpose for which it was built. As a result the city seems rather like the set for a huge stage performance which has ended, whose actors have sung their arias and gone and whose stage hands, of which there are very many, have emerged from backstage. They seem like the extras of a completely different play. This lack of correspondence between decorations and performances, between names and objects, constitutes the St Petersburg phenomenon.

This phenomenon is much less noticeable in the palaces, parks and estates in the suburbs of Leningrad. There you will find the greatest possible harmony between past and present. The high and immortal art of the past neutralises and overshadows the squalor of modern life that we so often come across in downtown Leningrad.

Peterhof-Petrodvorets: Situated 29 km (18 miles) to the west of the city is

Peterhof {*map reference* **29**}, one of the most splendid and impressive country estates of the 18th and 19th centuries. Since 1944, it has been officially known as **Petrodvorets**, but there is every reason to suppose that its previous name will soon be restored, just as it will also soon be necessary to write St Petersburg as the campaign for the restoration of the original names of Imperial Russia is translated into action.

The southern shore of the Gulf of Finland has been populated by Russians for a very long time and was part of the territory of Novgorod the Great. In 1617, however, it was seized by Sweden, thus depriving Russia of its Baltic coastline. Only the Northern War (1700–21), started by Peter I, restored to Russia its outlet to the sea. To protect the approaches to St Petersburg, founded in 1703, a fortress was built in the Gulf of Finland on a spit near the island of Kotlin (now Kronstadt). Peter often went there and a cottage was built for the Czar on the sea shore in 1705. The house was quite small – it had two rooms and was situated slightly to the west of the present-day park.

While the Northern War was in progress Peter did not concern himself much with the niceties of interior decorating, but after the battle of Poltava (1709) and the naval victories at Gangut (1714) and Grengam (1720) he decided to build a town as a memorial to Russia's victory over Sweden, then its greatest rival, near the new capital. He also wanted Peterhof, in all its finery, to demonstrate the power and wealth of the Russian Empire.

More than a copy of Versailles: During his trip to France at the end of the 17th century Peter had fallen under the spell of Versailles (the building of which, incidentally, cost France the entire annual income of its population, not to mention the deaths of 15,000 workers during its construction). Peter who, like many Russians, had a weakness for grandeur, ordered a "palace and kitchen-garden" (as he called the park and garden) to be built, "better than the French king's at Versailles."

To build parks and gardens on damp clay soil on the shore of the Gulf of Finland (i.e. 12 degrees north of Paris) required drainage work, the removal of layers of clay and the transport of earth and fertilizers to the site by barge. On Peter's orders tens of thousands of maples, lindens, chestnuts and fruit trees and bushes were brought to Peterhof from Europe. Floods and storms often destroyed the plantations, but they were replanted again and again. Ships brought building materials, fountain parts, wonderful statues, paintings and expensive damask fabrics to the estate.

One archive document, for example describes the delivery of "12 lead statues denoting each of the months of the year"; another document records the delivery of a lead statue, "half-man, half-fish".

About 4,000 soldiers and serfs worked on the canal for the fountains alone. They suffered from the lack of proper living quarters and food, from the cold and from infectious diseases which resulted in a high mortality rate. So, in this sense at least, Peterhof succeeded in surpassing Versailles.

Once the Northern War had ended Peter speeded up the construction work, taking part personally in the drawing up of plans and, according to his habit of putting the maximum amount of detail into each task, showing what and how he wanted things done. Here, for example, is just one quotation from one of his many orders: "Build a cart for Neptune and his four horses, from whose mouths water will flow in cascades, and put tritons on the ledges, so that it looks as if they are playing on horns, the tritons to be set in motion by water, playing various water games."

Peter not only thought up themes for groups of fountains, but also gave instructions for building ornamental paths. They were laid in such a way that not a single garden decoration was hidden from the sight of visitors. Peter chivied

Pavlovsk during the 18th century.

his craftsmen and ordered: "Appoint officers to keep an eye on every piece of work…"

Fountains galore: The talented Russian architects Peter Yeropkin and Mikhail Zemtsov played a major role in the building of Peterhof in the initial stages, while its system of fountains, one of the world's greatest, was constructed under the supervision of Russia's first hydraulic engineer, Vassili Tuvolkov.

In 1715, together with Vassili Suvorov (father of the future military commander), Tuvolkov was sent to France "to the places where canals, docks and harbours were built, so that they could get a look at the machines and the like." Returning to Russia at the end of 1720, he began the construction of hydraulic installations at such a fast pace that in eight months the first test-run took place to try out the fountains. The intricate piping system stretched from the so-called Ropsha Heights, 22 km (14 miles) away, and was appreciated by specialists as "a masterpiece of hydraulic art of the 18th century," while the beauty, grandeur and technically rational design of the fountains markedly surpassed that of the celebrated waterworks at Versailles.

In the following years such major Russian and West European architects and sculptors of the 18th century as Bartolomeo Carlo Rastrelli and his Russified son Varfolomei, Andrei Voronikhin, Mikhail Kozlovsky, Fyodor Shubin, Ivan Martos, Giacomo Quarenghi, Andrei Stakenschneider, Nikolai Benois and many others contributed to the creation of Peterhof's artistic appearance. With the help of these celebrated architects the Hermitage, Monplaisir Palace, Chateau de Marly and Bolshoi Palace, as well as new fountains and a number of park buildings, were all completed.

At the end of two centuries of construction work the famous Peterhof palace and park complex was finished, incorporating seven parks with a combined area of more than 600 hectares

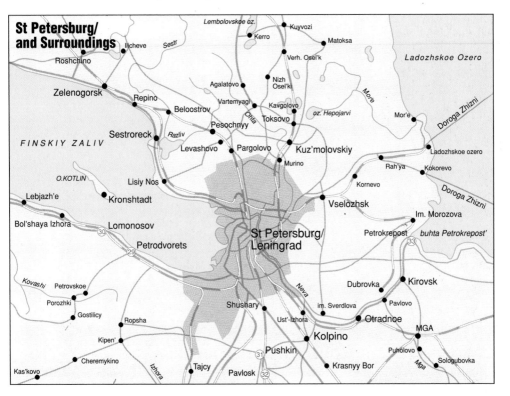

(1,500 acres) and more than 20 palaces and pavilions.

In 1734–35, Peterhof's largest fountain, **Samson**, was constructed at the base of the **Grand Cascade**. Peter wanted to immortalise the victory of Russia over Sweden in the form of the demigod Hercules "who wrestles with a nineheaded monster called the Hydra." But instead of Hercules a statue of the Biblical hero Samson, tearing open the lion's jaws, was put in the middle of the fountain. This sculpture allegorically portrayed the victory of the Russian forces over the Swedes in the decisive battle of the Northern War at Poltava, a battle which took place on Samson Day – 27 June 1709. The lion symbolises Sweden, taken from its coat-of-arms.

In the 18th century there were palisades all along the canal, from the sea to the palace, with recesses in which fountains on the theme of Aesop's fables were built. The so-called **Favourite Fountain**, built on the principle of Segner's wheel, was also installed: the

figures decorating this fountain portrayed a dog chasing ducks. The explanation for this fountain was as follows: "The favourite dog chases ducks in the water. Then the ducks tell him that he should not bother for he has the strength to chase them but not the strength to catch them." Many such humorous fountains adorn the avenues of Peterhof.

For two centuries the parks were out of bounds to the public. In the 18th century the guard at Peterhof was ordered "in no uncertain terms" to "make absolutely sure that the vulgar masses or, worse, beggars didn't wander around the garden and were not admitted under any circumstances."

After 1917, by special decree of the Council of People's Commissars, Peterhof's monuments were put in the care of the state, and on 18 May the first workers' excursion in the history of Peterhof passed through the halls of the Grand Palace carrying a red flag and revolutionary posters. The visit to the palace by these 500 people marked the beginning of the continuous great and productive work of the Peterhof palace-museums; the gardens and parks of this wonderful area outside Leningrad have became one of the favourite summer resting places of Leningraders and an obligatory stop for tourists from all corners of the globe.

The Grand Palace destroyed: In September 1941, Hitler's invading forces managed to break through to Peterhof, which they occupied for 27 months. As a result, the Grand Palace was destroyed, the fountains, statues, dams and sluices were wrecked and about 14,000 trees chopped down.

The restoration of Peterhof began as early as 1944. The restoration workers were helped by over 2,000 Leningraders every week, who went there on Sundays. They dismantled 300 dug-outs and bunkers, and filled in about 30 km (18 miles) of ditches and trenches. By June 1945 the Peterhof parks were open to visitors and the following spring the fountains were turned on. The resto-

View from Peterhof's Grand Palace.

ration work continued, however, for many more years. A new statue was erected in place of the figure of Samson, formerly at the base of the Grand Cascade but now stolen by Hitler's soldiers. Not far from Samson, at the crossroads of the Monplaisir and Marly avenues, had stood a bronze statue of Peter the Great erected in 1883 by the outstanding sculptor Mark Antokolsky. The Nazis stole this sculpture but it was recreated from a second copy kept in the Naval Museum in Leningrad.

Restoration: The restoration work at Peterhof was accompanied by extensive scientific research. For example, window glass, which in its external appearance does not differ from the few surviving ancient fragments, was made for the Monplaisir Palace with the help of the glass-working department of the Leningrad Technological Institute. The walls of one of the rooms of the Monplaisir Palace – the Japanese room – were decorated with wooden panels with intricate drawings, formerly thought to be made by Japanese and Chinese craftsmen. These panels were used as firewood by the invaders, and it was only by chance that the restoration workers found three surviving panels in a nearby bunker built by the Nazis.

It turned out that the panels were not, after all, the work of Oriental craftsmen, but rather of Russian icon-painters from the famous village of Palekh. Contemporary Palekh artists were able to recreate the works of their ancestors quite quickly. By contrast, it took over 10 years to restore, from old photographs and drawings, the 2.5-metre (8-ft) shining golden bowl on the roof of the Grand Palace, first put there more than 200 years ago but removed during the war. The list of such examples is endless.

What do the large numbers of visitors who set off for Peterhof between spring and autumn on suburban trains, tour buses and, most popular of all, on hydrofoils, see? First and foremost, of course, they see the **Grand Cascade** running down from the foot of the **Grand Palace** to the edges of the **Lower Park**. The Grand Cascade ensemble is made up of 17 steps, 39 gilded bronze statues, 29 bas-reliefs and 142 spurts from 64 water jets. On the upper level of the cascade is the group of sculptures called *Tritons Blowing into Sea Shells*. The streams of water from these shells fall on to the exquisite Basket Fountain.

The steps of the cascade are adorned with sculptures of ancient gods and heroes, in order to emphasise the theme of Russia's victory in the Northern War. For example, the sculpture of Perseus with the head of Medusa in his hand and the bas-relief *Perseus Saving Andromeda from the Sea Monsters* can be interpreted as an allegory of the liberation of the Izhora lands on the Baltic by the Russian army.

Several sculptures from the Grand Cascade serve as satirical allegories on the defeated Swedish King Charles XII. One of these sculptures is *The Frightened Actaeon, Running Away from His Own Dogs* – an allegoric depiction of

Golden sculptures adorn the waterworks.

Charles XII, abandoned by his allies after the defeat. Another sculpture ridicules the King's love for himself – *Narcissus, Turned into a Flower*. Almost every sculpture of the Grand Cascade is imbued with various allegorical meanings.

Less decorative, but still very interesting, are the cascades in the Lower Park, known as **Golden Hill** and **Chess Hill**. Wide avenues lead to the **Monplaisir Palace**, the **Hermitage Pavilion**, other cascades and the fountains known as **Adam and Eve**. The Great Fountains at the foot of the Golden Hill are of note – the water bursts from them in jets of up to 30-cm (12-in) in diameter. Not by chance were they called Menagerie (Economic) in the past – these powerful streams are hollow.

The variety of fountains in the Lower Park is striking. Here you can see the water jets of the **Roman Fountains** and the **Cup**, the 505 jets of the **Pyramid Fountain** and dozens of others: the golden shroud of bell-shaped waterfalls at the foot of the gilded statues in the Monplaisir Garden and around the **Marly Palace**; streams of water pouring out of the mouths of dragons, dolphins and sea shells held by marine gods, water streaming smoothly over the squares of Chess Hill, through the marble and gilt of Golden Hill; seething waterfalls rushong down the steps of the Grand Cascade and flowing together towards the basin, over which a wide stream of water foams at a height of 20 metres (65 ft) from the lion's jaws being torn open by Samson. The jets of water shooting upwards, the gleaming of the gilded statues and the miraculous intertwining of streams, above which tiny droplets of water create rainbows, all combine to make a magnificent sight.

In the amount of water it uses, the variety of forms and the length of time the fountains are in operation, Peterhof is second to none in the world. Despite the fact that, in one working season, over 30,000 litres (8,000 gallons) of water are used every second, the **Peterhof is an often used stage for period films.**

242

fountains can work for 10 to 12 hours a day for up to five months a year.

Peterhof is of course first and foremost about fountains, but there is more than this to see. This was the main country residence of the Czars, frequented especially in the 18th and in the early 20th centuries. For example, a few weeks before the outbreak of World War I, Raymond Poincaré stayed here as a guest of Czar Nicholas II. And now, too, the **Grand Palace** attracts the attention of millions of visitors to Peterhof.

There is, however, not just the one palace here. There are several dozen first-class buildings built in the 18th and 19th centuries, most of which are now museums. The last two of these to be opened were the memorial museum of the international Benois family (whose members did a lot over three centuries for the artistic appearance of the town), and the museum of wax sculptures opened in the summer of 1990. The ambitious creators of this museum intended, eventually, to make it more lavish than Madame Tussaud's in London.

Oranienbaum-Lomonosov (30): A group of historians is compiling a list of famous Jews: Disraeli, Heine, Spinoza, Pasternak… "Lomonosov!" one exclaims. "What do you mean? He wasn't a Jew; he was pure Russian," the second objects. "Didn't you know, he used to be called Oranienbaum."

This joke plays on the Soviet authorities' passion for changing names here, there and everywhere to suit the moment. Nevsky Prospekt was at one time called 25th October Street, Kirov Prospekt used to be Kamennoostrovsky (Stone Island Avenue), Bolshoi Prospekt was named Karl Liebknecht Prospekt, while the university has at various times been known as the St Petersburg Imperial University, Bubnov University and Zhdanov University. At the moment it is nameless, but it seems likely that it may soon be named after Mendeleyev, Vernadsky or Peter the Great himself.

If you leave Peterhof (Petrodvorets) and travel along the shore of the Gulf of

The Samson fountain.

Finland for another 10 km (6 miles) you will come to **Oranienbaum**, 40 km (25 miles) west of Leningrad. This palace was founded in 1707 by Peter the Great's favourite, Alexander Menshikov, and renamed in 1948 in honour of "the father of Russian science", Mikhail Lomonosov, who opened a factory here in the middle of the 18th century.

It was often the case with the former pastry-cook, the dazzling Prince Menshikov, that his own residences significantly outshone the court of Peter the Great in size and splendour – as does the Menshikov Palace on the University Embankment in Leningrad.

Similarly, the Oranienbaum Palace, built on the Izhora lands which he received as a gift from Peter I, turned out to be significantly bigger and more splendid than the palace built at Peterhof by the Russian Czar at the same time. Of course, the Peterhof palace was soon extended, and this main seashore residence of the Czar later overshadowed Oranienbaum, which remained in the possession of the Czar's distant relatives (specifically, the Mecklenburg-Streletskys). However, Oranienbaum has at least one very important distinction – it was the only country palace in Leningrad not to have been destroyed by the Nazis, and therefore it has been preserved in its original form rather than as a reconstruction.

The most important building at Oranienbaum is the **Grand Palace**, built in 1710–25 by architects Gottfried Schädel and Giovanni Fontana, on the crest of the ridge along the shore. The building consists of a central section and side wings which were naturally extended into octagonal pavilions. A church was situated in the western pavilion, while the eastern pavilion housed a Japanese hall. Terraces sloping down from the palace to the sea are adorned with balustrades and sculptures.

In front of the palace, on the empty shore of the Gulf of Finland, a **Lower Park** was built with fountains, statues, greenhouses and menageries. The strict

There is beauty in every detail.

geometrical planning of the park (the so-called regular style) was embellished with a man-made canal which, according to legend, was dug by 9,000 serfs in three days.

The most significant buildings of the middle of the 18th century, when Oranienbaum belonged to the husband of the future Catherine II, are the two-storey palace of Peter III, situated on the high right bank of the River Karost in the eastern part of the **Upper Park**, and also the **Kamenny (Stone) Hall**, the **Opera House** and the entire **fortress of Peterstadt**.

The final stage in the creation of the architectural ensemble at Oranienbaum was the construction, in 1762–68, of the famous **Chinese Palace** with its suite of ceremonial rooms, including the **Hall of Muses**, the **Blue Drawing Room**, the **Bead Study**, the **Great Hall**, the **Lilac Drawing Room** and the **Great and Small Studies**.

For two centuries visitors have been amazed by the fineness and exquisite-ness of the interior decor: the murals and painted panels (the work of Stefano Torelli and Serafin Barozzi), the delicate stucco work, the embroidery and, finally, the parquet floors made of thin layers of maple, oak, ash, walnut, boxwood, larch, rosewood and mahogany.

One of the most remarkable rooms in terms of artistic decoration is the **Bead Study**, with its mosaic floor of coloured smalt (a glass-like alloy). This art, which is rooted in the ancient Orient, owes its revival to Lomonosov. Unfortunately, however, only a part of this masterpiece has survived to be seen by visitors.

There is one more principal sight at Oranienbaum – the fine architecture of the white and blue **Toboggan Hill (Katalnaya Gorka)** in the northwestern section of the Upper Park. Such pavilions are purely Russian structures dating back to the 18th century when they formed one of the most popular attractions on public holidays. The design of the Oranienbaum buildings is severe and at the same time grand. This

Children love to roam this history-laden environment.

impression is created by the stepped silhouette of the buildings, the delicate colonnade on the ground floor, the smooth semi-circular cornices and slender, elegant dome.

Tsarskoye Selo – Pushkin {31}: The foundation of this town 25 km (16 km) south of Leningrad dates back to the beginning of the 18th century when royal country residences and summer cottages for nobles were being built around the growing capital. The first to be built here was the small country estate of **Saari-Mois** (meaning "elevated place" in Finnish) which comes out as Saarskaya Myza in Russian.

In 1710 Peter the Great presented the lands of this estate to his wife, the future Catherine I. From that time the place was called Saarskoye Selo, and after 1725, **Tsarskoye Selo (Tsar's Village)**. In 1918, its name was changed again, for obvious reasons, to **Detskoye Selo (Children's Village)** and in 1937 the town was renamed yet again; it is now called **Pushkin**, in honour of the great Russian poet.

Stone palaces with 16 front rooms were built for the first owners of Saarskaya Myza (on the site of the future Grand Palace). Serfs from the surrounding villages dug ponds, laid out gardens and built greenhouses and menageries – these were always included in Czars' country residences – where hunts were organised.

One of the most significant dates in the history of Tsarskoye Selo was the middle of the 18th century when this place became the main summer residence of the royal family (it remained so until 1917). In the 1740s and '50s, thousands of workers, serfs, soldiers and sailors extended and planned the parks and constructed the grandiose building of the **Grand (Catherine) Palace**, designed by the Russian architects Andrei Kvasov and Savva Chevakinsky. The building was completed during the third quarter of the 18th century when the task was entrusted to the most outstanding architect of those days,

Bartolomeo Rastrelli. As a result a magnificent building was created, astounding the contemporary population by its beauty and exquisite form.

The turquoise, white and gold facade, stretching for 306 metres (1,000 ft), is noted for its splendid decoration, the monumental rhythm of its columns and sculptures and its more than 200 types of stucco ornamentation.

The building is made even more grandiose by the large square in front of it, enveloped by two semi-circles of single-storey auxiliary buildings. The palace's golden suite of ceremonial rooms, including the world-famous **Amber Hall**, the **Great Hall**, the **Picture Gallery**, the **Green Dining Room**, the **Lyons Parlour**, the **Blue Study**, the **Blue Drawing Room** and the **Maple Bedroom** have all gone down in the history of art as matchless examples of Russian baroque architecture and for two centuries they have stunned visitors by their richness, originality, artistic scope and tastefulness. Second only in

Left, the ironwork is of a special quality. **Right**, a classical sculpture in Pushkin.

this respect to the Winter Palace in St Petersburg, the Catherine Palace is a valuable treasure house of decorative and applied art.

By the beginning of the 19th century a few more dazzling buildings had appeared in Tsarskoye Selo: the **Hermitage**, intended for palace banquets, the **Grotto Pavilion**, the Island **Concert Hall** and other structures in the clear, severe, laconic style of Russian classicism which replaced the decorative forms of baroque. Meanwhile the natural "landscape" style dominated in the planning of the famous ponds and the extension of the parks, which now cover 600 hectares (1,500 acres). At this time the **Alexander Palace** and **Lyceum** (from where Alexander Pushkin graduated in 1817), the **Agate Rooms** and the **Cameron Gallery** were built. Particularly striking is the great architectural brainchild of the outstanding architect Giacomo Quarenghi – the Alexander Palace, which was completed in 1796.

The famous historian Igor Grabar was to write a century later: "In St Petersburg and its suburbs there are palaces that are bigger and more regal than this one, but none can surpass the magnificence of its architecture. Suffice it to mention the mighty double colonnade joining the two wings of the palace! In terms of the artistic scope of its composition and the refinement of detail, this is a masterpiece of world architecture." It is a great shame that for several decades visitors have not been able to visit the interior of the palace: up until recently it was "occupied" by a military department, and now it is under restoration.

The next most significant building after the Alexander Palace is the Cameron Gallery. The base of the building is made out of huge blocks of deliberately coarsely hewn grey stone, which forms the ground floor. In stark contrast to this heavy foundation the architect, Charles Cameron, built a light, airy gallery with pale, graceful colonnades and open sunny terraces.

Crowning the whole composition a **The renovated facade of the Catherine Palace.**

wide staircase, with curved steps in the upper section, leads down to the **Great Lake**, uniting architecture and nature. On the high stone pylons on both sides of the staircase stand bronze statues of Hercules and Flora, made in 1786 in the Academy of Arts foundry and based on models by Fyodor Gordeyev, while on the terraces of the gallery there are 54 sculpted busts of ancient Greek and Roman statesmen, scientists, philosophers and mythological characters. These are first-class copies of the ancient originals.

Further building and finishing touches in the Tsarskoye Selo palace and park ensemble have brought us such masterpieces as the **Triumphal Gates** in honour of Russia's victory over Napoleon (architect Vassili Stasov), the **Evening Hall** (designed by Ivan Neyelov), the **Granite Terrace** (architect Luigi Rusca) and the bronze **Girl with a Jug** (sculptor Pavel Sokolov).

The rapid development of Tsarskoye Selo and its expansion into a sizeable town in the environs of the capital city were encouraged both by the natural desire of many members of St Petersburg's upper classes to be nearer to the imperial family in summer, and by the construction in 1836 of the first regular railway in Russia, linking the town with St Petersburg, on the one hand, and Pavlovsk, on the other. A whole town quickly sprang up around the railway station, while the St Petersburg nobility built themselves summer cottages along the Pavlovsk highway. In 1887 a model water supply and sewerage system started functioning in Tsarskoye Selo and there was an electric power station – this was actually one of the first towns in Europe to be fully illuminated by electricity.

Life was particularly animated here during the time of the last Russian Emperor, Nicholas II. He always spent at least six months at a time here with his family, even in winter. Accordingly this palace is the largest of all the country residences around St Petersburg and the balls here overshadowed even those held in the Winter Palace. The Empress's favourite, Grigori Rasputin, was a frequent guest here (he was actually buried in the park here after his murder, but then removed from his grave by revolutionary soldiers). This is where Nicholas II lived as a private citizen, after his abdication, and it was from here that he and his family were taken into exile to the Urals, where they were villainously killed in 1918.

The town suffered terribly during World War II, for it found itself in the front line for nearly two years. Thousands of trees were chopped down, houses and pavilions were burned, bridges were destroyed, and much of the museum's treasures that were left after the evacuation were stolen. This includes the famous Amber Hall, which has not been found to this day.

Pavlovsk {32}: For many years, after the foundation of the town of Tsarskoye Selo in the 18th century, the forested area to the south was used by the rulers of Russia as a hunting ground. In 1777, Catherine the Great made a gift of this area to her adult son Pavel so that he might build his country cottage there. The creation of the future park began shortly after this with the felling of trees, the clearing of thickets to make way for roads and paths and the draining of marshland. With the arrival of the Scottish architect, Charles Cameron, plans were drawn up to construct a large palace and an enormous park that would occupy a territory of 600 hectares (1,500 acres) located 26 km (16 miles) to the south of St Petersburg. The result was to be a splendid example of the art of garden and park design and the most outstanding feature of Pavlovsk.

Work was intensified shortly after Pavel I came to the throne in 1796, when Pavlovsk received the status of a city and became the Czar's official summer residence. V. Brenna was invited to replace Cameron as architect. His task was to make the palace and park larger and still more magnificent.

The third period of construction covers the first quarter of the 19th century when Pavlovsk park was given an artistic completeness akin to that of a landscape painting. Fruitful cooperation between Pietro Gonzaga, Carlo Rossi, Andrei Voronikhin and the reinstated Cameron fortified the expressive quality of the Pavlovsk landscape. With amazing skill and talent, they created a harmony between the buildings and nature and turned Pavlovsk into a priceless ensemble of park and garden art.

The compositional centre of this ensemble is the **Grand Palace** which can easily be seen from all parts of the park. It is a high stone building crowned with a dome with 64 colonnades. The central block and one-storey galleries leading off it to the side wings were designed by Cameron and built between 1782 and 1789. The construction of the square side blocks and the addition of front yard pavilions was completed in the 1790s by Brenna. Veronikhin began decorating the rooms of the palace in

1803 and Rossi added a library to the north-westerly part of the palace in 1822.

The decorations and furniture of the palace rooms are of particular value. Sculptures and paintings, marble and gilt and artistic fabrics were all used by the architects to adorn the rooms. Most splendid of all are the **Italian**, **Greek**, **Cavaliere** and **Throne Rooms**, the **War and Peace Rooms** and the ceremonial northern and southern suites.

When the Nazi occupation forces set fire to the palace much was destroyed. The rooms' architectural decorations, however, remained intact and the palace was once again opened to visitors in the early 1960s.

Let us now, however, return to the park. Its beauty is unique. If the characteristic feature of 18th-century country residences, such as Peterhof and Yekaterininsky and Tsarskoye Selo, is their geometrically correct avenues and paths running through flower beds and the regularity of the trees planted at equal distances from each other, then **Pavlovsk Park** is distinguished by its beautiful landscapes that create pictures of nature in a natural setting.

The greater part of the park's avenues and paths have free curves and winding along them you can see not strategically pruned and symmetrically positioned lines of trees but freely growing flower beds and trees standing all alone, grouped in such a way as to display the natural beauty of their leaves and crowns. The reservoirs of Pavlovsk Park look like forest lakes with reeds at their banks, while the meandering river is like a quiet stream towards which silver willows incline. The woodlands of the park remind one of a forest in a Russian fairytale with their dark thickets and sunny glades. It is no accident that there are elks still living in Pavlovsk Park while, in the lilac thickets, the trill of the nightingale can be heard.

Gatchina: References to the village of Gatchina can be traced back to 15th-century manuscripts. At the beginning of the 18th century it was the site of the

The Catherine palace is laden with objets d'art.

estate of Peter the Great's sister Natalia, yet true fame came to Gatchina only after Catherine II came to the throne and presented it to her favourite, Grigori Orlov; he, together with his brothers, had played the most active part in bringing her to the throne while her husband, Peter II, was still alive. From 1766 to 1772 Gatchina was made into a vast hunting park and a palace was built there by architect Antonio Rinaldi.

In 1782 the palace and park ensemble, located 45 km (28 miles) from St Petersburg, and thus the furthest from the capital, came into the hands of Catherine II's son, Pavel I. Pavel duly created a military town-fortress in the Prussian style. At the same time the palace itself was rebuilt according to the design of architect Brenna and took on the appearance of a medieval castle complete with moat and water, underground bridges and stone bastions.

After Pavel's murder, life at Gatchina came to a halt and the palace, as we might say today, became an object of preservation. In 1881 it became the Czar's residence once again, with Alexander III staying there almost uninterruptedly for 13 years.

After 1917 (or as Anna Akhmatova used to say "after what happened happened") Gatchina, like all other royal residences, was nationalised and became a museum.

There are many things well worth seeing at Gatchina concentrated around the **White Lake**, down to whose banks stretches a picturesque park that has been planted with much art. When its trees were planted the height to which they would grow was taken into account, as was the colour of the leaves and the time at which they would fall. Strange twisting paths, reservoirs, sunny glades and shady groves have given the park the appearance of untouched "naturalness," in contrast to the formal gardens with their straight avenues, carefully pruned tree tops, fountains and statues.

The **Upper Garden** is located nearby

The golden towers of the Catherine Palace.

and is modelled on Italian gardens, which were traditionally arranged in terraces along the slopes of hills. Among the interesting buildings to be found in the park is the **Chesme obelisk**, which was erected in honour of the victory of the Russian fleet over the Turks in 1770. Also to be seen are the **Eagle Pavilion**, **Venus Pavilion** and the **Admiralty** where tiny warships were built to be sailed on Gatchina's lakes, the site of make-believe "sea battles" that included broadsides and on-board skirmishes.

The palace building stands looking over the gardens and the entire park. According to the design made out by Antonio Rinaldi, the author of the original project, the main facade was built facing the park with a wide staircase decorated with marble sculptures and five-angled towers.

Among the numerous well-preserved buildings, the **Prioratsky Palace of the Malta Order**, built by architect Nikolai Lvov in 1798, deserves special mention. That year Pavel I became patron of this order and was elected its Grandmaster. The palace has the appearance of a medieval castle and it is interesting to note that it was finished in just three months. Lvov's method was to use wooden moulds which were filled with layers of clay and then compressed. The building has stood the test of time and proved the wisdom of its builder.

Penaty: If you drive along Primorskoye Highway, you pass Ilya Repin's country estate, **Penaty**. This is where the famous Russian painter lived from 1900 to 1930 and where he created many of his masterpieces, including *Pushkin's Examination* and *Bloody Sunday*. Today you can stroll through the park, visit his studio and living rooms, and get a good feeling for the style of living at the beginning of the century.

Shlisselburg-Petrokrepost {33}: The Neva, as anyone who visits Leningrad will see, is a deep and full-flowing river. Yet not everyone knows that the Neva is, in fact, very short, beginning only 70 km (44 miles) to the east of Leningrad

where it flows out of Lake Ladoga, the largest lake in Europe. In the middle of the Neva, at the point where it leaves Lake Ladoga, lies the small island of **Oreshek**. Here, way back in 1323, the citizens of Novgorod built a fortress as defence against the constant attacks launched by their northern neighbours.

In 1611, during the Time of Troubles, this region was seized by the Swedes and Oreshek became the Swedish fortress of **Noteborg**. It was only in 1702 that the Russians finally stormed the fortress, which Peter I duly renamed **Shlisselburg** (from the Germany "Schlüsselburg", Key Town).

Six months later the foundations of St Petersburg were laid at the mouth of the river Neva. Shlisselburg, like the Peter and Paul Fortress around which the new Russian capital grew up, no longer played a role in deciding the military fate of the country and was turned (again like the Peter and Paul Fortress) into a prison for political prisoners.

Its location on a lonely island in the

Ilya Repin, Russia's great painter.

252

middle of a wide river with a fast current and its high fortress walls with watch-towers made this prison a most reliable place for confinement. In the course of its entire history no one ever managed to escape. Its proximity to the capital was considered by the government to be of a particular convenience.

In the 18th century the prisoners at Shlisselburg were mostly members of the royal family and representatives of the upper classes. During the reign of Peter I, Maria Alexeyevna, who had joined in the Czar's son's plot against his father, languished here in captivity for five years until she refused to accept food and died.

After Peter's death his widow, Catherine I, had Peter's first wife, Evdokia Lopukhina, hidden away here. Under Anna Ioannovna, Prince Golitsyn found himself in the fortress for advocating that the rights of the Empress be curtailed. Ivan VI spent the last eight years of his confinement here until he was ultimately put to death, despite be-ing innocent of any crime. Having been proclaimed Czar in his infancy, Ivan VI became the unfortunate pawn of palace intrigues before he was dethroned and thrown into a dungeon where he languished for 24 years.

The 19th century increasingly witnessed the imprisonment of convinced opponents of autocracy. These included certain Decembrists, many members of the People's Will Organization and large numbers of revolutionaries. Some of them, like Nikolai Morozov – landowner, revolutionary and scholar – spent more than 25 years in solitary confinement, while Valerian Lukasinsky, a Pole, languished under similar conditions for a total of 37 years.

After the February Revolution of 1917 all prisoners were liberated and the prison buildings burnt down. The ancient fortress once more acquired military significance during the siege of Leningrad in the Great Patriotic War (World War II). Oreshek Island and the right bank of the Neva were in the full

Penaty, Ilya Repin's country estate.

sense of the word a "key" to the Ladoga and it was through here that the only supply line to besieged Leningrad passed. Today the small industrial town of **Petrokrepost** stands on both banks of the Neva. Since 1928 the island has housed a branch of the Leningrad Museum of the Revolution.

Kizhi: Reach the eastern coast of Lake Onega and you are already in **Karelia**, famous for its stern and magnificent northern beauty. Earlier it was called "subcapital Siberia," a reference to this region of peaceful birds, blue lakes, bubbling rivers and innumerable islands overgrown with woods.

Petrozavodsk, the capital of Karelia, is located approximately 300 km (190 miles) from Leningrad on the most westerly bay of Lake Onega, the second biggest in Europe after Lake Ladoga. Sixty-eight km (42 miles) from Petrozavodsk lies the **island of Kizhi**, not the biggest but the most famous of all the 1,650 islands in Lake Onega.

The name of the island in Karelian means "playground." In heathen days celebrations took place here. Later Kizhi became an ecclesiastical centre and in the 18th century, to commemorate the victory over the Swedes, the wooden **Churches of the Transfiguration** and of the **Protecting Veil of the Most Holy Mother of God** were built here. In 1960, a museum-cum-nature reserve was created on Kizhi. From different parts of Karelia various buildings dating from the 14th to the 19th centuries were brought here, including the ancient **St Lazarius Church** from Muromsky Island, houses from previous centuries, barns and an eight-sailed windmill.

In Russia wood has been and remains the most widely used of building materials. Unfortunately, because the life of wood is relatively short and because of frequent fires, many buildings have not survived until our own time. This makes the museum-reserve on Kizhi even more unique, for here may be seen the great skill of local craftsmen who created the most wonderful masterpieces

Families love to bring their children to Schlisselburg.

in wood with the most simple of tools.

The uniqueness of the buildings lies in the fact that they were built without nails. The craftsmen, moreover, used only the simplest tools – with a carpenter's axe and chisel they fitted the logs together in such a way that the solidity of the buildings was ensured.

The most ancient of the preserved churches are reminiscent of peasant houses in that they both evolved from primitive timber shell-like structures (incidentally, this type of peasant hut still remains a fundamental feature of modern peasant life). Later on, in order to create more space in their houses, they began to erect timber huts with numerous corners to them and, in such a way, octagonal timber huts and churches with side altars and annexes appeared. In the 16th century churches with domed and tiered roofs appeared, consisting of a number of timber frames put one on top of the other and gradually diminishing in size.

The wooden churches of Kizhi are built without nails.

The museum's main attraction is the 22-domed Church of the Transfiguration, and it is well worth saying a few more words about it here. Who exactly the builder was is not known. Legend attributes the glory to Nestor who, the story goes, threw his axe into Onega Lake when he had finished the construction work with the words: "This church was built by the master Nestor. There never has been and never will be anything like it evermore."

It was built in 1714 to celebrate the victory of the Russian army in the Northern War. At first sight the building seems a very complex one. Suffice it to say that it is as high as a 12-storey house. The church has survived in such a good state of repair because it was made out of especially tough, dry and resinous pine. It has no facade; to the octagonal timber structure four side altars are attached corresponding to the four points of the compass. To these, five tiers of cupolas are "threaded." The cupolas are of different sizes, something that lends the church its harmonious proportions.

GETTING THERE

BY AIR

International airlines connect Leningrad directly with 16 European countries. Some, however, operate only during the summer months. Aeroflot has the most international flights to and from the city and operates internal flights linking Leningrad with 105 cities in the USSR. Its fleet of aircraft has been designed primarily for military purposes and hence lacks the comfort of western carriers.

Aeroflot is now buying the European Airbus which will soon be in service on certain international routes.

Fares within the USSR are very reasonable, though flights have to be booked far in advance since there is a far greater demand than there is capacity.

Check-in at Aeroflot counters starts 1½ hours and ends half an hour before departure. Foreigners have to pay for their tickets in hard currency.

Foreign Airline Offices in Leningrad:
Finnair, Ulitsa Gogolya 19. Tel: 315 9736, 312 8987.
Pan-American, Ulitsa Gertsena 36. Tel: 311 5819/20/22.
Air France, **British Airways**, **KLM**, **Lufthansa** and **LOT** have offices in Pulkovo 2 Airport. Information: tel: 930 927.

Aeroflot Offices in Leningrad:
Aeroflot Information, tel: 293 90 21; International Department, tel: 314 6943. The **Central Aeroflot Office** is at **Nevsky Prospekt 7–9**, tel: 211 7980; reservation for domestic flights: **Aprelskaya Ulitsa 5**, tel: 293 9021.

Other Aeroflot Offices in the USSR:
Moscow: 37, Leningrad Highway. Tel: 155 0922

Kiev: 66, Boulevard Shevchenko. Tel: 774 4223
Minsk: 18/28, Karl Marx St. Tel: 224 232
Yerevan: 2, Tumanyan St. Tel: 582 422
Tbilisi: 2, Javakhishvily St. Tel: 932 744
Vilnius: 21, Lenin Prospekt. Tel: 756 175
Khabarovsk: 5, Amursky Blvd. Tel: 332 071

Aeroflot's International Offices:
Amsterdam: Singel 540. Tel: 245 715
Athens: Ksenofontis 14. Tel: 322 1022
Bangkok: 7 Silom Rd. Tel: 233 6965
Berlin: Unter den Linden 51/53. Tel: 229 1592
Bombay: 7th Brabourn Stadium, Vir Nariman Rd. Tel: 221 682
Brussels: Rue des Colonies 54. Tel: 218 6046
Bucharest: 35 Boulevard Nicolae Balcescu. Tel: 167 431
Budapest: 4 Waci. Tel: 185 892
Copenhagen: 1–3 Vester Farimasgade. Tel: 126 338
Delhi: 18 Barakhamba Rd. Tel: 40 426
Frankfurt: Theaterplatz 2. Tel, 230 771
Helsinki: Mannerheimintie 5. Tel, 659 655
Lisbon: Av. Antonio Augusto de Aguiar 2H–3E. Tel: 561 296
London: 69–72 Piccadilly. Tel: 492 1756
Madrid: 25 Calle Princesa. Tel: 241 9934
Milan: 19 Via Vittor Pisani. Tel: 669 985
Munich: Ludwigstr. 6. Tel: 288 261
Paris: 33 Avenue des Champs Elysees. Tel: 225 4381
Peking: 2–2–42, Jianguomenwai. Tel: 523 581
Prague: 15 Vaclavske Namesti. Tel: 260 862
Rome: 27 Via Leonida Bissolati. Tel: 475 7704
Singapore: 55 Market St. Tel: 336 1757
Sofia: 2 Russky Blvd. Tel: 879 080
Tokyo: 3–19, 1-chome Yaesu, chuo-ku. Tel: 272 8351
Vienna: 10 Parkring. Tel: 521 501
Warsaw: 29 Allee Jerozolimskie. Tel: 281 710
Zurich: 9 Usteristr. Tel: 211 4633

FROM THE AIRPORT TO TOWN

Leningrad's international airport, **Pulkovo 2**, is just 10 minutes by bus from the domestic airport **Pulkovo 1**. If you go to town by bus, tickets are 5 and 10 kopecks. The official taxi fare to the city vary between 3 and 15 roubles depending on the distance and the category of car (municipal or co-operative).

The Leningrad Air Terminal is at Nevsky Prospekt 7/9; buses for the airports leave from the nearby bus stop at Kirpichnyy Pereulok 3.

BY SEA

Leningrad can be reached by regular passenger ship from London, Bremerhaven, Helsinki, Copenhagen, Göteborg, Stockholm, Montreal and New York. Intourist and Morflot offices will provide detailed information about sea routes, schedules and bookings. The **Sea Terminal** with the **Passenger Port** is on Vasilyevsky Island and the **River transport booking office** is at Rechnoy Vokzal, Prospekt Obukhovskoy Oborony 195. Tel: 262 1318 (information), 262 5511 (booking office).

BY RAIL

Railway Terminal Information. Tel: 168 0111.
Within the European part of the USSR railways are the most important means of passenger transportation. Railways connect Leningrad with the largest Soviet cities (Moscow, Kiev, Minsk) and Western European capitals. If you can spare the time you can travel in a comfortable first class sleeping-car, the pride of the Soviet Railways.

From Central Europe the train takes two days to reach Leningrad with a change of gauge at the junction with the railway system of the USSR. The Helsinki-Leningrad route (departure 1 p.m. arrival 9 p.m.) is the most popular rail route between the west and the USSR.

Travelling time from:
Berlin: 33 hrs
Paris: 48 hrs
Warsaw: 22 hrs

If you want to travel within the USSR by train, there are transcontinental rail routes, such as those from Moscow to Vladivostok and from Moscow to Hanoi. They demand an adventurous spirit and a week spent in the train contemplating the endless Siberian and Transsiberian (Baikal) landscapes. Food for the trip should be taken along since station buffet food is often not to the liking of weary travellers.

Leningrad has five large stations: The **Baltic Station** with trains to the southern suburbs and Petrodvorets, the **Finland Station** with trains to Vyborg and Finland, the **Moscow Station**, with trains to Moscow, the northeast and the south of Russia, the **Vitebsk Station** with trains to the Ukraine and Byelorussia and to Pushkin and Pavlovsk and the **Warsaw Station** with trains to Tallin and Riga.

BY BUS

There are no international bus lines to Leningrad, but special bus tours operate from the UK, West Germany and Finland.

The long-distance **Bus Terminal** is at Sadovaya Ulitsa 37.

BY CAR

If you intend to visit Leningrad by car you should first get into contact with Intourist as they have worked out a number of routes through the European part of the Soviet Union which can easily be negotiated with your own vehicle.

The ideal route to Leningrad is via Helsinki which can be reached comfortably by car ferry.

If you intend to continue within European Russia you can drive to Moscow, the Caucasus and the Black Sea, ferrying the car across to Yalta or Odessa and crossing the Ukraine to Czechoslovakia or Poland. Details for this and other routes (across the Baltic States, Byelorussia or Moldavia) can be found in the book *Motorists' Guide to the Soviet Union*, Progress Publishers Moscow, 1980. It gives details about fueling stations, repair shops, overnight stops as well as emergency procedures.

Since crossing the border into Turkey is now possible, you can also exit or enter via Anatolia. Whether this route remains open, however, depends on the changing political conditions in the Caucasus.

Sovinterautoservice are the specialists for car travel in the USSR. They solve nearly every problem a foreigner is likely to experience on Russian roads. Write or phone for detailed information: **Institutski Pereulok** 2–1, Moscow. Tel: (007095) 101 496.

During the last few years marked changes have taken place in the quality of services along Soviet roads. Leningrad now boasts new service and repair stations for non-Soviet cars. But you should still be cautious of the state of Soviet roads. Diverting from the highways (which is still not permitted if the diversion is not on your officially approved itinerary) might get you into some unexpected adventures.

Entry points to the USSR are: Brusnichnoe and Torfyanovka from Finland; Brest and Shegini from Poland; Chop when coming from Czechoslovakia and Hungary, and Porubnoe and Leusheny from Rumania. You can also ship your car directly to Leningrad.

Below are the routes to Leningrad which you can use driving your own car. You will, however, have to stick to your schedule, staying overnight only at pre-booked hotels or campsites. You are not permitted to deviate from your planned route. Intourist will make the necessary arrangements.

From Finland: Torfyanovka-Vyborg-Leningrad From Western Europe: Brest-Minsk-Smolensk-Moscow and Chop-Uzhgorod-Lvov-Kiev-Orel-Moscow-Leningrad.

YOUTH TRAVEL

The USSR does not have an extensive system of youth hostels. Some big cities have youth hotels belonging to **Sputnik**, the Bureau of International Youth Tourism, once a part of Comsomol but now acting independently. During the summer months, when demand exceeds hostel capacity, Sputnik falls back on unused, inexpensive university dormitories. For information write to: **Sputnik** International Youth Travel Bureau, 4, Ulitsa Chapygina.

The **MIR International Centre**, tel: (007812) 542 2845, fax: (007812) 315 1701, is a specialist youth travel agent and arranges inexpensive individual and group tours to Leningrad and the USSR. For anyone who wants to avoid Intourist arrangements this is the best address.

TRAVEL ESSENTIALS

VISAS & PASSPORTS

You will need a valid passport, an official application form, confirmation of your hotel reservations (for both business travellers and tourists) and three passport photographs, to get your visa from a Soviet embassy or consulate. If you apply individually, rather than through a travel agency, you should allow ample time, as it might take up to a month or so to check your papers.

According to the new regulations, this term can be shortened to 48 hours if an applicant is a business traveller or if he or she has a written invitation (telex and fax are also accepted) from a Soviet host. However, it might take the Soviet counterpart some time to have the invitation stamped by the local authority.

The visa is not stamped into the passport but onto a separate sheet of paper, consisting of three sections. The first part is removed when a person enters the country, and the last is taken out when leaving the country.

There are several types of visas. Transit visas (for not more than 48 hours), tourist, ordinary and multiple entry visas (for two or more visits).

If you go to the USSR at the invitation of relatives or friends, you can get a visa for a private journey which presupposes that no hotel reservation is needed. Individual tourists should have their trip organised through Intourist, Mir, Sputnik or their Soviet hosts. They need an itinerary listing, in detail, times, places and overnight reservations.

You should carry your passport at all times while you are in the USSR. Without it you might be prohibited entry to your hotel, your embassy and many other places.

Intourist hotels will give you a special hotel card that serves as a permit to enter the hotel and to use its restaurant and currency exchange office.

HEALTH REGULATIONS

Visitors from the USA, Canada, European countries and Japan need no health certificate. Visitors from regions infected with yellow fever, especially from Africa and South America, need an international certificate of vaccination against yellow fever. A cholera and tetanus vaccination certificate may also be required. Visitors from certain AIDS-infected regions who are planning to stay in the USSR for an extended period can be subjected to an AIDS test.

CUSTOMS

When entering the USSR you will have to fill in the customs declaration which must be kept as carefully as a passport during the whole period of your stay on Soviet territory. It must be returned to the customs office, along with another declaration, which you fill in on leaving the country.

USSR customs regulations have been revised several times in the last few years. Customs authorities want to find a compromise between conforming to international customs regulations in the epoch of openness and of preventing the export of large batches of goods bought cheaply in Soviet shops for resale in other countries.

The latest edition of the Soviet customs regulations prohibits the import and export of weapons and ammunition (excluding approved fowling-pieces and hunting-tackle), and of drugs and devices for their use. It is prohibited to export antiquities and art objects except for those which the visitor imported to the country and declared on entry.

It is permitted to import free and without limitation: 1) gold and the other valuable metals except for gold coins, whose import is prohibited 2) materials of historic, scientific, and cultural value 3) articles approved by the licensees of V/O Vneshposyltorg 4) foreign currency and foreign currency documents 5) personal property except for computers and other technical devices (*see below*).

Limited duty-free import:
1) Gifts with a total value less then 500 roubles (about US$770). If you want to bring gifts, which are highly appreciated among Soviet people, it is best to choose ballpoint pens, elegant business note books, calcula-

tors, electronic watches and the other inexpensive items. You are recommended not to have more than 10 units of an article if you want to escape time-consuming questions from customs officers.

2) Cars and motorcycles approved according to International Traffic Convention, no more than 1 unit per family, with the obligation to export the vehicle.

3) Spare parts for the vehicles insured by the Soviet international insurance company Ingosstrakh and approved by the documents of Ingosstrakh or Intourist (for other spare parts duty must be paid).

4) Medicines not registered in the list of the Soviet Ministry of Health Protection must be approved by the Soviet medical institutions.

5) Personal computers, photocopying apparatus, video-recorders, TVSat systems with the obligation to export (if the obligation is broken and the article is sold in the USSR, duty must be paid).

6) Alcohol (limited to persons over 21) spirits – 1.5 litres, wines – 2 litres.

7) Tobacco (limited to persons over 16) 200 cigarettes or 200 grammes of tobacco per person.

Duty-free export:
1) Articles imported by the visitor.

2) Articles bought in Soviet hard currency shops or in rouble-shops for legally exchanged Soviet currency (with some limitations – *see below*).

3) Food stuffs with a total value of no more than 5 roubles.

4) Alcohol (over 21) spirits 1.5 litres, wines 2 litres per person.

5) Tobacco (over 16) 100 cigarettes or 100 grammes of tobacco.

It is prohibited to export the following articles bought in rouble shops: electric cable, instruments, building materials, fur, cloth, carpets, leather clothes, linen, knitted fabric, socks and stockings, umbrellas, plates and dishes, medicines and perfumes, sewing machines, refrigerators, bicycles, cameras, vacuum cleaners, washing machines, children's clothes and boots, all articles produced abroad, valuable metals and jewels.

Some of the customs officers are indeed quite severe in their observation of these regulations. Therefore when you enter or leave the country you must expect a careful examination of all your luggage and you will be asked if any personal items are intended for sale in the USSR (if the answer is yes, you will have to pay duty).

MONEY MATTERS

Roubles can neither be imported nor exported to or from the USSR. The newly established exchange rate for tourists has lessened the importance of the former black market. There is no limit to the import of hard currency, which, however, has to be declared on entry. The amount exported should not exceed the amount declared when entering the country. Officially documented but unspent roubles can be reconverted at the hotel exchange counter or at the Pulkovo 2 airport bank. If you intend to do this, you should reckon on spending at least half an hour, since there always seem to be long queues at the bank counters before international flights leave.

All Intourist hotels have an official exchange counter where you can buy roubles with hard currency cash, traveller's cheques and credit cards. You need your customs declaration form where all your money transactions have to be recorded. You will need to present this form when leaving the country and you should, as with your passport, make sure not to lose it. Most major hotels have bars, restaurants and shops were you can only pay with hard currency, but these transactions do not need to be recorded on your exchange certificate. Leaving the country, customs will check that you have officially exchanged money for the goods you bought and export from the country and that you are not exporting more hard currency than you have imported.

CREDIT CARDS

Most tourist-related businesses accept major credit cards. American Express runs two cash dispensers in Moscow where card holders can either receive roubles or US dollar traveller's cheques. They are located at 21 A Sadovokudrinskaya Street and at the Sovincentr, Mezhdunarodnaya Hotel, 12 Krasnoprenskaya Embankment. No such service is available in Leningrad.

Intourist hotels, restaurants and co-operative cafés that accept credit cards usually have a notice to this effect at the entrance. As well as American Express, Diners Club, Visa, Eurocard and Mastercard are also accepted.

LOCAL CURRENCY

Banknotes in the USSR are available in the following denominations: 1, 3, 5, 10 and 25 roubles. In 1991, 50 and 100 rouble notes were removed from circulation. One rouble is divided into 100 kopecks and they are issued in denominations of 1, 2, 3, 5, 10, 15, 20 and 50 kopecks. Platinum and golden coins of 150 and 200 roubles are more the object of numismatists, than a matter of real circulation. You should not neglect small coins of 5, 3 and 2 kopecks. You will need 5 kopecks to travel by Metro (any distance and in any direction); for 3 kopecks you can drink a glass of water from the *automat* and for 2 kopecks you can make a telephone call.

The present Soviet exchange rate, which is called the "commercial rate" has nothing in common with the "tourist rate"; in fact, you get three times fewer roubles at the tourist rate than at the commercial rate. Foreign visitors are sometimes still exposed to propositions from black market dealers, the most active of whom are taxi drivers and restaurant waiters. The black market rate is published regularly by the newly established non-governmental newspaper, *Commersant*, which is also published in English.

In spite of the fact that rouble banknotes carry an inscription saying that they are accepted for "all fees within the USSR's territory" porters and taxi drivers sometimes demand hard currency payment. You should remember that currency black market activities are unlawful and culprits can be punished severely.

THE "MAJORS" OF LENINGRAD

Leningrad also has a unique breed of illegal "businessmen". People who call themselves "majors" operate both in the city's main thoroughfares and on the highways in the suburbs. They flag down buses and cars with foreign plates and offer to buy or sell currency, liquor, cigarettes, military uniforms, icons and many other things. As a rule, both sides are satisfied. Sometimes, however, the Russian "merchants" do not pay for your goods, showing the trusting foreigner a gun or an ugly-looking knife instead.

Do not be surprised to see youngsters who offer to "change money" in many languages on the streets. They also know such terms as "chewing gum" and "cigarettes". Don't fall for their hustle – the money they beg from you will most probably end up in the pockets of their elders, who will then send them out into the streets again. The press' description of old ladies out to make a buck in their own manner: they beg (mainly from soft-hearted foreign women) and then sell your dollars to dubious characters at lucrative rates.

BLACK MARKET MONEY

As everyone knows, dealing in convertible currency is against the law; the most serious crimes of this type are investigated by the KGB. Nevertheless, as soon as you set foot on Soviet soil you'll be showered with attractive propositions. A bottle of vodka costs less than a dollar at black market rates (provided, of course, that you can find a shop where vodka is on sale without standing in line or being asked for a coupon).

By way of consolation, it is true to say that no foreign national has yet been punished for violating currency regulations. As for the speculators, they do not even attempt to hide – in part because they know that their crime is difficult to prove, in part because they pay off the militia. Even so, think twice before you agree to do business with a "major". Foreigners are often conned with money that has been withdrawn from circulation (50 and 100 rouble notes in 1991) or through sleight of hand (money is counted as you watch, but only half of the agreed sum – at best – will make its way into your pocket). There have also been cases where Finnish tourists, who came to buy cheap liquor, were sold water instead of vodka in what appeared to be factory-sealed bottles.

The best way to catch the eye of a taxi driver or doorman who pretends that you do not exist is to take a pack of Marlboro or Camel cigarettes out of your pocket. You can also show them a couple of dollars. This is illegal, but virtually every cabby, waiter and prostitute is openly involved in the black market and currency business.

GETTING ACQUAINTED

STREET NAMES

Looking at the map of any Soviet city you will find a standard set of names. Streets under these names can be found in almost every city. They have been changed in different periods of the short but intensive Soviet history. During Lenin's government, streets were named after Karl Marx and other revolutionaries and ethnic groups. The more exotic the revolutionary to be immortalised in a street name, the better it was.

Stalin's time was also marked with the compulsory use of the name of Karl Marx. But then a new standardisation was used since some foreign revolutionaries were suspected of being followers of heresies. The champions during this period were Lenin and Stalin himself (the names of the final points of a tram route that crossed Kiev looked like this: Stalin Square to Stalinka) and the members of Stalin's gang: Voroshilov, Kaganovich, Zhdanov, Beriya, etc. The present tendency is to bring back the original pre-Revolutionary names.

Who were the men immortalised on Soviet city maps? Leading names are Lenin, Marx and Engels. They are known by people the world over. In addition there are:

Chernyshevsky, Nikolai (1828–1889) – revolutionary-democrat, publisher and literary critic. The author of novel *What to do?* revered by Lenin.

Dzerzhinsky, Felix (1877–1926) – revolutionary, the associate of Lenin. After the revolution he became chief of the VeCheKa, the Bolshevik's special department, the forerunner of the KGB.

Gogol, Nikolai (1809–1852) – famous Russian writer, the author of the prose poem *Dead Souls* and a series of stories in which Ukrainian mythological plots are used.

Gorky, Maxim (1868–1936) – well-known writer, author of the novels *The Life of Klim*

Samgin and *Mother* as well as of romantic short stories. Proclaimed as the father of so-called "socialist realism" in literature.

Kirov, Sergei (1886–1934) – revolutionary, after the Revolution the 1st Secretary of the Leningrad Regional Party Committee. His assassination, instigated by Stalin, became a cloak for starting the repressions of the 1930s.

Ordzhonikidze, Sergo (1886–1937) – revolutionary, associate and friend of Stalin. After the Revolution appointed the People's Commissar of Heavy Industry. Shot by Stalin.

Pushkin, Alexander (1799–1837) – famous Russian poet and writer, author of "the novel in verses", *Evgeny Onegin* and of many poems, essays and stories.

Shevchenko, Taras (1814–1861) – famous Ukrainian poet, writer and painter, revolutionary-democrat.

Sverdlov, Yakov – revolutionary, the associate of Lenin. After the Revolution appointed the chairman of the All-Russian Executive Committee. He is believed to have given the order for the czar's family to be shot and he developed the policy of exterminating the Cossacks.

COUNTRY PROFILE

Area: 8,649,498 sq. miles (22.4 million sq. km).

Population 1988: 286,435,000. Population density: 33 per sq. mile (86 per sq. km).

GNP per capita: US$8,734, (cf. USA, US$18,951).

Demographics:
Population growth: 0.80 percent
Population 2000: 315,175,000
Age distribution: Under 15   26.0 percent
                 15–65   64.9 percent
                 Over 65   9.1 percent
Health:
Life expectancy (M): 65 years
Life expectancy (F): 74 years
Infant mortality: 25.4 per 1000
Politics:
Type of a State: Union of Republics
Government Leader: President Gorbachev, Mikhail Sergeyevich. Major Parties: Communist Party of the Soviet Union, Democratic Platform (Social-Democracy), Russian People's Front, Rukh, Sayudis.
Languages: Russian, Ukrainian, Turkish languages, Caucasian languages.

Ethnic Groups: Russians 52 percent, Ukrainians 16 percent, others 32 percent.
Religions: Orthodox 18 percent, Muslims 9 percent, Jews 3 percent, atheists 70 percent (including other confessions like Buddhists, Hare Krishnas etc.).
Natural Resources: crude oil, natural gas, coal, timber, manganese, gold, lead, zinc, nickel, potash, phosphates, mercury.
Agriculture: wheat, rye, oats, potatoes, sugar beets, linseed, sunflower seeds, cotton, flax, cattle, pigs, sheep.
Major Industries: mining, metallurgy, fuels, building materials, chemicals, machinery, aerospace.

CITY PROFILE

Leningrad is on the same latitude as the southern part of Greenland and Alaska and consists of 101 islands separated by 65 rivers, channels and streams, totalling 160 km/100 miles in length and spanned by 365 bridges, of which 20 are movable. It covers an area of 1,400 sq. km/540 sq. miles. Its population is now 4.9 million and includes over 100 different nationalities and ethnic groups.

In Leningrad there are some 30,000 weddings and 50,000 births per year; it has 1,455 health care institutions and is home to 41 institutions of higher learning, 450 research institutes and 2,500 libraries with over 150 million books and journals.

The city has 34 large stadiums and **Kavgolovo** (34km/22 miles away) is the ski capital of the USSR with a 70-metre (230-ft) high ski-jump. There are more than 300 soccer fields and 1,700 basketball, volleyball and tennis courts.

The Leningrad seaport is the country's largest and, even though the Baltic freezes over during winter, icebreakers keep the port open all year round.

Leningrad's twin cities are: Bombay, Dresden, Gdansk, Göteborg, Le Havre, Manchester, Turku, Zagreb, Milan, Osaka and Rotterdam.

CLIMATE

Leningrad has a maritime climate with cold winters (minus 25°C/minus 13°F) and hot summers (30°C/86°F), the average temperatures, however, lie between minus 7.7°C and 17.5°C (18.5°F and 63.5°F). On 222 days the temperature rises above zero (32°F) and it rains an average of 126 days per year. Most precipitation is in August, and the least in March. The bathing season on the Gulf of Finland lasts from mid-June to the end of August. Water temperatures are between 10°C and 24°C (52°F and 79°F).

WHAT TO WEAR

Today Leningrad is visited by many visitors who demonstrate all the caprices of fashion. Therefore the old guide book phrase, "when going to the USSR, follow a modest and classic style of clothes," is somewhat outdated. You may dress as you would at home.

Coming to Leningrad in the cold months (November to March) you should not be surprised to meet temperatures of 25°C to 30°C below zero (–13°F to –22°F). Waterproof shoes are a necessity in winter, since the traditional Russian frost is not as frosty anymore and is often interrupted by periods of thaw. For business meetings formal dress is obligatory. The dress code is as rigorously enforced as in the west and compliance with it is an important matter of status.

WHITE NIGHTS

The "White Nights", when it never becomes really dark, start on 25 May and last until 20 July. Their peak is between 11 June and 2 July. The **White Nights Festival of Arts** lasts from 21 June to 29 June.

TIME ZONES

Leningrad time is GMT plus 3 hours. The same time is adopted nearly everywhere west of the Urals, although Western Ukrainians and the people of the Baltic states prefer to use the Mean European Time (GMT plus 1 hour) in their daily life to demonstrate their independence.

DURATION OF A HOTEL DAY

The hotel day is counted from noon to noon. Exceptions are seldom made, especially in hotels that cater for large groups. Still, ask your receptionist or the house-lady of your floor if you want to stay longer; maybe the next group is not due until the evening.

ELECTRICITY

Electrical current in Leningrad tourist hotels is normally 220 volts AC. Elsewhere in the USSR it can vary. In some remote places you will also find 127 volts. Sockets require a continental type plug, but no Schuko plug. It is best to have a set of adaptors with you. The same is true for batteries. If your appliances depend on a supply of batteries, bring plenty with you, since they might not be available in the USSR, not even for hard currency.

TIPPING

Though the Soviet Union has been a Socialist state for 70 years, tipping, one of the capitalist sins, is still an accepted practice. Waiters, porters, taxi drivers, especially in Moscow and Leningrad, have always appreciated tips. As anywhere in the west, 10 percent is the accepted rule. However, do not tip guides, interpreters or other Intourist personnel. If you want to show your gratitude they will surely appreciate a small souvenir or gift.

OFFICIAL HOLIDAYS

1 January, New Year Holiday.
23 February, Soviet Army Day.
8 March, International Women's Day.
1 and 2 May, Day of International Solidarity of Working People.
9 May, Victory Day.
October 7, Constitution Day.
7 and 8 November, October Revolution Anniversary.
On 23 February, 1 May, 9 May, 7 November and 12 April (Cosmonaut's Day) there are fireworks in the evenings.

RELIGIOUS HOLIDAYS

The greatest religious holidays of the year include Christmas (celebrated by the Orthodox Church on 7 January) and Easter (a movable holiday usually celebrated in March–April). Religious holidays are still not acknowledged officially, but they are recognised by the many people who participate in religious services.

Nowadays local factory and government administrators negotiate with believers, offering compromises like shifting the days off to the days of religious festivals or granting free time which can be worked later.

RELIGIOUS SERVICES

Russian Orthodox
Alexander Nevsky Monastery, Monastyrik Embankment.
St Nikolas Marine Cathedral, Kommunarov Square 1/3.
Spaso-Preobrazensky Cathedral, Radischeva Square 1.
Vladimirskoi Ikon God's Mother, Vladimirskaya Square 20.

Catholic
The Catholic Church, Kovensky Pereulok 7.

Baptist
The Baptist Church, 29a Bolshaya Ozernaya Ulitsa.

Mosque
Mechet, Proyzed Maksima Gorkogo 7.

Synagogue
The Synagogue, 2 Lermontovsky Proyzed.

COMMUNICATIONS

MEDIA

Kiosks in Intourist hotels carry the main western daily newspapers (though mostly more than a day late). *Pravda*, the official paper of the Communist Party of the USSR, appears in an English-language translation.

Moscow News, an informative English-language weekly, is a liberal paper published in Moscow. The first independent Soviet-American weekly newspaper is *We*, a joint venture between Izvestia and the Hearst Corporation. *Travel to the USSR* is a bimonthly illustrated magazine, published in Russian, German, English and French, that carries many interesting tips and infor-

mation about fast-changing travel conditions in the country.

Pravda and *Izvestia* are the leading Russian-language national government newspapers. Local newspapers are the *Leningradskaya Pravda*, the *Vecherni Leningrad*, the *Smena* and the *Leningradskaya Rabochi*. The monthly *Novy Mir* and the weekly *Ogonyok* are critical papers that thrive on the ideas of *glasnost*. The Russian language Leningrad TV show, *600 seconds*, is reputed to be the most critical in the whole country.

POSTAL SERVICES

The opening times of post offices vary, but most of them open from 8 a.m. till 7 p.m. or 8 p.m. during the week and from 9 a.m. to 6 p.m. on Saturdays. They are closed on Sundays. Some post offices, however, work only one shift a day, from 9 a.m. to 3 p.m. or from 2 p.m. to 8 p.m. The mail service in the USSR is constantly understaffed.

Not all post offices accept international mail larger than a standard letter. Postal delivery is quite slow, and it may take some two or three weeks for a letter from Moscow to reach Western Europe and sometimes even a month or more to reach the USA. A standard letter up to 20 grams costs 50 kopecks and a postcard costs 35 kopecks to any country of the world.

Central Post office: 9 Ulitsa Soyuza Svyazi. Open: 9 a.m.–9.pm, Sunday 10 a.m.–8 p.m.
Oktyabrskaya Hotel Post Office: 10 Ligovsky Prospekt (opposite Moscow Railway Station).
Post office 400: 6 Nevsky Prospekt.
Poste restante address: C-400, 6 Nevsky Prospekt, Leningrad.

CABLES & TELEGRAMS

Cables to addresses within the USSR can be sent from any post office or by phone. International cables can be sent from nearly all post offices, but not by phone.

Central Telegraph office: 24 Ulitsa Gertsena. Tel: 314 3757.

TELEPHONE

From a pay phone a local call costs 2 kopecks per 3 minutes. The coin must be inserted before dialling. If you hear a bip-bip tone during the conversation it's time to insert another coin.

For long-distance calls within the USSR there are specially marked phones which accept 15 kopeck coins. First dial 8, than the area code and the number.

International calls must be booked in advance or at the hotel service bureau: the charge per minute to the US is six roubles, to Western European countries four roubles. Express calls are charged double.

Area codes within the USSR:

Alma-Ata	327
Ashkhabad	363
Baku	892
Bukhara	365
Donetsk	062
Dushanbe	377
Yerevan	296
Kiev	044
Kishinev	042
Kharkov	057
Lvov	032
Minsk	017
Moscow	095
Novosibirsk	383
Odessa	048
Riga	013
Rostov on Don	863
Samarkand	366
Tallinn	014
Tashkent	371
Tbilisi	883
Vilnius	012
Yalta	060

If you are calling Leningrad from abroad be prepared to try often; the lines are not too good and are always very busy. The direct dial code for Leningrad is 007812.

TELEX & FAX

All official institutions and major business representatives have telex numbers and the majority of them now also have telefax. Moscow has a public fax and telex service, where you can send a fax or telex or register a number by which you can be reached if you plan to stay in the city for a long period. Any incoming message will be forwarded either by phone or by local mail. It is the only way to beat the slow mail service. The telex access code for the USSR is 871.

EMERGENCIES

These numbers can be dialled free of charge from public telephones.

Fire Guards (Pozharnaya okhrana)	01
Police (Militsia)	02
Ambulance (Skoraya pomoshch)	03
Gas Emergency (Sluzhba gaza)	04
Time	08
Information (Spravochnaya)	09

Aeroflot Information: tel: 239 9021
Railway Information: tel: 168 0111

Officials responding to these calls speak little English, so you will require a minimal knowledge of Russian to make yourself understood.

CRIME

In 1989, crime rose by 33.2 percent as compared to 1988. The number of murders, rapes, grievous injuries, robberies and muggings has gone up by 70–80 percent. Despite all the efforts of law enforcement agencies, the crime rate remains high in the 1990s.

Gone are the days when you could walk the streets of Leningrad at night or leave your valuables unprotected in your hotel room. Criminals want their share of the currency loaf. Foreigners are habitually robbed in hotels, taxis, private cars. Think of your safety.

Avoid private cabbies, who are certain to pester you with offers of their services in the international airport or at the hotel. Sometimes they take too much – everything you have, in fact. Be wary of the ladies of the night – many of them are just waiting for you to fall asleep. When you wake up, your things and money may be gone. Do not open your door to people you do not know.

Leningrad is a beautiful northern city. It is particularly eye-catching between the end of May and the middle of July – the season of white nights. Even though you would be right to rely on the friendliness of the majority of the people you'll meet here – foreigners are still treated with particular respect in Russia – keep our advice in mind. Then your stay in the former Russian capital is certain to be a pleasant one.

MEDICAL SERVICES

Medical services for tourists are free of charge except for drugs from chemist's shops and in-patient treatment. Doctors at the big hotels speak foreign languages.

Outpatient clinic for tourists: 2 Moskovsky Prospekt. Tel: 292 3877.

Leningrad's tap water is drinkable but for people with stomach problems, it is advisable to drink bottled mineral water. Note that ice in bars and coffee shops is also made from tap water.

GETTING AROUND

LOCAL TRANSPORT

The subway dazzles with the beauty of its stations, particularly those that were built in the 1950s. But the initial rapture quickly disappears at the sight of the crowds which cram the cars like the proverbial sardines. And the subway will not necessarily take you anywhere you want to go. The extensive network of surface transport – buses, trolleys and trams – can also let you down, even though the fares are incredibly cheap – only 5 kopecks.

If you are alone in town, you may find it hard to find your way, particularly if you have to travel far. You also have to bear in mind that in Leningrad, as indeed all over the USSR, transport does not run in accordance with a rigid schedule, and you may have to wait a while (then three buses will come, if it is any consolation). So the best thing to do is to take a taxi and be ready to give a large tip (the official rate is 20 kopecks per kilometer).

Car rental facilities have recently appeared in Leningrad. A Ford or a Volvo can be had for US$3 an hour (petrol is charged separately). Unfortunately Leningrad is a nightmare for the first-time driver. The map will do little to help. The rudeness of local drivers is notorious. Nor will you like the roads – the asphalt surface cracks as the snow thaws and freezes, leaving the road full of holes, particularly where there are tram rails. The best thing to do (unless, of course, you have a friend with a car) is to rent one with a chauffeur (US$6 per hour).

You can always try for a taxi, of course. Once your service bureau gets hold of one for you, be sure not to let it go until you return from your outing. It is almost impossible to catch a taxi in town. Don't get mad if no one stops. Several "green lights" (signifying vacancy) are certain to cruise by. Be patient – sooner or later, a cab is bound to stop. You will be asked where you want to go, and how much you are willing to pay. Offer to pay "two meters", that is double the fare, if you know what's good for you.

As for the private cars, which have no taxicab markings, you should be extra careful. These people often want dollars, cigarettes or clothes. You should not get in if the driver is not alone: anything can happen (you could get robbed), and the driver would then explain to the militia that his "unknown companion" is to blame for everything (the companion will have disappeared by that time, of course). There have been several cases when foreigners were driven out of town, robbed and left on the road.

CAR RENTAL

MIR charges US$6 per hour between 6 a.m. and midnight for a car with a driver; US$5 per hour if it is rented for more than three hours. Intourist has also a rent-a-car service.

SERVICE STATIONS

In Leningrad there are service stations that are used to dealing with foreigners at: 5 Pervaya Staroderevenskaya Ulitsa, tel: 233 6930 Open: 8 a.m.–8 p.m. and at 69 Prospekt Kosmonavtov, tel: 299 6302. Open: 8 a.m.–9 p.m.

PARKING

Parking is free where there is no prohibitive sign. Protected parking, which costs 30 kopecks per day, is available at Isaakiyevskaya Ploshchad, next to the Astoria Hotel, on the Vyborg side at 5 Pervaya Staroderevenskaya Ulitsa.

BRIDGES

Bridges across the Neva are raised during the night to let ships pass. During this time you cannot cross from one side of Leningrad to the other except by Metro.

Alexander Nevskogo Bridge, 2.35 a.m.–4.50 a.m.
Bolsheokthinski Bridge, 2.45 a.m.–4.45 a.m.
Liteiny Bridge, 2.10 a.m.–4.40 a.m.
Kirovsky Bridge, 2 a.m.–4.40 a.m.
Volodarsky Bridge, 2.05 a.m.–3.45 am and 4.30 a.m.–5.45 a.m.
Dvortsovy Bridge, 1.55 a.m.–3.05 a.m. and 3.15 a.m.–4.45 a.m.
Leitenanta Schmidta Bridge, 1.55 a.m.–2.55 a.m. and 3.15 a.m.–4.50 a.m.

The bridges are not raised on national holidays.

RULES OF THE ROAD

The USSR is a signatory to the International Traffic Convention. Rules of the road and road signs correspond in general to international standards. The basic rules, however, are worth mentioning.
1) In the USSR traffic drives on the right.
2) It is prohibited to drive a car after consuming, even the smallest amount of alcohol. If the driver shows a positive alcohol test, the consequences may be very serious. It is also prohibited to drive a car under the effect of drugs or drastic medicines.
3) The driver must have an international driving licence and documents verifying his right to drive the car. These papers must be in Russian and are issued by Intourist.
4) Vehicles, except for those rented from Intourist, must carry the national registration code. All must have a national licence plate.
5) The use of the horn is prohibited within city limits except in emergencies.
6) The use of seat belts for the driver and front seat passenger is compulsory.
7) The speed limit in populated areas (marked by blue coloured signs indicating "town") is 60 kph (37 mph); on most arterial roads the limit is 90 kph (55.5 mph). On highways different limits apply and these are shown on road signs.
8) You can insure your car in the USSR through **Ingosstrakh**, the national insurance company.
9) Foreigners still need a permit to drive more than 40 km/25 miles beyond city limits and must follow the routes established by Intourist. Permits may be checked by traffic police when exiting the city.

PUBLIC TRANSPORT

Trolley buses and buses run from 6 a.m. to 1 a.m. and cost 4 kopecks and 5 kopecks respectively. Trams and the Metro run from 5.30 a.m. to 1.00 a.m. and cost 3 kopecks and 5 kopecks respectively.

Taxis and collective cars are available 24 hours and cost 20 kopecks and 15 kopecks per kilometer respectively.

If you are using buses, you should be sure to carry enough change with you, since you buy the tickets on a self-service basis inside the buses. You also can buy booklets in advance at newspaper kiosks.

METRO

The most convenient local transport is Leningrad's Metro. Construction started before the war and was completed in 1955. All Intourist hotels and most others have Metro stations marked "**M**", nearby.

On 15 November 1955, the first Metro line was opened from Uprising Square to Avtovo, covering some 10.8 km/6.7 miles. Now the lines total 60 km/38 miles, and trains run at speeds of 40 kph (25 mph);

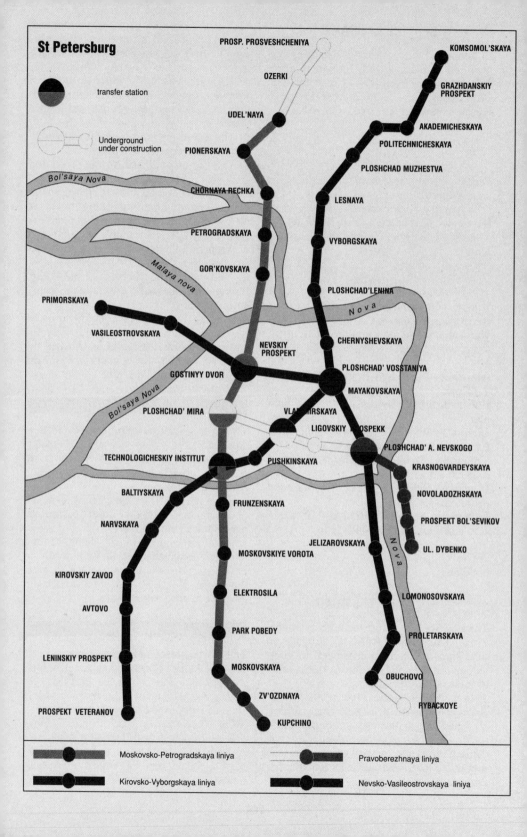

during the rush hours trains arrive at intervals of 1½ minutes.

There are three lines in operation (a fourth one is under construction): The **Moskovsko-Petrogradskaya Line**, the **Kirovsko-Vyborgskaya Line** and the **Nevsko-Vasileostovskaya Line**.

The stations were built in many architectural styles. Some of the most impressive are: Avtovo, Kirovsky Zavod, Narvskaya, Baliskaya, Ploshchad Vosstaniya and Ploshchad Muzhestva on the Kirovsko-Vyborgskaya Line. On the Moskovsko-Petrogradskaya Line, the Park Pobedy station actually has no boarding platform but is equipped with a "horizontal lift". Nevsky Prospekt and Petrogradskaya are impressive for their optimal use of space. The Nevsko-Vasileostrovskaya Line brings you from the Pribaltiyskaya Hotel to Nevsky Prospekt. At the Gostiny Dvor station there is no surface station; the exits lead directly into the department store. At Ploshchad Alexandra Nevskogo the exit leads into the Moskva Hotel.

The transfer stations, where you can change from one line to the other are **Gostiny Dvor**, **Ploshchad Vosstaniya** and **Technological Institute**.

TOUR OPERATORS

Intourist

Leningrad Intourist Office: Isaakievskaya Ploshchad 11.

Between June and September Intourist runs a **Cultural Centre** in the Palace of Culture to acquaint visitors with the Soviet way of life: 32, Prospekt Obukhovskoi Oborony.

Intourist cooperates with more than 700 foreign firms who are agents for Intourist in their respective countries. It offers services in more than 200 cities in all the 15 Soviet republics and runs numerous hotels, motels, campsites and restaurants. On Intourist's itinerary are more than 600 different tours within the USSR. They include local sightseeing trips, thematic tours for history, art and nature lovers, as well as arrangements for recreation and medical treatment, sporting and hunting tours. A visit to the nearest Intourist office will give you a good overall impression of their diversified offerings.

In addition to its tours Intourist also runs a car rental service, with and without driver, in larger cities. Lada, Chaika and Volga cars as well as Ikarus coaches and LAZ, PAZ and RAF buses for 9 to 42 people can be hired.

Intourist also manages 110 hotels, motels and campsites for 55,000 guests. A variety of hotels are now being built and reconstructed in cooperation with foreign partners, including Leningrad's Astoria Hotel, which is operated jointly with the Finnish INFA Hotel company and Finnair.

Over 5,000 guide-interpreters, speaking more than 30 languages, work for Intourist. Since cooperatives are now permitted, Intourist is no longer a monopoly tourist agency; a few small and independent firms have sprung up during the last few years which now serve special interest groups. The most prominent of them, having its headquarters in Leningrad, is Mir International Centre. But since the itinerary of a journey to the USSR has to be confirmed in advance, and submitted together with the visa application, Intourist, with its worldwide net of sales agents, is still carrying out most of the business.

Besides group tours, Intourist also arranges individual journeys to the USSR. These trips must be planned on a day-by-day basis in advance, and Intourist arranges transport, accommodation and food. Judging by accommodation prices in those Intourist hotels that are available to foreigners, such individual travel is, however, not inexpensive.

ALTERNATIVE TOUR OPERATOR

MIR International Centre: Tel: (007812) 542 2845, Fax: (007812) 315 1701, Telex: 121 425 TURBO SU, arranges inexpensive group travel, special interest tours, Russian language courses and international group exchange. They are one of the new co-operatives who try hard to compete with Intourist. They can send out invitations for individual visas, arrange hotel and private accommodation, and make out of the way travel arrangements. They have interpreters, rent cars with or without drivers and organise symposiums. Their speciality is the organisation of individual trips to the USSR, especially Leningrad where they have their head office.

In Leningrad they arrange for theatre tickets, restaurant reservations and individually guided city and museum tours.

WHERE TO STAY

HOTELS

Hotels in Leningrad only accept convertible currency from foreigners. The **Pribaltiyskaya Hotel** (built by a Swedish company with a view of the Gulf of Finland) has rooms at between 93 (individuals) and 20 (groups) convertible roubles per day. Be warned: service leaves much to be desired, even in the best rooms. Don't be surprised if the hot water disappears, and no one comes to clean your room. And don't count on drinking coffee in bed.

Two five-star hotels in midtown Leningrad have undergone refurbishment – the **Astoria** and **Hotel Europe**. Rooms will be more expensive there, but quality will be guaranteed – or so the Soviet, Swedish and Finnish managers of the projects say. Hotel personnel were sent abroad for training.

A good example of what such cooperation brings is the floating Soviet-Swedish **Olympia Hotel**. The staff are attentive and the place is always clean. You can watch European stations on TV and there is no line in front of the doors of the restaurant. There is also a popular, but expensive, night club with a casino and a bar.

When checking into a Soviet hotel you will receive a guest card which you should carry with you all the time. Each hotel has a service bureau which will assist you in all small matters, from medical help to calling a taxi or obtaining theatre tickets, restaurant reservations or arranging international telephone calls. Each floor has a floor clerk who will call a porter, get your laundry done, etc. He or she will also keep your room key while you are away.

Astoria (Intourist), Ulitsa Gertsena 39. Tel: 219 1100.
Baltiyskaya, Nevsky Prospekt 57. Tel: 277 7731.

Gavan, Sredny Prospekt 88. Tel: 356 8504.
Karelia (Intourist), Ulitsa Tukhachevskovo 27/2. Tel: 226 5701.
Kievskaya, Dnepropetrovskaya Ulitsa 49. Tel: 166 0456.
Ladoga, Prospekt Shaumyana 26. Tel: 528 5628.
Leningrad (Intourist), Vyborgskaya Naberezhnaya 5/2. Tel: 542 9031.
Mir, Ulitsa Gastello 17. Tel: 293 0092.
Moskva (Intourist), Ploshchad Alexandra Nevskovo 2. Tel: 274 2051.
Neva, Ulitsa Chaikovskovo 17. Tel: 278 0504.
Oktyabrskaya, Ligovsky Prospekt 10. Tel: 315 5362.
Pribaltiyskaya (Intourist), Ulitsa Korablestroiteley 14. Tel: 356 5112.
Pulkovskaya (Intourist), Ulitsa Pobedy 1. Tel: 264 5100.
Rossia, Ploshchad Chernyshevskovo 11. Tel: 296 7349.
Sovetskaya, Lermontovsky Prospekt 43/1. Tel: 259 2552.
Sputnik, Prospekt Toreza 34. Tel: 552 8330.
Tourist, Ulitsa Sevastyanova 3. Tel: 297 8252.
Vyborgskaya, Torzhkovskaya Ulitsa 3. Tel: 246 9141.
Yevropeyskaya, Ulitsa Brodskovo 1/7. Tel: 210 3149.

CAMPING

Camping Site, Klenovaya Ulitsa 9, Repino.
Olgino Motel and Campingsite (Intourist), Primorskoe Shosse 5 Tel. 238 3551.

PRIVATE

Many Leningradians like to rent out their apartment for hard currency. This can be a very personal and inexpensive way of staying in the city for a longer period and of avoiding the high Intourist hotel charges. Such private accommodation can be arranged through the MIR International Centre (*see Alternative Tour Operators*).

FOOD DIGEST

WHERE TO EAT

It is not easy to eat out in an ordinary (rouble) restaurant in Leningrad. It is difficult to book a table even at the hotel where you are staying. There are simply not enough restaurants, so if you want to have supper, book a table after breakfast and be ready to wait for 30 minutes or so for the waiter. But nearly every hotel has hard-currency restaurants and bars. If you pay in hard currency, the service immediately improves. Prices may be high, however. Another option is to go to the co-ops (private restaurants) in town. They accept roubles and hard currency. If you choose to pay in convertible currency, you will get wonderful-looking and tasty food. Look for ads for the most popular co-op cafés (their number is growing) in the lobby of your hotel. The best known at the moment are **Tbilisi**, the Soviet-Canadian **Nevskiye Melodii** (it is rather far away, in Okhta), **Tête-a-Tête** (Bolshoi Prospekt on the Petrograd Side), and the Soviet-German **Schwab House**. A bottle of Soviet champagne will cost you around 12 roubles, and a main course around 20.

If it is both Russian cuisine and action you crave, book a table in the restaurant of the **Sovetskaya Hotel**, the **Leningrad** or the **Troika**, a restaurant in Zagorodny Prospekt, all of which offer noisy, colourful variety shows à la Russe. By the way, you ought to know that if there is an orchestra in a restaurant, it always plays too loud.

Try Russian cuisine at the **Sadko**, Hotel Yevropeiskaya, tel: 210 3667, or eat romantically aboard an old schooner at the **Kronwerk**, close to the Peter and Paul Fortress. Inside the fort at Peter's Gate is the **Austeria**, tel: 238 4262. The **Fregat**, at 14 Bolshoi Prospekt, serves food cooked according to recipes from the time of Peter the Great. The **Metropol**, Ulitsa Sadovaya 22,

tel: 310 2281, is famous for its Russian cuisine and so is the **Na Fontanka**, 77 Naberezhnaya reki Fontanki, tel: 310 2547.

NATIONAL CUISINES

Aragvi (Georgian cuisine), Ulitsa Tukhachevskovo 41. Tel: 225 0336.
Baku (Azerbaijan cuisine), Ulitsa Sadovaya 12. Tel: 311 2751.
Bukhara (Uzbek cuisine), Prospekt Nepokoryonnykh 74. Tel: 538 4553.
Kavkazsky (Caucasian cuisine), Nevsky Prospekt 25. Tel: 214 6663.

Other restaurants with Russian and European cuisines
Belaya Loshad (White Horse Beer Restaurant), Chkalovsky Prospekt 16. Tel: 235 1113.
Troika, Ulitsa Zagorodnaya 27. Tel: 113 5343.
Admiralteysky, Ulitsa Gertsena 27. Tel: 315 5661.
Demyanova Ukha, Prospekt Gorkovo 53. Tel: 232 8090.
Neva, Nevsky Prospekt 46. Tel: 210 3466.
Nevsky, Nevsky Prospekt 71. Tel: 311 3093.
Okean, Primorsky Prospekt 15. Tel: 239 6984.

CAFÉS & BARS

Korchma (wine), Prospekt Engelsa 83.
Leningrad (dairy dishes), Nevsky Prospekt 96.
Literaturnoe Café, Nevsky Prospekt 18. Tel: 312 8536.
Pogrebok, Ulitsa Gogolya 7. Tel: 315 5371.
Rakushka (seafood), Prospekt Maklina 44.
Shokoladnitsa, Moskovsky Prospekt 200.
Pizzerias: Budapeshtskaya Ulitsa 71; Moskovsky Prospekt 73; Nevsky Prospekt 44; Ulitsa Rubinshtejna 30.

BEER PUBS

Beer addicts will have a tough time in Leningrad (as just about everywhere else in the USSR). There are no real pubs here. The few restaurants that do serve beer (**Petropol** in Sredniy Prospekt on Vasilievsky Island, **Pushkar** and **Belaya Loshad** on Petrogradskaya Side) will probably leave you in shock at the poor quality of both the drink and food. It is next to impossible to drink the beer they sell in kiosks. Do not let the long lines fool you: kiosks are something of a debating club, a Leningrad version of London's Hyde Park Corner (they are also the ideal place to meet the natives – but you have to know the language). However, as always, you'll be saved by a glass of cold Heineken in the hard-currency bar at your hotel, or a can of Carlsberg at the nearest Beriozka shop

Akvarium, Budapeshtskaya Ulitsa 44, korp. 1.
Gavan, Srednegavansky Prospekt 9.
Medved, Potemkinskaya Ulitsa 7.
Petropol, Sredny Prospekt 18.
Staraya Zastava, Ploshchad Mira 7.

WHAT TO EAT

Most of the different ethnic groups populating the USSR claim to have their national cuisine, and some of them do genuinely have them. Within this diversity, experts say Georgian, Ukrainian, Russian and Central Asian cuisines are the best.

GEORGIAN

With *perestroika* Georgian food came to the rest of the USSR (served at restaurants like the traditional Kavkaz in Leningrad). Many co-operatives run by people from the Caucasus opened restaurants serving Georgian food. The Georgian cuisine is famous for its *shashlyk*, *tsyplyata tabaka* (chicken fried under pressure), *basturma* (specially fried meat), *suluguni* (salted cheese) and *satsyvi* (chicken). It can be served with *lavash* (a special kind of bread) or with *khachapuri* (a roll stuffed with cheese).

UKRAINIAN

Ukrainians are traditionally regarded as people who eat a lot – but also well. Among their favourite dishes are *borshch* (beetroot soup with cabbage, meat, mushrooms and other ingredients), *galushky* (small boiled dumplings) and *varenyky zvyshneyu* (curd dumplings with red cherries served with sugar and sour cream). Chicken Kiev (or Kiev Cutlet), known throughout the world, is prepared with different spices and garlic. Loved by

everyone in the Ukraine is *salo* (salted raw lard spiced with garlic). It is served with black bread. *Kovbasa* (different kinds of smoked sausages) is also very popular.

RUSSIAN

Famous dishes include beef Stroganov and Beluga caviar. Russian cuisine includes less refined but no less popular dishes like *bliny* (pancakes served with butter and sour cream, caviar, meat, jam etc.), *shchi* (sour cabbage soup with meat; gourmets prefer this with mustard), *pelmeni* (boiled dumplings with meat) and *kasha* (gruel or porridge of different grains).

CENTRAL ASIAN

The cuisine is represented by a variety of pilaws or rice dishes.

DRINKING NOTES

Everyone knows what they drink in Russia: vodka (only available with a ration card since 1991) and tea from the samovar. This is only half the truth. There are numerous other drinks within different national cuisines, though it is not so easy to get these national specialities in Leningrad.

The Ukrainian traditional alcoholic drink is *gorilka* which resembles vodka. More popular, and more refined, is *gorilka z pertsem*, i.e. gorilka with a small red pepper. The traditional non-alcoholic drink is *uzvar* (made of stewed fruit).

Georgians drink different dry and semi-dry wines especially *Tsinandali*, *Mukuzani*, *Kinzmarauli*, *Alazan Valley*, and *Tvishi* (reported to have been the favourite wine of Stalin). Non-alcoholic drinks from Georgia are represented by the best in the USSR's mineral water such as *Borzhomi* and the so-called *vody Lagidze* (mineral water with various syrup mixtures).

In summer Russians prefer to drink *kvas*, an enigmatic refreshing drink prepared from bread fermented with water and yeast.

Central Asians drink *geok chaj* (green tea), the best treatment for a thirst in the hot Central Asian climate.

CULTURE PLUS

MUSEUMS

Leningrad itself is a huge museum of 18th and 19th-century architecture and sculpture. The city also houses many small and large museums which can be divided into three groups: **(1) Museums of Arts & Literature, (2) Museums of History** and **(3) Scientific Museums.** The art museums includes two of the world's greatest collections, the **Hermitage** in the Winter Palace on Dvortsovaya Ploshchad (the entrance is on Dvortsovaya Naberezhnaya 34, tel: 311 3465), and the **Russian Museum** in the Mikhailovsky Palace, Inzhenernaya Ulitsa 4–2, tel: 314 3448. Other museums include:

Museum of the Academy of Arts
Universitetskaya Naberezhnaya 17.

Brodsky Museum-Flat
Ploshchad Iskusstv 3.

City Sculpture Museum
Ploshchad Alexandra Nevskovo 1.

Necropolis of Alexander Nevsky Lavra
Ulitsa Rasstannaya 30.

Literatorskie Mostki
Necropolis. This museum also takes care of all the old sculptures around the city.

Menshikov Palace-Museum
Universitetskaya Naberezhnaya 15.

Dostoevsky Museum-Flat
Kuznechny Pereulok 5/2.

Pushkin Museum
Naberezhnaya Mojki 12 (Pushkin's Flat) and Ulitsa Komsomolskaya 2.

Pushkin town (Liceum)
Repin Museum-Estate
Primorskoe Shosse 411.

Repino town
Russian Literature Museum
Naberezhnaya Makarova 4.

Museum of Theatre
Ploshchad Ostrovskovo 6.

HISTORY MUSEUMS

Museums in the Peter and Paul Fortress.
Museum of the History of Leningrad
14 Naberezhnaya Krasnogo Flota.

Cathedral of the Holy Virgin of Kazan (Museum of the History of Religion and Atheism)
2 Kazanskaya Ploshchad.

Peter the Great's Cottage
6 Petrovskaya Naberezhnaya.

Museum of History and Regional Studies
Komsomolskaya Ulitsa 22, Pushkin town.

REVOLUTIONARY MUSEUMS

Aurora Cruiser
Near the Leningrad Hotel, Vyborgskaya Naberezhnaya.

Lenin's Museum
Ulitsa Khalturina 5–1.

Lenin's Hut
next to Razliv Lake.

Museum of the History of Artillery and Communications
Lenin Park.

Naval Museum
Pushkinskaya Ploshchad 4.

Museum of the Great October Revolution
4, Ulitsa Kuibysheva.

SCIENTIFIC MUSEUMS

Museum of Anthropology and Ethnography (Kunstkammer)
Universitetskaya Naberezhnaya 3.

Museum of the Arctic and Antarctic
Ulitsa Marata 24a.

Meteorological Museum
Ulitsa Belinskovo 6–46.

Popov Museum-Flat
Ulitsa Professora Popova 5.

Dokuchayev Central Soil Science Museum
Vasilyevsky Ostrov 6, Birzhevoi Proyezd.

THEATRES & CONCERT HALLS

In any hotel, you can order tickets to the most
prestigious performances. A small amount
of hard currency will guarantee you good
seats in the famous Kirov Theatre. The services of a professional guide cost between
$10 and $50 (book through the hotel service
bureau).

Theatre performances normally start at
7.30 p.m. and concerts at 8 p.m. There is no
admission once the performance has started.

Oktyabrsky Concert Hall
6 Ligovsky Prospekt.

Gorky Academic Bolshoi Drama Theatre
65 Naberezhnaya reki Fontanki.

Pushkin Academic Drama Theatre
2 Ploshchad Ostrovskogo.

Glinka Academic Capella
20 Naberezhnaya reki Moiki.

Comedy Theatre
56 Nevsky Prospekt.

Maly Theatre of Opera and Ballet
1 Ploshchad Iskusstv.

**Kirov Academic Theatre of Opera
and Ballet**
1 Teatralnaya Ploshchad.

Komissarzhevskaya Drama Theatre
19 Ulitsa Rakova.

Komsomol Theatre
4 Park Imeni Lenina.

Lensoviet Theatre
12 Vladimirsky Prospekt.

Puppet Theatre
10 Ulitsa Nekrasova.

Theatre of Musical Comedy
13 Ulitsa Rakovba.

Children's Theatre
1 Pionerskaya Ploshchad.

Leningrad Philharmonia
2 Ulitsa Brotskogo.

State Circus
3 Naberezhnaya reki Fontanki.

Mali Theatre of Drama
18 Ulitsa Rubinshteina.

State Conservatory
3 Teatralnaya Ploshchad.

CINEMAS

Cinemas open at 9 a.m. or 10 a.m. and show
films all day long. The entrance fee is between 30 and 70 kopecks. Up to 4 p.m.
tickets are sold at half price.

Avror, 60 Nevsky Prospekt.
Baltika, Vasilyevsky Ostrov, 34 Sedmaya
Linya.
Khodozhestvenny, 67 Nevsky Prospekt.
Leningrad, 4 Potyomkinskaya Ulitsa.
Moskva, Prospekt Gaza.
Nevsky, 4 Narodnaya Ulitsa.

SOVIET ROCK

Young people who are interested in rock
music will find themselves in the epicentre
of this art. Soviet rock was born here, in the
rock club in **Rubinshtein Street**. Don't miss
it. You can buy tickets for roubles in town or
directly before the concert. Such trips may
bring unexpected closeness (both pleasant
and otherwise) to your neighbours, who are
not always calm and rational. Take your
local friends with you – they will help you
choose a good concert and, if need be, save
you from the militiamen at the entrance who
do not like it when people have a beer or two
to get into the mood.

SHOPPING

BUSINESS HOURS

The absence of even the most basic goods very often determines the opening hours of shops. If there are no goods, the shop need not be open!

Many small shops have a one-hour lunchbreak sometime between noon and 5 p.m. Larger shops are continuously open from Monday to Saturday from between 7 a.m. and 9 a.m. and 8 p.m. and 9 p.m; certain food stores might be open until 10 p.m. Book shops and other specialty shops open around 10 a.m. or 11 a.m. and are open until 7 p.m. or 8 p.m., with a break usually between 2 p.m. and 3 p.m. On Sundays all shops, with the exception of some food stores, are closed.

SHOPS FOR FOREIGNERS

For foreigners who are horrified by the empty counters of Soviet shops there are special shops where they can buy nearly everything for a hard currency. There are now different chains of such shops in hotels, international airports and at certain points in the big cities called *Beriozka* (birch tree), *Sadko*, etc. The sales personnel in these shops usually speak English, French or German.

They offer Soviet goods of comparatively good quality. Furs, glass, ceramics, vodka, Crimean and Georgian wines, and many goods that are hard to come by in other city shops are all available if paid for in hard currency.

Beriozka prices are based on the so called *invalyutny rouble* and correspond with prices in Western European countries, though they are lower for Russian goods than for imported ones. These hard currency shops accept cash, traveller's cheques as well as most credit cards.

SOUVENIRS

Inexpensive souvenirs, toys and other knick-knacks abound on Soviet streets. Many co-operatives prefer not to rack their brains with such difficult matters as food production or the maintenance of computers. Instead they produce souvenirs, hair combs and belts. They also imitate the labels of designer jeans, so Soviet youngsters can sew them onto their pants to get an imitation feeling of freedom.

All this cheap stuff is sold on the streets, in the vicinity of department stores and in co-operative markets. In Leningrad the market is on Ostrovsky Square where you can also have your portrait drawn. Souvenirs abound also in special shops for foreigners, art-salons and curio shops. But beware of the problems waiting for you at customs: according to the new Soviet regulations, antiquities and art works may not be exported, nor may a whole list of other goods purchased in rouble stores (*see Customs section*). The danger of confiscation is quite real. For all goods bought in a Soviet shop, including those you bought at "Beriozka", you must keep the receipt to show that you paid in hard currency and that the goods are not antique.

Beriozka (hard currency shops)
Are at Pulkovo 2 Airport and in the following Intourist Hotels: Hotel Astoria, Hotel Leningrad, Hotel Oktyabrskaya, Hotel Pribaltiyskaya, Hotel Sovietskaya and Hotel Yevropeiskaya; also at Ulitsa Gertsena 26.

Beriozka jewellery shop is at Nevsky Prospekt 7–9.

Gostiny Dvor Department Store
Nevsky Prospekt 35.

Dom Leningradskoy Torgovli Department Store
Ulitsa Zhelyabova 21.

Dom Knigi (house of books)
Nevsky Prospekt 28.

Heritage Art Salon
Junction of Nevsky Prospekt and Ploshchad Vosstania.

You can buy records at Nevsky Prospekt 32–34; Sheet Music at 13 Ulitsa Zhelyabova;

photographic goods at 61 Liteiny Prospekt and 92 Nevsky Prospekt; applied art at 45, Nevsky Prospekt; crystal at 34 Nevsky Prospekt and prints at 72 Nevsky Prospekt.

Markets
Kuznechny Market
Kuznechny Pereulok 3.

Torzhkovsky Market
Torzhkovskaya Ulitsa 20.

Vasileostrovsky Market
Bolshoi Prospekt 18.

ART

The last few years have seen a boom in the type of art which has never had anything to do with "socialist realism". Theatre and especially painting, has just emerged from the underground. Artists who were banned are now openly exhibited; on Nevsky there are hundreds (if not thousands) of hitherto undiscovered paintings. Some artists have already found a way to sell their works in the West. Others will gladly sell their paintings for several hundred roubles. Bear in mind that such paintings may cost several thousand dollars in Western Europe. Naturally, the streets are full of cheap stuff – moons over ponds, imitation icons, portraits of rock stars, Gorby cartoons and naked women – but you may also run into something interesting.

SPORTS

SPECTATOR

Kirov Stadium, Primorsky Park Pobedy.
Lenin Stadium, Petrovsky Ostrov (island).
Yubileyny Palace of Sports, Prospekt Dobrolyubova 18.
Winter Stadium, Manezhnaya Ploshchad 6.
Cycle-track, Prospekt Engelsa 81.

PARTICIPANT

The Pribaltiyskaya and the Pulkovskaya Hotels have their own swimming pools and gyms.
SKA Swimming Pool, Litovskaya Ulitsa 3.
Spartak Swimming Pool, Konstantinovsky Prospekt 19.
Chigorin Chess Club, Ulitsa Zhelyabova 25.
Yacht Club, Petrovskaya Kosa 7.
Tennis Courts, Naberezhnaya Fontanki 33.

PHOTOGRAPHY

The diplomat services agency (UPDK) and some newly appearing co-operative laboratories develop Agfa, Kodak and Fuji films (E6 process). Ask at your hotel service counter or at the photography shops at 61 Liteiny Prospekt or 92 Nevsky Prospekt. Some Beriozka shops sell Ektachrome and Fuji films. Kodachrome, which needs a special development process, is not officially available.

You should not take photographs of military installations or from aeroplanes and it is also not recommended to take them from the train. The interpretation of what constitutes a military installation rests with the officials. You will have to be cautious and if possible ask your guide or interpreter before you take a picture of a bridge, a railway station, an airport or anything else that might be assessed as a special security object.

LANGUAGE

ENGLISH/RUSSIAN

Russian is one of the 130 languages used by the peoples of the USSR. It is the mother tongue of some 150 million Russians and the state language the Russian Federation (RSFSR). Talking to anybody in the USSR in Russian, you will be understood by most Soviet citizens.

It is important when speaking Russian that you reproduce the accent (marked here before each stressed vowel with the sign ') correctly to be understood well.

From a linguistic point of view, Russian belongs to the Slavonic branch of the Indo-European family of languages; English, German, French, Spanish and Hindi are its relatives.

Historically Russian is a comparatively young language. The appearance of the language in its present shape, based on the spoken language of the Eastern Slavs and the Church-Slavonic written language, is attributed to the 11th to 14th centuries.

Modern Russian has absorbed numerous foreign words and they form a considerable group within the Russian vocabulary. Very few tourists will be puzzled by Russian words like telefon, televizor, teatr, otel, restoran, kafe, taxi, metro or aeroport.

The thing that usually intimidates people on their first encounter with Russian is the alphabet. In fact it is easy to come to terms with after a little practice, and the effort is worthwhile if you want to make out the names of streets and shop signs.

The Russian (or Cyrillic) alphabet was created by two brothers, philosophers and public figures, Constantine (St Cyril) and Methodius; both were born in Solun (now Thessaloniki in Greece). Their purpose was to facilitate the spread of Greek liturgical books in Slavonic speaking countries. Today the Cyrillic alphabet, with different modifications, is used in the Ukrainian, Byelorussian, Bulgarian, Serbian and in some other languages.

ALPHABET

printed letter	sounds, as in	Russian name of a letter
А а	a, archaeology	a
Б б	b, buddy	be
В в	v, vow	v
Г г	g, glad	ge
Д д	d, dot (the tip of the tongue close to the teeth, not the alveoli)	de
Е е	e, get	ye
Ё ё	yo, yoke	yo
Ж ж	zh, composure	zhe
З з	z, zest	ze
И и	i, ink	i
Й й	j, yes	jot
К к	k, kind	ka
Л л	l, life (but a bit harder)	el'
М м	m, memory	em
Н н	n, nut	en
О о	o, optimum	o
П п	p, party	pe
Р р	r (rumbling, as in Italian, the tip of the tongue is vibrating)	er
С с	s, sound	es
Т т	t, title (the tip of the tongue close to the teeth, not the alveoli)	te
У у	u, nook	u
Ф ф	f, flower	ef
Х х	kh, hawk	ha
Ц ц	ts (pronounced conjointly)	tse
Ч ч	ch, charter	che
Ш ш	sh, shy	sha
Щ щ	shch (pronounced shcha conjointly)	
ъ	(the hard sign)	
Ы ы	y (pronounced with the same position of a tongue as when pronouncing G,K)	y
	(the soft sign)	
Э э	e, ensign	e
Ю ю	yu, you	yu
Я я	ya, yard	ya

NUMBERS

1	adín	один
2	dva	два
3	tri	три
4	chityri	четыре
5	pyat'	пять
6	shes't'	шесть
7	sem	семь
8	vósim	восемь
9	d'évit'	девять
10	d'ésit'	десять
11	adínatsat'	одиннадцать
12	dvinátsat'	двенадцать
13	trinátsat'	тринадцать
14	chityrnatsat'	четырнадцать
15	pitnátsat'	пятнадцать
16	shysnátsat'	шестнадцать
17	simnátsat'	семнадцать
18	vasimnátsat'	восемнадцать
19	divitnátsat'	девятнадцать
20	dvátsat'	двадцать
21	dvatsat' adin	двадцать один
30	trítsat'	тридцать
40	sórak	сорок
50	pidisyat	пятьдесят
60	shyz'disyat	шестьдесят
70	s'émdisyat	семьдесят
80	vósimdisyat	восемьдесят
90	divinósta	девяносто
100	sto	сто
101	sto adin	сто один
200	dv'és'ti	двести
300	trísta	триста
400	chityrista	четыреста
500	pitsót	пятьсот
600	shyssót	шестьсот
700	simsót	семьсот
800	vasimsót	восемьсот
900	divitsót	девятьсот
1,000	tysicha	тысяча
2,000	dve tysichi	две тысячи
10,000	d'ésit' tysich	десять тысяч
100,000	sto tysich	сто тысяч
1,000,000	milión	миллион
1,000,000,000	miliárd	миллиард

PRONOUNS

I/We
ya/my
я/мы

You
ty (singular, informal)/
vy (plural, or formal singular)
ты /вы

He/She/They
on/aná/aní
он/она/они

My/Mine
moj (object masculine)/
mayá (object feminine)/
mayó (neutral or without marking the gender)/
maí (plural)
мой/моя/моё/мои

Our/Ours
nash/násha/náshe/náshy (resp.)
наш/наша/наше/наши

Your/Yours
tvoj etc. (see My)
vash etc. (see Our)
твой/ваш

His/Her, Hers/Their, Theirs
jivó/jiyó/ikh
его/её/их

Who?
khto?
Кто?

What?
shto?
Что?

FORMS OF GREETING

Forms of Address: Modern Russian has no established and universally used forms of address. The old revolutionary form *tavárishch* (comrade), still used amongst some party members, lacks its popularity in the rest of the population.

One way is to say: *Izviníte, skazhíte pozhálsta...* (Excuse me, tell me, please...) or *Izvinite, mózhna sprasít'...* (Excuse me, can I ask you...).

If you want to look original and to show your penetration into the depths of history of courteous forms, you can appeal to the man *súdar'* (sir), and to the woman *sudárynya* (madam). Many people want to restore these pre-revolutionary forms of address in modern Russian society. If you know the name of the father of the person you talk to, the best and the most neutral way is to use these both when addressing him (her): "Mikhál Sirgéich" to Mr Gorbachev and "Raísa Maxímavna" to his spouse.

In business circles you can use forms *gaspadín* to a man and *gaspazhá* to a woman. The English forms of address "Mister" or "Sir" are also acceptable.

You can hear common parlance forms *Maladói chilavék!* (Young man!) and *Dévushka!* (Girl!) to a person of any age and also *Zhénshchina!* (Woman!) to women in the bus, in the shop or at the market. These forms should be avoided in conversation.

Hello!
zdrástvuti (neutral, often accompanied by shaking hands, but it is not necessary)
Здравствуйте!

alo! (by telephone only)
Алло!

zdrástvuj (to one person, informal)
Здравствуй!

priv'ét! (informal)
Привет!

Good afternoon/Good evening
dóbry den'/dobry véchir
Добрый день/Добрый вечер

Good morning/Good night
dobrae útra/dobraj nóchi (= Sleep well)
Доброе утро/Доброй ночи

Good bye
dasvidán'ye (neutral)
До свиданья

chao! (informal)
Чао!

paká! (informal, literally means "until")
Пока!

Good luck to you!
shchislíva!
Счастливо!

What is your name?
kak vas (tibya) zavút?/kak váshe ímya ótchistva? (the second is formal)

Как вас (тебя) зовут?/Как ваще имя и отчество?

My name is… /I am…
minya zavut… /ya…
Меня зовут… /Я…

It's a pleasure
óchin' priyatna
Очень приятно

Good/Excellent
kharashó/privaskhódna
хорощо/отлично

Do you speak English?
vy gavaríti pa anglíski?
Вы говорите по-английски?

I don't understand/I didn't understand
ya ni panimáyu/ya ni pónyal
Я не понимаю/Я не понял

Repeat, please
pavtaríti pazhálsta
Повторите, пожалуйста

What do you call this?
kak vy éta nazyváiti?
Как вы это называете?

How do you say…?
kak vy gavaríti…?
Как вы говорите…?

Please/Thank you (very much)
pazhálsta/(bal'shóe) spasíba
Пожалуйста/(Большщое) спасибо

Excuse me
izviníti
Извините

GETTING AROUND

Where is the… ?
gd'e (nakhóditsa)… ?
Где находится… ?

beach
plyazh
…пляж

bathroom
vánnaya
...ванная

bus station
aftóbusnaya stántsyja/aftavakzál
...автобусная станция/автовокзал

bus stop
astanófka aftóbusa
...остановка автобуса

airport
airapórt
...аэропорт

railway station
vakzál/stántsyja (in small towns)
...вокзал/станция

post office
póchta
...почта

police station
...milítsyja
...милиция

ticket office
bil'étnaya kássa
...билетная касса

marketplace
rynak/bazár
...рынок/базар

embassy/consulate
pasól'stva/kónsul'stva
...посольство/консульство

Where is there a...?
gd'e z'd'es'...?
Где здесь...?

currency exchange
abm'én val'úty
...обмен валюты

pharmacy
apt'éka
...аптека

(good) hotel
(kharóshyj) atél'/(kharoshaya) gastínitsa
...(хороший)отель(хорошая)гостиница

restaurant
ristarán
...ресторан

bar
bar
...бар

taxi stand
stayanka taxí
...стоянка такси

subway station
mitró
...метро

service station
aftazaprávachnaya stantsyja/aftasárvis
...автозаправочная станция

newsstand
gaz'étnyj kiósk
...газетный киоск

public telephone
tilifón
...телефон

hard currency shop
val'útnyj magazín
...валютный магазин

supermarket
univirsám
...универсам

department store
univirmák
...универмаг

hairdresser
parikmákhirskaya
...парикмахерская

jeweller
yuvilírnyj magazin
...ювелирный магазин

hospital
bal'nítsa
...больница

Do you have...?
u vas jes't'...?
У вас ес...

282

I (don't) want…
ya (ni) khachyu…
Я (не) хо чу…

I want to buy…
ya khachyu kupít'…
Я хочу купить…

Where can I buy…?
gd'e ya magú kupít'…?
Где я могу купить…?

cigarettes
sigaréty
…сигареты

wine
vinó
…вино

film
fotoplyonku
…фотоплёнку

a ticket for…
bilét na…
…билет на…

this
éta
…это

postcards/envelopes
atkrytki/kanv'érty
…открытки/конверты

a pen/a pencil
rúchku/karandásh
…ручку/карандаш

soap/shampoo
myla/shampún'
…мыло/шампунь
aspirin
aspirn
…аспирин

I need…
mn'e núzhna…
Мне нужно…

I need a doctor/a mechanic
mn'e núzhyn dóktar/aftamikhánik
Мне нужен доктор/автомеханик

I need help
mn'e nuzhná pómashch'
Мне нужна помощь

Car/Plane/Train/Ship
mashyna/samal'yot/póist/karábl'
маъшина/самолёт/поезд/корабль

A ticket to…
bil'ét do…
билет до…

How can I get to…
kak ya magu dabrátsa do…
Как я могу добраться до…

Please, take me to…
pazhalsta atvizíti minya…
Пожалуйста, отвезите меня…

What is this place called?
kak nazyváitsa eta m'ésta?
Как называется это место?

Where are we?
gd'e my?
Где мы?

Stop here
astanavíti z'd'es'
Остановите здесь

Please wait
padazhdíti pazhalsta
Подождите, пожалуйста

When does the train [plane] leave?
kagdá atpravl'yaitsa poist [samalyot]?
Когда отправляется поезд (самолёт)?

I want to check my luggage
ya khachyu prav'érit' bagázh
Я хочу проверить багаж

Where does this bus go?
kudá id'yot état aftóbus?
Куда идёт этот автобус?

SHOPPING

How much does it cost?
skól'ka eta stóit?
Сколько это стоит?

That's very expensive
eta óchin' dóraga
Это о чень дорого

A lot, many/A little, few
mnóga/mála
много/мало

It (doesn't) fits me
eta mn'e (ni) padkhódit
Это мне (не) подходит

AT THE HOTEL

I have a reservation
u minya zakázana m'esta
У меня заказана комната

I want to make a reservation
ya khachyu zakazát' m'esta
Я хочу заказать место

A single (double) room
adnam'éstnuyu (dvukhmestnuyu) kómnatu
одноместную (двухместную) комнату

I want to see the room
ya khachyu pasmatrét' nómer
Я хо чу посмотреть номер

Key/Suitcase/Bag
klyuch/chimadán/súmka
ключ /чемодан/сумка

AT THE RESTAURANT

Waiter/Menu
afitsyánt/minyu
официант/меню

I want to order…
ya khachyu zakazat'…
Я хочу заказать

breakfast/lunch/supper
záftrak/ab'ét/úzhyn
завтрак/обед/ужин

the house specialty
fírminnaya blyuda
фирменное блюдо

mineral water/juice
minirál'naya vadá/sok
минерал'ьная вода/сок

coffee/tea/beer
kófe/chai/píva
кофе/ чай/пиво

What do you have to drink (alcoholic)?
shto u vas jes't' vypit'?
Что у вас есть выпить?

Ice/Fruit/Dessert
marózhynaya/frúkty/disért
можо еное/фрукты/дессерт

Salt/Pepper/Sugar
sol'/périts/sákhar
соль/перец/сахар

Beef/Pork/Chicken/Fish/Shrimp
gavyadina/svinína/kúritsa/ryba/kriv'étki
говядина/свинина/курица/рыба/ креветки

Vegetables/Rice/Potatoes
óvashchi/ris/kartófil'
овощи/рис/картофель

Bread/Butter/Eggs
khleb/másla/yajtsa
хлеб/масло/яйца

Soup/Salad/Sandwich/Pizza
sup/salát/butyrbrót/pitsa
суп/салат/бутерброд/пицца

a plate/a glass/a cup/a napkin
tar'élka/stakán/cháshka/salf'étka
тарелка/стакан/чашка/салфетка

The bill, please
shchyot pazhalsta
Счёт, пожалуйста

Well done/Not so good
fkúsna/ták sibe
вкусно/так себе

I want my change, please
zdáchu pazhalsta
Сдачу, пожалуйста

MONEY

I want to exchange currency (money)
ya khachyu abmin'át' val'yutu (d'én'gi)
Я хочу обменять валюту (деньги)

Do you accept credit cards?
vy prinimáiti kridítnyi kártachki?
Вы принимаете кредитные карточки?

Can you cash a traveller's cheque?
vy mózhyti razminyat' darózhnyj chek?
Вы можете разменять дорожный чек?

What is the exchange rate?
kakój kurs?
Какой курс?

TIME

What time is it?
katóryj chas?
Который час?

Just a moment, please
adnú minútachku
Одну минуточку

How long does it take?
skól'ka vrémini eta zanimáit?
Сколько времени это занимает?

Hour/day/week/month
chas/den'/nid'élya/m'ésits
час/день/неделя/месяц

At what time?
f kakóe vrémya?
В какое время?

At 1:00/at 8 a.m./at 6 p.m.
f chas/ v vósim utrá/f shés't' chisóf v'échira
в час/в восемь утравшестьчасоввечера

This (last, next) week
eta (próshlaya, sl'édujshchiya) nid'elya
эта (прошлая, следующая) неделя

Yesterday/Today/Tomorrow
fchirá/sivód'nya/záftra
вчера/сегодня/завтра

Sunday
vaskris'én'je
воскресенье

Monday
panid'él'nik
понедельник

Tuesday
ftórnik
вторник

Wednesday
sridá
среда

Thursday
chitv'érk
четверг

Friday
pyatnitsa
пятница

Saturday
subóta
суббота

The weekend
vykhadnyi dni
выходные дни

SIGNS & INSCRIPTIONS

вход/выход/входа нет
fkhot/vykhat/fkhóda n'et
Entrance/Exit/No Entrance

туалет/уборная
tual'ét/ubórnaya
Toilet/Lavatory

Ж (З) / М (М)
dlya zhén'shchin/dlya mushchín
Ladies/Gentlemen

зал ожидания
zal azhidán'ya
Waiting hall

занято/свободно
zánita/svabódna
Occupied/Free

касса
kassa
Booking office/cash desk

медпункт
mitpúnt
Medical Services

справочное бюро
správachnae bzuro
Information

вода для питья
vadá dlya pit'ya
Drinking Water

вокзал
vakzál
Terminal/Railway station

открыто/закрыто
atkryta/zakryta
Open/Closed

запрещается/опасно
zaprishchyaitsa/apásna
Prohibited/Danger

продукты/гастроном
pradúkty/gastranóm
Grocery

булочная/кондитерская
búlachnaya/kan'dítirskaya
Bakery/Confectionery

закусочная/столовая
zakúsachnaya/stalóvaya
Refreshment room/Canteen

самообслуживание
samaapslúzhivan'je
Self-service

баня/прачечная/химчистка
bánya/práchichnaya/khimchístka
Bath-House/Laundry/Chemical Cleaning

книги/культтовары
knígi/kul'taváry
Books/Stationery

мясо/птица
m'ása/ptítsa
Meat/Poultry

обувь
óbuf'
Shoe-Store

овощи/фрукты
óvashchi/frúkty
Green-Grocery/Fruits

универмаг/универсам
univirmák/univirsám
Department Store/Supermarket

ткани/цветы
tkani/tsvity
Fabrics/Flowers

FURTHER READING

HISTORY

Catherine the Great, by J.T. Alexander. Oxford University Press, 1989.
Stalin, Man of Contradiction, by K.N. Cameron. Strong Oak Press, 1989.
History of Soviet Russia, by E.H. Carr. Pelican, 3 vols, first published 1953.
A History of the Soviet Union, by G. Hosking. Fontana/Collins, 1990.
The Making of Modern Russia, by L. Kochan and R. Abraham. Penguin, 1983.
The Blackwell Encyclopaedia of the Russian Revolution, ed. by H. Shukman. Blackwell, 1989.

POLITICS

Voices of Glasnost, by S. Cohen and K. van den Heuvel. Norton, 1989.
The Other Russia, by Michael Glenny and Norman Stone. Faber & Faber, 1990.
Perestroika, by M.S. Gorbachev. Fontana, 1987.
Towards a Better World, by M.S. Gorbachev. Richardson and Steirman, 1987.
Soviet Union: Politics, Economics and Society, by R.J. Hill. Pinter Publishers, 1989.
Glasnost in Action, by A. Nove. Unwin Hyman, 1989.
Against the Grain, by Boris Yeltsin. Jonathan Cape, 1990.

BIOGRAPHY/MEMOIRS

The Making of Andrei Sakharov, by G. Bailey. Penguin, 1990.

Alone Together, by Elena Bonner. Collins Harvill, 1986.

An English Lady at the Court of Catherine the Great, ed. by A.G. Gross. Crest Publications, 1989.

On the Estate: Memoirs of Russia Before the Revolution, ed. by Olga Davydoff Bax. Thames & Hudson, 1986.

Into the Whirlwind and *Within a Whirlwind*, by Eugenia Ginzburg. Collins Harvill, 1989.

In the Beginning, by Irina Ratushinskaya. Hodder & Stoughton, 1990.

Ten Days that Shook the World, by John Reed. Penguin, first published 1919.

The Gulag Archipelago, by Alexander Solzhenitsyn. Collins Harvill, 1988.

Russia: Despatches from the Guardian Correspondent in Moscow, by Martin Walker. Abacus, 1989.

ART

A History of Russian Painting, by A. Bird. Phaidon, 1987.

Russian Art of the Avant Garde, by J.E. Bowlt. Thames & Hudson, 1988.

New Worlds: Russian Art and Society 1900–37, by D. Elliot. Thames & Hudson, 1986.

The Kremlin and its Treasures, by Rodimzeva, Rachmanov and Raimann. Phaidon, 1989.

Russian Art from Neoclassicism to the Avant Garde, by D.V. Sarabianov. Thames & Hudson, 1990.

Street Art of the Revolution, by V. Tolstoy, I. Bibikova and C. Cooke. Thames & Hudson, 1990.

The Art of Central Asia. Aurora Art Publishers, 1988.

Folk Art in the Soviet Union. Abrams/Aurora, 1990.

The Hermitage. Aurora, 1987.

Masterworks of Russian Painting in Soviet Museums. Aurora, 1989.

TRAVEL, GEOGRAPHY & NATURAL HISTORY

First Russia, Then Tibet, by Robert Byron. Penguin, first published 1905.

Caucasian Journey, by Negley Farson. Penguin, first published 1951.

Sailing to Leningrad, by Roger Foxall. Grafton, 1990.

The Natural History of the USSR, by Algirdas Kynstautas. Century Hutchinson, 1987.

Portrait of the Soviet Union, by Fitzroy McLean. Wwidenfeld and Nicolson, 1988.

Atlas of Russia and the Soviet Union, by R. Millner-Gulland with N. Dejevsky. Phaidon, 1989.

The Big Red Train, by Eric Newby. Picador, 1989.

The USSR: From an Original Idea by Karl Marx. Faber & Faber, 1983.

Journey into Russia, by Laurens van der Post. Penguin, first published 1964.

Among the Russians, by Colin Thubron. Penguin, first published 1983.

Ustinov in Russia, by Peter Ustinov. Michael O Mara Books, 1987.

Motorist's Guide to the Soviet Union, Progress Publishers, 1980.

The Nature of the Soviet Union: Landscapes, Flora and Fauna. Mokslas Publishing 1987.

Russia. Bracken Books, 1989.

USSR: The Economist Guide. Hutchinson Business Books, 1990.

LITERATURE

The Russia House, by John le Carré. Coronet, 1990.

The Brothers Karamazov; The Idiot, by Fyodor Dostoevsky.

Doctor Zhivago, by Boris Pasternak.

Children of the Arbat, by Anatoli Rybakov. Hutchinson, 1988.

And Quiet Flows the Don; The Don Flows Home to the Sea, by Mikhail Sholokov.

War and Peace; Anna Karenina, by Leo Tolstoy.

USEFUL ADDRESSES

SOVIET MISSIONS ABROAD

Argentina
1741 Rodriges Penya
Buenos Aires
Tel: 421 552

Australia
Griffis
70 Canberra Ave
Canberra
Tel: 956 6408

Austria
45–47 Reisnerstr.
Vienna
Tel: 721 229

Belgium
66 Avenue de Fre
1180 Bruxelles
Tel: 373 3569, 374 3406

Canada
285 Sharlotta Street
Ottawa
Tel: 235 4341

Denmark
3–5 Christianiagade
Copenhagen
Tel: 125 585

Finland
6 Tehtaankatu
Helsinki
Tel: 661 876

France
16 Boulevard Lann 40/50
Paris
Tel: 450 40550

Germany
Embassy:
2 Waldstr. 42
5300 Bonn
Tel: 312 086
Consulate:
76 Am Feenteich
2000 Hamburg
Tel: 229 5301

Greece
28 Nikiforu Litra Street
Paleo Psyhico
Athens
Tel: 672 6130, 672 5235

India
Shantipath Street
Chanakiapury
Delhi
Tel: 606 026

Ireland
186 Orwell Road
Dublin
Tel: 975 748

Italy
5 Via Gaeta
Rome
Tel: 494 1681

Japan
Minato-ku
Adzabu-dai 2-1-1, T-106
Tokyo
Tel: 583 4224

Netherlands
2 Andries Bickerweh
The Hague
Tel: 345 1300

New Zealand
Carory
57 Messines Road
Wellington
Tel: 766 113

Norway
2 Dramensveien 74
Oslo
Tel: 553 278

Singapore
51 Nassim Road
Singapore 1025
Tel: 235 1834

Spain
6 & 14 Maestro Ripol
Madrid
Tel: 411 0706, 262 2264

Sweden
31 Ervelsgatan
Stockholm
Tel: 813 0440

Switzerland
37 Brunnadenrein 3006
Bern
Tel: 440 566

Thailand
108 Sathorn Nua
Bangkok
Tel: 258 0628

Turkey
Caryagdy, Soc. 5
Ankara
Tel: 139 2122

United Kingdom
5, 13 & 18 Kensington Palace Gardens
London
Tel: (71) 229 3628

USA
Embassy:
1125 16th Street
20036 Washington DC
Tel: 628 7551, 628 8548, 628 6412
Consulate:
2790 Green Street
San Francisco
Tel: 922 6644

CONSULATES IN LENINGRAD

Bulgaria
Ulitsa Ryleeva 27
Tel: 273 7347.

China
3-Linia 12
Tel: 218 1721, 218 3492, 218 7953

Cuba
Ulitsa Ryleeva 37
Tel: 279 0492

Finland
Ulitsa Chaikovskovo 71
Tel: 273 7321

France
Naberezhnaya Moiki 15
Tel: 314 1443, 312 1130

Germany
Ulitsa Petra Lavrova 39
Tel: 273 5598, 273 5731, 273 5937

Hungary
Ulitsa Marata 15
Tel: 312 6458, 312 6753

Italy
Teatralnaya Ploshchad 10
Tel: 312 2896

Japan
Naberezhnaya Moiki 29
Tel: 314 1434, 314 1418

Mongolia
Saperny Pereulok 11
Tel: 243 4522

Poland
Ulitsa Sovetskaya 12
Tel: 274 4331, 274 4170

Sweden
10th line (VO)
Tel: 218 3526/27/28

USA
Ulitsa Petra Lavrova 15
Tel: 274 8235

FOREIGN MISSIONS IN THE USSR

If you are a citizen of the following countries, which do not have diplomatic representation in Leningrad, you should consult their embassies at the Moscow addresses given below:

Argentina
Sadovaya-Triumfalnaya Ulitsa 4/10
Tel: 299 0367

Australia
Kropotkinsky Pereulok 13
Tel: 246 5012

Austria
Starokonyushenny Pereulok 1
Tel: 201 7317

Canada
Starokonyushenny Pereulok 23
Tel: 241 5070

Czechoslovakia
Ulitsa Fuchika 12/14
Tel: 250 2225

Denmark
Pereulok Ostrovskovo 9
Tel: 201 7868

Greece
Ulitsa Stanislavskovo 4
Tel: 290 2274

India
Ulitsa Obukha 6–8
Tel: 297 1841

Ireland
Grokhol'sky Pereulok 5
Tel: 288 4101

Luxembourg
Khrushchevsky Pereulok 3
Tel. 202 2171

Malaysia
Mosfilmovskaya Ulitsa 50
Tel: 147 1415

Netherlands
Kalashny Pereulok 7
Tel: 291 2999

New Zealand
Ulitsa Vorovskovo 44
Tel: 290 3485

Norway
Ulitsa Vorovskovo 7
Tel: 290 3872

Portugal
Grokholsky Pereulok 3/1
Tel: 230 2435

Rumania
Mosfilmovskaya Ulitsa 64
Tel: 143 0424

Singapore
Pereulok Voevodina 5
Tel: 241 3702

Spain
Ulitsa Gertsena 50/8
Tel: 291 9004

Switzerland
Pereulok Stopani 2/5
Tel: 925 5322

Thailand
Eropkinsky Pereulok 3
Tel: 201 4893

Turkey
Vadkovsky Pereulok 7/37
Tel: 972 6900

United Kingdom
Naberezhnaya Morisa Toreza 14
Tel: 231 8511

INTOURIST OFFICES ABROAD

Amsterdam
Honthorststr. 42
Tel: 798 964

Athens
Stadiou 3, Syntagma Sq.
Tel: 323 3776

Berlin
Friedrichstr. 153A
Tel: 229 1948 and
15 Kurfürstendamm 63
Tel: 880 070

Budapest
Felszabadulas ter. 1
Tel: 180 098

Brussels
Galerie Ravenstein 2
Tel: 513 8234

Copenhagen
Vester Farimagsgade 6
Tel: 112 527

Delhi
Plot 6/7, Block 50-E
Njaja Marg Chanakiapuri
Tel: 609 145

Frankfurt
Stephanstr. 1
Tel: 285 776

Helsinki
Etela Esplanaadi 14
Tel: 631 875

London
292 Regent St
Tel: (71) 631 1252.

Montreal
801 McGill College Ave
Suite 630
Tel: 849 6394

New York
630 Fifth Ave, Suite 868
Tel: 757 3884

Paris
7, Boulevard de Capucines
Tel: 474-24740

Prague
Stepanska 47
Tel: 267 162

Rome
Piazza Buenos Aires 6/7
Tel: 863 892

Sydney
Underwood House
37–49 Pitt St
Tel: 277 652

Tokyo
Roppongi Heights, 1–16
4-chome Roppongi, Minato-ku
Tel: 584 6617

Vienna
Schwedenplatz 3–4
Tel: 639 547.

Zurich
Usteristr. 9
Tel: 211 3335

OTHER TRAVEL AGENTS

USA
Four Winds Travel
175 Fifth Ave
New York, NY 10010

Lindblad Travel Inc.
1 Sylvan Rd North
Westport, CT 06880

Russian Travel Bureau Inc.
245 E. 44th St
New York, NY 10017

UK
American Express Co. Inc.
6 Haymarket
London SW1

Voyages Jules Verne
10 Glentworth St
London NW1 5 PG

P & O Holidays
77 New Oxford St
London WC1

London Walkabout Club
20–22 Craven Terrace
Lancaster Gate
London W2

Germany
Hansa Tourist
Hamburger Str. 132
Hamburg 76

Lindex Reisen
Rauchstr. 5
8000 München

Intratours
Eiserne Hand 19
6000 Frankfurt 1

GeBeCo-Reisen
Eckernförder Str. 93
2300 Kiel

Singapore
Folke von Knobloch
126 Telok Ayer
#02-01 Gat House
Singapore

ART/PHOTO CREDITS

INDEX

T

U – V

W – Y

Z